Politicking Online

Politicking Online

The Transformation of Election Campaign Communications

EDITED BY
COSTAS PANAGOPOULOS

RUTGERS UNIVERSITY PRESS

NEW BRUNSWICK, NEW JERSEY, AND LONDON

LIBRARY OF CONGRESS CATALOGING-IN-PUBLICATION DATA

Politicking online : the transformation of election campaign communications /
edited by Costas Panagopoulos.
    p.   cm.
Includes bibliographical references and index.
ISBN 978–0–8135–4488–5 (hardcover : alk. paper)
ISBN 978–0–8135–4489–2 (pbk. : alk. paper)
    1. Internet in political campaigns.   2. Political campaigns—Effect of
technological innovations on.   3. Elections—Effect of technological innovations
on.   4. Information technology.   5. Telecommunication.   I. Panagopoulos,
Costas, 1972–
    JF2112.C3P66   2009
    324.7'302854678—dc22   2008029195

A British Cataloging-in-Publication record for this book is available
from the British Library.

Visit our Web site: http://rutgerspress.rutgers.edu

Manufactured in the United States of America

CONTENTS

v

PREFACE AND ACKNOWLEDGMENTS

I recall vividly, in 1992, when I was a candidate for the Massachusetts state legislature, asking a kind, elderly volunteer to help create a database of voters in the district from a printout hundreds of sheets long that the campaign had obtained from the local election board. Patiently, for many months, the volunteer typed in the names, addresses, phone numbers, and party affiliations of the nearly thirty thousand voters who resided in the district. At the time, we could not simply download voter files online at the click of a button. One had to visit the Board of Elections in person and secure a disk or a printout. I also remember that volunteers were not so easy to recruit. We could not simply attract friends or post invitations on Facebook or MySpace. Money was even tougher to come by, and it usually required a personal appeal—a call or a visit—a mailing, or an event. Donors could not simply go to a Web site and make a contribution.

Although this was only about fifteen years ago, there has been a sea change in political campaigning that has been driven by technological developments. Electioneering, like politics and society as a whole, is now operating in a brand-new environment that provides candidates, parties, and organizations with unprecedented opportunities. This volume explores how political campaigns are adapting to the technological advancements, primarily in interpersonal communications, that have taken place over the past decade.

The volume would not have been possible without the support of many colleagues and friends. First and foremost, I thank the authors. The keen insights and meticulous analyses they each contributed make the volume a top-rate piece of research that will appeal to a wide audience. I also thank G. David Garson, editor of *Social Science Computer Review*, who asked me to serve as guest editor of a special issue of the journal devoted to this topic. Several of the selections included in this volume appear in that issue.

I am grateful to colleagues in the Department of Political Science at Fordham University for their strong support of my scholarly endeavors. In particular, Jeffrey Cohen and Richard Fleisher constantly express their encouragement and support, and I appreciate it greatly. Bruce Berg was also very supportive and delighted that the volume is being published by Rutgers University Press.

I am also thankful to Marlie Wasserman at Rutgers University Press for her vision and encouragement and for embracing this project so enthusiastically. She and her staff at RUP, especially Christina Brianik, are consummate professionals, and it has been a joy to work with them.

Finally, although I did not win the election in 1992, I am forever indebted to the many volunteers in that election cycle who worked tirelessly—and without the advantages of modern technology—to promote my candidacy. I dedicate this work to them.

Politicking Online

1

Technology and the Modern Political Campaign

The Digital Pulse of the 2008 Campaigns

COSTAS PANAGOPOULOS

On January 20, 2007, New York Senator Hillary Rodham Clinton formally announced her intention to seek the Democratic Party's 2008 nomination for president via the Internet. The Clinton announcement, delivered in a video featured on her Web site, followed a statement a few days earlier by Illinois Democratic Senator Barack Obama about his plans for a presidential run and was launched on the same day that New Mexico Governor Bill Richardson, another hopeful for the Democratic presidential nomination, declared his intentions—all on the Internet. In the 2006 midterm elections in the United States, Republican Senator George Allen's bid for reelection in Virginia was seriously damaged by widespread online viewing of a speech on YouTube and other popular videosharing Web sites in which he referred to a young man of Indian ancestry associated with an opponent's campaign as a "macaca," a derogatory term. Allen eventually lost the election, narrowly. These unprecedented events signaled the start of a new era for the use of the Internet in political campaigns and marked the growing dominance of the medium as a political tool (MacAskill 2007).

A wide range of technological developments, most notably although not exclusively the Internet, has transformed the landscape of modern political campaigns. Technology has increasingly been featured in political campaigns throughout the world in prominent and unprecedented ways. Campaigns have capitalized on advancements in technology to inform, target and mobilize voters. Strategists, for example, increasingly rely on database management and Web-based tools to identify, monitor, and communicate with voters. Campaigns use software tools to recruit and manage staff and volunteers and to execute elaborate campaign plans. Software helps track campaign contributions and expenditures, facilitating required disclosure of such details to the appropriate regulatory authorities. Pollsters turn regularly to Web-based tools for interviewing purposes.

The Internet, generally, has revolutionized political campaign communications. As public access to the Internet has surged past 70 percent of the U.S. population, the Internet has claimed front-and-center status in campaign strategies. This volume assembles views and scholarship from leading experts and academics to explore innovative uses of technology for electioneering purposes in contemporary campaigns and to reflect on their impact. Overall, this is an intriguing area of inquiry for readers interested in the linkages between technology and elections.

New Technology and the 2008 Presidential Election Cycle: A Watershed Year

The 2008 presidential race, above and beyond developments over the past few election cycles in the United States, fueled intense political analysis and media buzz about the potential effects of an online political revolution. From the start, campaigns posted speech clips to YouTube, creating "groups," "events," and advertisements on Facebook, making announcements through online videos, and desperately seeking new ways to reach out to voters through social networking tools on the Web. In many ways, such efforts have proved to be rewarding. Some candidates, including Ron Paul and Barack Obama, achieved tremendous success building buzz because of their internet tactics; the Ron Paul camp connected supporters through the networking and organizational tools on MeetUp.com, an approach that resulted in raising an unprecedented $4.2 million dollars online in twenty-four hours for the Republican candidate; the Obama campaign took a step further and built its own social networking site, MyBarackObama.com, which allows millions of supporters to create profiles, connect to other Obama fans, plan and attend events, and help raise money for the senator. Consequently, both Obama's and Paul's official campaign Web sites maintained significantly higher traffic than many other candidate Web sites (Techpresident.com 2008a). On the other hand, Rudy Giuliani, whose campaign made little effort to connect to voters through Internet platforms, was an early Republican casualty.

Undoubtedly, new media strategies have the capacity to exert measurable impact on elections, and there is little disagreement that the landscape of campaigns and elections is changing rapidly. At this moment in politics, candidates have strong incentives to take advantage of new media technologies and to implement at least some new media approaches. Clearly, the Internet is a powerful tool, and those who use it successfully allow themselves an advantage in getting their message to the masses. But just how much is truly at stake on the Web? What are the early lessons analysts and operatives can draw from the pioneering uses of the Internet in electoral settings? And what are the broad implications for democracy and representation?

Insights into these questions can be gleaned from developments in the 2008 campaign as election strategists realize the Web's true potential and gain new ideas about how to gauge the relative influence of new media campaign tactics on vote choice. Not only has the Internet become a vital aspect of campaign strategy, but it has revolutionized the way analysts, candidates, and ordinary citizens think about and deal with politics. There still exist vast uncharted territories within the World Wide Web, and one can only speculate about the future exploration of new media election strategies. Nonetheless, the 2008 election cycle, in particular, sheds valuable light on trends and developments in at least five important areas that are revolutionizing campaigns.

Online Fund-Raising

Money in campaigns coffers often translates into power and respect and can be a signal of support and credibility. In the past, candidates with friends with the deepest pockets may have had an edge in their election bids. But thanks in part to the Internet, this is changing change. Several of the 2008 presidential campaigns have raised the bar in regard to campaign financing using new, inventive, and more efficient means of reaching hoards more donors than was ever before possible with traditional fund-raising methods.

Some of the most effective approaches incorporate the use of online videos, personal messages, and other new media outlets as a great way to convey a sense of "informality" between the candidates and their supporters. Candidates often send brief, unedited videos along with their e-mail blasts to give people a peek into parts of their lives that are normally undocumented. One example is the Obama campaign e-mail containing a ten-minute video of a dinner in which he met with five different small donors; it showed him chatting with them about everything from comic books to his children. Such efforts are designed to spark connections with ordinary voters by reinforcing a candidate's down-to-earth image. By creating this sense of intimacy, candidates are able to draw support from ordinary people, who may be less enthusiastic about politics, and to garner a large online base of small first-time donors.

Indeed, fund-raising is an area that has been forever altered by the access the Internet provides to small donors like the ones who give to the various Obama, Clinton, and Paul Web-drives. Although less than 5 percent of donations in the 2006 cycle were collected online (E.politics.com 2006, in the most recent campaign Barack Obama has collected more than a third of his funds via online donation (Luo 2007). The Web allows candidates to reach more donors, even if they aren't particularly wealthy or known to give to political operations. Many of the campaigns devised creative ways to provide incentives that cost them little or nothing in their Internet fund-raising efforts in order to increase their number of donors. Candidates had the chance to be "gimmicky," and such techniques that work especially well with fund-raising. In the early primary season, Clinton's campaign offered the opportunity for a small donor to travel with her campaign for a day; Obama offered five people the chance for a personal dinner with him. Despite the fact that the lion's share of campaign money continues to come from donors who give at or near maximum permissible levels, most of the donations received via the Internet are not from the usual ritzy donors who attend formal fund-raisers at $2,300 per head. Online fund-raising has proven its worth by soliciting donors who "have demonstrated a willingness to give again and again" and including citizens who would have never given to a campaign in the past (Luo 2007).

Campaigns that utilize the Internet wisely to raise money and create buzz are likely to benefit from a return on the money they invested to implement an effective online fund-raising strategy. According to campaign finance reports, Senator John McCain raised more than $4 for every $1 spent in an attempt to raise money online (Schatz 2007). As 2007 came to an end, the only Democratic candidate who had spent more than $1 million on his or her Internet operation was Senator Clinton. (TheHotlineBlog 2007). Recent "Web-warring" between the leading Democratic candidates has caught the attention of the international media and blogosphere, as online fund-raising hauls have produced unprecedented returns in the first quarter 2008. Twenty-eight million of the record-breaking $32 million Senator Obama raised in January 2008 was raised online (M. Sifry 2008), with more than 85 percent of the money donated via MyBarackObama.com (Melber 2008). The week of Super Tuesday, Obama raised a remarkable $7.9 million in a two-day online fund-raising heave, part of a larger Internet drive supplemented by major grassroots organizations like MoveOn.org (Melber 2008). Hillary Clinton cashed in on the Internet donor bank as well; her campaign reported that she had raised an average of $1 million online per day in the month of February 2008 (Marre 2008). Clearly, the Internet provides campaigns with the ability to reach out to voters and solicit money much more cheaply than tactics like the direct mail campaigns used in previous elections. Candidates have been able to spend small amounts online and generate substantial grassroots support, favorable reviews from bloggers, free publicity from mainstream media, and collect massive amounts of information from their followers at the same time. The recent success of online grassroots fund-raising suggests campaigns may, at least over time, become less beholden to wealthy donors or private interests groups

Viral Video

The importance of digital video cannot be understated; it is at the forefront of new media campaign strategies and can make or break a candidate. The online audience is vast, and with "video on demand" (VOD) users have a sense of viewing freedom that regular TV has yet to offer. Clips can be viewed repeatedly, edited, and spread around various networks via URLs or by embedding players. More than one hundred million video clips are viewed every day on YouTube (Seelye 2007). And as of February 2008 about 1,500 political videos had been posted by the presidential candidates (YouTube. com 2008); combined, they had been watched more than forty-eight million times (Techpresident.com 2008b).

Some of the 2008 presidential hopefuls understood the power of online videos from the get-go. Both of the two final Democratic competitors—Obama and Clinton—announced their candidacies in online videos. Nearly all of the candidates showed their appreciation for digital video by participating in the landmark Democratic and Republican debates sponsored by CNN and YouTube that allowed regular users to upload questions they wanted the candidates to answer. These are just a few examples that demonstrate the value of new media approaches to connecting with voters.

Not surprisingly, the most edgy and imaginative videos are the ones that have the most success for their Web-strategies. This is not the standard thirty-second television spot anymore, and ads built for that format often seem flat on an interface like YouChoose (YouTube's official channel for the 2008 presidential candidates). The videos that most often garner attention and go "viral" are those that are extremely funny or show a different side of the candidate. If a campaign can create a video that does both, chances are it will strike a responsive chord and be forwarded around via e-mail or picked up by the mainstream media.

For example, Senator Clinton's "Choose My Theme Song" campaign was a big Web hit in 2007. It started with a concept that was simple enough—allowing Internet users to listen to certain songs and vote on which one they thought was the best. First, she made a humorous video that poked fun at her own singing abilities and asked voters to take action. Then, a few weeks later, she released another video spliced with feedback (mostly negative) from the YouTube community, and again asked people to vote on the remaining songs. Finally, she and her husband, Bill, spoofed the much-discussed finale of *The Sopranos* to reveal the winning song. The effort was, by many assessments and at least in some respects, a triumph for at least three reasons. First, by acknowledging her critics and referencing pop culture, Clinton showed the public a rare glimpse of her sense of humor. As Michael Crowley of *The New Republic* put it, "[s]he's sort of the embodiment in modern American politics of control-freakery and micro-calculation, but the videos were fun and she seemed likable and funny, and she doesn't get many opportunities to come across that way" (quoted in Newman 2007). Second, she encouraged public discourse and incorporated "regular people" into her videos. Third, she was able to direct users to her Web site, where at least some visitors likely browsed to learn more about the candidate after voting for their preferred song. Senator Clinton was able to earn massive amounts of free publicity and steal buzz from Obama just by being creative.

Candidates can benefit from the videos their supporters post as well. Senator Obama has enjoyed massive free publicity and celebrity endorsements in the popular "Yes We Can" music video, which was viewed more than four million times since it began circulating on YouTube (Youtube.com 2008). The clip contains footage and audio of Obama's now famous "Yes We Can" speech, spliced with celebrity cameos reciting the speech and layered with vocal harmonies singing along to the speech. Compiled and produced by Will.I.Am. of the Black Eyed Peas, the clip also features R&B singer John Legend, actress Scarlett Johansson, members of the cast of the TV series *Grey's Anatomy*, and rapper/actor Common—an appealing group for younger voters especially. The clip even sparked a spoof mocking Republican John McCain: set to the same style and tune, a group of actors are shown reading McCain's "A Time of War" speech, then reacting with confusion as the candidate references the Beach Boys singing "bomb, bomb, bomb, bomb, bomb Iran."

This attack on McCain, however, illustrates the inevitable downside to viral video: it leaves no one safe. One of the most notorious (and moving) ads in the 2008 election was the "Clinton 1984" clip made by an unaffiliated Obama supporter, which compared the former first lady to Big Brother. This attack on Senator Clinton was viewed by more than five million people on YouTube and appeared on countless other Web site and on television news programs. Once a video gets out there and goes viral, it is very difficult for a campaign to stop it. Another example is Obama's "Just Words" speech plagiarism scandal. After Senator Obama was accused of plagiarizing pieces of Massachusetts Governor Deval Patrick's 2006 speech, videos of both speeches, to highlight the similarities, were running rampant on YouTube. This proves that anyone with Internet access and a creative idea now has the ability to make a splash in the upcoming election. Although most will view this development as a positive for the political process, it can hinder a campaign's ability to promote and control its official platform and, in the parlance of political operatives, to "control the message." But just as the Internet provides a platform for opponents to craft a viral video attack, it also gives candidates the chance to push back in the same manner. The informal nature and low cost of the Internet allows candidates to respond to attack clips with funny and edgy comeback videos.

Recent advancements in live streaming Web-video technology have helped give Internet users the power to broadcast live wherever there's a camera and an Internet connection. The Mike Gravel camp took advantage of this technology when MSNBC denied Gravel, widely perceived as a fringe candidate, an invitation to the Drexel University Democratic debate in Philadelphia during the 2008 campaign. Gravel and his supporters set up at a café down the street from Drexel and broadcast their own debate live on the Internet via UStream. As this and other examples suggest, technological developments that facilitate the creation and dissemination of visual content can be deployed in meaningful ways on the campaign trail. They also have powerful implications for the electoral process overall. By eliminating financial barriers, giving partial control of media to ordinary people, and allowing candidates new tools to enhance their image, personality, and character, digital video is a viable alternative to traditional media during election time. When asked in one survey in 2007 about the sources of political news, 43 percent of likely voters said the Internet—"placing digital video increasingly at the center of every campaign, every election" (Sender 2007).

Blogs, Citizen Journalism, Online News Sources

It seems so odd to think that just four years ago having a "blog" on a campaign Web site was considered forward-thinking. To give some perspective, the total number of blogs at the end of the 2004 election was estimated to be less than 1.4 million. In April 2007, that number stood at over 71 million and continues to grow at an estimated rate of 120,000 new blogs created worldwide each day (D. Sifry 2007).

From the onset of the 2008 campaign, Internet tactics of the major presidential candidates have been examined, critiqued, and dissected by the blogs, the mainstream media, and the other candidates. Web sites like Technocrati, TechPresident, New Politics Institute, and countless others are devoted to helping track the impact of Internet campaigning by charting hits, views, and content relating to the 2008 presidential candidates and analyzing the latest trends and changes. Such sites are often a valuable resource for campaign advisors, who realize it is imperative to have a successful Internet strategy, not only to improve credibility among the younger, hipper crowds, but also to show an understanding and appreciation for the sense of grassroots change that can come from the Web.

Campaigns can benefit from blogs by incorporating them into their candidate Web sites and by reaching out to independent bloggers and blog readers with a smart marketing plan. Most of the users who view political content on the Internet are those who are seeking it out in the first place. But there are clever ways to bring voters who were not necessarily looking for information about a candidate to his or her Web site. For example, Senator John McCain used paid Internet advertisements to garner more than forty million unique impressions to his Web site (MarketingCharts.com 2007). Candidates can also gain exposure by creating "linked buttons" for blogs and online news sites. Well-known bloggers can display their support for Obama by adding an image link leading to the candidate's Web site on their blog page, which might inspire loyal readers to click and learn more.

Obviously, campaigns will continue to use blogs to promote their messages, track down supporters, and build up their base. But perhaps more important is the way blogs will continue to shape campaigns. Many independent bloggers and group blogs have become credible news sources (for example, DailyKos and The Drudge Report). The Huffington Post, one of the most widely read left-wing online news Web sites and blog aggregators, demonstrates how much the credibility and content quality of news-blogging is continuously improving. The "Off the Bus" section of the Huffington Post offered extensive coverage of the 2008 election by well-known bloggers and allows for a wide range of opinions from the public in the "comments" section. Catering to some of these Web sites can really boost the profile of lesser-known candidates and build recognition. One of the most beneficial things about blogs is that they are often willing to work (for free) for the candidates they support. They find and post favorable articles, create fundraising drives, and build awareness to support the politicians of their choice. In the future, these blogs will continue to have a substantial impact on the electoral process, as they can be the opinion leaders in today's political climate.

Blogs also provide a social aspect for their readers. Many like-minded individuals visit the Web sites not only to receive information but also to present it. People enjoy posting and debating on the sites, and they discuss events that are important to the election. Citizen journalism platforms (such as GroundReport, Global Voices Online) encourage ordinary citizens to report the news as they witness it and publish to the international Web-community; many who are disillusioned with the mainstream media turn to these sources for alternative political coverage. Big media's crucial role in campaigns is now supplemented by the easily accessible and unregulated nature of Internet news blogs, which had a massive impact on the 2008 race.

Web sites like MyDD.org, OpenDebates.org, and WhyTuesday.org invite Internet users to help keep tabs on politicians and mainstream media spinners, and they encourage their readers to join in causes aimed at improving democracy. For example, many bloggers and watchdog Web sites blew the whistle on CNN when the network failed to ask any questions about global warming during a CNN presidential debate sponsored by the coal front group Americans for Balanced Energy Choices (ThinkProgress.org 2008). The charges were refuted by CNN, which claimed that sponsors had no influence on the debate questions—but these statements only prompted further criticism on Web discussion boards and comment walls. Such developments suggest the influence of big media (and big business) on election coverage may be changing. Even as citizens and observers often question the reliability of information disseminated through these new vehicles, the blogosphere and the online participatory journalism community are not only the new watchdogs of the media; they also have the capacity to democratize and decentralize election news and information.

Social Networking

Social scientists have long recognized the importance of social networks in influencing political behavior (Huckfeldt and Sprague 1995). In recent years, advances in Web-based technology have enabled the formation of online social networks that operate much like traditional communities in which members meet (virtually), discuss ideas, exchange information, and even impel each other to action. These online social networks, facilitated by Web sites like MySpace, MeetUp, Facebook, and YouTube, engage all sorts of topics and events, and politics is no exception. The creation of sizable online networks formed around candidates, issues, and ideas without regard to geographic boundaries is a feature of modern campaigns that cannot be ignored. Creating a profile on the largest social networking sites like Facebook and MySpace (as most of the 2008 presidential candidates did) can bring the campaign to some supporters who would not necessarily seek out the candidate's Web site on their own. The ultimate goal after finding "friends" on these networks is to bring them back to the original campaign Web site and encourage them to interact with others and sign up for e-mails.

Candidates can also interact with supporters through applications on social networking sites. The creation of a Hillary Clinton interactive Facebook application, or group, which could be mounted on a Facebook user's profile, could spark the interest of the user's "friends" as the additions appear in their social network minifeed. The ABC News Facebook application allowed users to participate in debates, answer surveys about the election, voice their support for a candidate, discuss important issues, and even have the chance to get their responses aired during an ABC News broadcast. Not only was the information collected from applications like this useful in analyzing the importance of certain issues and the concerns of voters, it also helped candidates to tap into a voter base that may not have been so interested in politics.

Countless "groups" have also been created on the major social networks aimed at garnering support for specific candidates, and many have enhanced the legitimacy of their causes by attracting a large membership. When comedian Stephen Colbert announced his presidential candidacy in October 2007, a sixteen-year-old high school student from Alabama created the "1 Million Strong for Colbert" Facebook group, joined by more than 1.1 million members in one week (Stelter 2007). The high volume of wall posts, group participants, and discussion boards caused the site to remove the group temporarily, and it reached the attention of the mainstream media. The Caucus (the political blog of the *New York Times*) echoed the importance of user-driven networks in generating intensity around just about any cause, reporting, "Stephen Colbert's presidential candidacy may be phony, but his supporters are very, very real" (Stelter 2007). Of course, this type of intensity can be directed against candidates as well as for them, like the "Stop Hillary Clinton" Facebook group, which, in early 2008, was just shy of its goal of reaching a million members by Election Day 2008. This is just a consequence of user-generated content.

Users visit Facebook and MySpace primarily to check up on their friends, keep in touch, and post personal photos. For this reason, the impact of social network sites like MySpace and Facebook will remain limited in some respects. Even if candidates have whip-smart profiles and generate impressive numbers of friends, this may not necessarily translate into votes. In a social environment like Facebook, there is still not much in the way of political discourse. Users on social networking sites are more concerned with detagging unflattering pictures of themselves; they are not seeking the answers to difficult political questions. If candidates can find a way to translate a Facebook group into something more tangible (like a MeetUp. com group that allows users with similar interests in defined geographies to meet), the potential for impact may increase.

The creation of MyBarackObama.com in the 2008 presidential election cycle was a pioneering example along these lines. The Obama campaign capitalized on the benefits of a social networking site while simultaneously maintaining control over content. Obama supporters were able to connect to one another, recruit friends, organize meetings, rallies, and fund-raising drives, and offer feedback to the candidate, all while providing the campaign with a mass of information about their supporter base. Social networking sites in general can benefit a campaign by cultivating and nurturing a relationship with its base supporters. By going to the platforms where supporters are, candidates provide voters with a connection to the campaign at no cost to the user. They do not have to open a specific Web page and search for Hillary Clinton; instead, they can simply sign into their MySpace page—just as they do regularly—and find the latest information on Senator Clinton's profile if they so choose. Other candidates are likely to adopt this model as they develop their social networks. These networks are changing politics, as election events flood the Internet social scene and users achieve "friend" status with the candidates and their teams.

Interaction and Information

Besides encouraging fund-raising from first-time donors, a smartly designed Web site and new media strategy also give a campaign ample opportunity to track and communicate with its most ardent supporters. In the past, candidates would craft their voter lists by going door-to-door or having volunteers stand in a park, and patching the pieces together in a central database. While some might have been hesitant to give out their personal information to strangers in the past, the Internet has become a place where many feel secure offering up cell phone numbers and e-mail addresses. Campaigns obviously initially track their supporters when they visit the site and sign up for e-mails, but there are many other ways to find them online as well. Once people are on the e-mail or texting list, candidates can send out e-mails encouraging specific actions on an issue and see how well it plays with their base supporters. If the campaign tracks the reaction and notices response is high, the campaign may infer that it would be wise to emphasize a specific issue or quality. Used correctly, these blast e-mails can be used to gain at least some understanding of what voters care about.

For many campaigns, a key benefit of new media and the Web is the massive amount of information they can provide to potential voters at the click of a button. If there is a particularly vicious (or false) attack made on a candidate, the Internet provides a platform to dispel the claim. Campaigns can use their e-mail lists to send a message or a text to supporters urging them to take action. Never before has there been a way to reach out to so many people so quickly. Supporters often enjoy being involved and being asked to take action, and capitalizing on this interactivity can also be used to build enthusiasm. Campaigns generally welcome this interaction and encourage posts on their official blogs. In fact, candidates in 2008 (for example, Barack Obama and John McCain) even "favorited" user-generated videos on their YouChoose'08 profiles in an effort to show that ordinary citizens are a crucial part of the operation and to recognize these users' contributions. Senator Obama's official Web site even had a section simply called "People" where users can click on a group like "Faith" or "Students" to watch stories about volunteers. Campaigns realize it is crucial to provide information to voters, but it is also useful to absorb it from them as well. As Howard Dean, a pioneer in using online technology in his 2004 presidential bid, has put it, "it's not about communicating our message to you anymore; it's about listening to you first before we formulate the message" (Schulman 2007). Campaigns that figure out ways to involve voters in the process will likely reap rewards for doing so.

Moreover, one of the keys about the Internet and other new media is just how personal they can be. Ordinary people can visit blogs and citizen-news platforms like MyDD, GroundReport, and Global Voices Online and find other people who are disenfranchised with mainstream media coverage. Voters might view video profiles of volunteers on Obama's Web site and really connect with a story about "Betty in Arkansas." Clinton supporters in New York can receive a text message alerting them to an upcoming appearance where the senator will speak to them and hundreds of other union members. Successful campaigns will continue to utilize all of the information they have available to micro-target and personalize as many messages as possible.

Looking Ahead

The 2004 Dean campaign and its Internet revolutionary leader, Joe Trippi, recognized the power of the Internet and tools like blogging and social networking to create a grassroots movement previously unseen in presidential elections. Now, the 2008 presidential candidates are taking these strategies above and beyond.

Critics of the Internet and new media strategies are mindful of the medium's limitations. Perhaps the most challenging critique is the debate about access: the digital divide remains palpable. And even for those with online access, using the Internet for political purposes is not a guarantee. A June 2007 survey conducted by Nucleus Research and KnowledgeStorm found that that just 5 percent of respondents reported using YouTube as a source of election information; only 19 percent visit candidates' Web sites, and 72 percent still prefer sources such as newspapers and magazines (Nucleus Research and KnowledgeStorm 2007). Many voters, particularly older Americans, who also happen to vote with greater frequency, are simply not watching online videos, using text messages, or even accessing the Internet. Thus, candidates are wise to continue to rely on old-fashioned techniques like door-to-door canvassing, stump speeches, and the good old thirty-second television spots in combination with new media strategies.

Nonetheless, the Internet is influencing elections and campaigns in ways that cannot be ignored. So how can candidates adapt and benefit from these developments? The 2008 election suggests that the Internet now stands on its own as a valuable medium that can influence a nontrivial number of voters. Obviously, campaigns may be unwise to rely exclusively on the Web for electioneering purposes, but campaign organizations that use the Internet to supplement the mainstream media efforts may achieve maximum impact at the polls.

The inevitable downside of the Internet for campaigns is that the days of complete message control may be at an end. Campaigns must now be vigilant to monitor and respond to losses of message control or damaging information that may be rooted in online exchanges or activity. Campaign organizations ignore these attacks at their peril. Political operations must also find balance and not alienate their supporters by oversaturating them with online communications.

The Internet and associated technology that are transforming the landscape of contemporary campaigns and elections are here to stay. Campaign organizations that toss off new media tricks as gimmicks to persuade young voters will risk being left behind. In 2000, 36 percent of voters aged eighteen to twenty-four voted, and by 2004, 47 percent of the same age bracket participated (Sender 2007). As the generational shift to a voter pool made up increasingly of voters who have grown up relying on the Internet occurs, the online electioneering will continue to take on a whole new meaning in campaigns. Jarvis (2007) reports that one in three voters under the age of thirty-six relies on the Internet as their main source of political information. But it is not just about young voters. Increasingly, older Americans are turning to the Internet for political purposes. One study conducted in January 2008 by the Pew Research Center for the People and the Press revealed that 29 percent of likely primary voters aged fifty to sixty-five had viewed online videos about candidates or the election (Pew 2008). These trends are likely to continue.

In the end, candidates and campaign operatives will need to accept that they may no longer be able to dominate and direct the online discourse. They can do their best to participate and keep up, but, ultimately, the Internet is a medium for the people and by the people. Faceless, nameless bloggers can wreak havoc on entire candidacies. Simply put, in this brave new world, there are many cooks in the kitchen. Candidates will have to be on their best behavior twenty-four hours a day; any minor flub caught on video can be spliced, edited, and aired over and over, causing irreparable damage to a campaign. Certainly, there are times when an efficiently run operation will guide political conversations, but at other times it will spend months trying to downplay harmful comments taken out of context (examples from the 2008 presidential election cycle include Mike Huckabee's comments on HIV and Ron Paul's remarks about racism), or a *Saturday Night Live* drag queen skit gone wrong. This is simultaneously the blessing and the curse of

the Internet, and many advocates for democracy might say this is exactly as
it should be.

Organization of This Volume

Surely there are many other important ways in which technology and the
Internet are revolutionizing contemporary political campaigns all over the
world. This chapter has focused on key developments taking place in the
context of the spirited, 2008 presidential campaign in the United States to
highlight five broad areas in which technology appears to be exerting the
greatest impact on political campaigns. The main lesson from the 2008 election cycle, during which the Internet and related technology have arguably
been most mature, is that the technology offers campaigns unprecedented
opportunities but also has limitations and potential pitfalls. In a word, campaigns are wise to proceed enthusiastically but with caution.

In the chapters that follow, the authors reflect more directly on many
of these trends and developments and probe several additional aspects of
this phenomenon and its implications. This book is organized into four
main sections. Part 1 will discuss developments in candidate Web sites,
the main adaptation political campaigns have widely embraced. Part 2 will
present details about the effectiveness of technology-enabled mechanisms
designed to mobilize voters to vote or to contribute to political campaigns.
Part 3 will offer readers a comparative perspective by focusing on the ways
in which technology is being used cross-nationally. Part 4 will discuss the
newest developments (blogs and social networking sites including Facebook,
MySpace and YouTube) in interpersonal communications technology that
are being utilized by campaigns.

Part 1 of the volume begins with a series of selections that examine
the most direct form of candidate communications online—candidate Web
sites. Three chapters explore how candidates for political office at various
levels and across time use Web sites to promote their candidacies. James
Druckman, Martin Kifer and Michael Parkin analyze how, and perhaps more
importantly, why, U.S. congressional candidates used Web innovations in the
2002 and 2004 campaigns. In a similar study that offers some insights about
developments over time, Jeff Gulati and Christine Williams examine candidate Web sites in the 2006 elections. Taken together, the chapters reveal
similarities as well as key differences, even within the relatively short span
of three election cycles. The subsequent chapter, by Chapman Rackaway,
investigates how candidates for state legislative office use technology in
their campaigns. Rackaway also explores the factors that determine technology use in these campaigns and assesses the impact of the use of technology-
specific variables on electoral outcomes. The final chapter in this section,

by Hun Park and James Perry, examines evidence about the relationship between campaign Web sites and civic engagement, broadly defined.

In Part 2, the contributors investigate how technology-enabled tools—including e-mails, text messages, Web site features, and online political advertising—mobilize voters to political action. In the area of political fund-raising, the Internet has created new opportunities for campaigns in recent election cycles, and candidates at all levels have been capitalizing on this technology to raise unparalleled sums online. In the first chapter of Part 2, Daniel Bergan and I examine online fund-raising in the 2004 presidential election. We compare the demographic, socioeconomic, and political characteristics of online and offline donors and consider the degree to which online fund-raising has affected the composition of the donor pool. We also comment on how campaigns are mobilizing donors to contribute online.

Web-based communications also provide political campaigns with fresh tools to mobilize voters. David Nickerson reports the findings of a series of field experiments conducted to investigate the extent to which e-mail communications can boost registration and turnout rates. Another field experiment, described by Allison Dale and Aaron Strauss in the next chapter, explores whether text messaging can effectively mobilize voters to action. In the final chapter in this part of the volume, Michael Cornfield and Kate Kaye comment on developments in campaigns' use of online political advertising and on its effectiveness.

Two chapters in Part 3 offer readers some international perspective about how political campaigns abroad are adapting to incorporate advancements in technology. Steffen Albrecht, Maren Lübcke, and Rasco Hartig-Perschke of Hamburg University, investigate how Weblogs were used in Germany's 2005 Bundestag elections. In the next selection, Sandra Suárez analyzes how text messaging was used in the 2004 elections in Spain. Contributors in Part 4 reflect on the latest developments in interpersonal communications technology that are being utilized. Kevin Pirch offers some observations about the impact of blogs in the 2006 U.S. Senate race in Connecticut. In the following chapter, Vassia Gueorguieva, discusses the benefits, challenges, and influence of social networking Web sites on election campaigns, focusing on YouTube and MySpace. Allison Slotnick's chapter focuses on Facebook in the context of the 2008 presidential nomination race. The next chapter, by Christine Williams and Jeff Gulati, explores more systematically the impact of social networking sites on election outcomes.

Taken together, the chapters in this volume treat a wide range of specialized topics that provide insights about the ways in which technology is influencing political campaigns. The authors explore campaigns at many levels, over time, and cross-nationally, and they advance analyses that utilize a range of sophisticated methodologies. The selections blend theory, description, and rigorous empirical analysis that offer readers comprehensive and reliable assessments and contribute meaningfully to readers' understanding of the realities associated with the adoption of technological advancements for electoral purposes. By and large, the selections in the volume reveal both the opportunities and the limitations of the use of technology in campaigns. Even as some critics may contend that the Internet remains a work in progress, "far from being a decisive political force" (Kerbel 2005, 89), the chapters demonstrate that it is a formidable medium that has inspired tremendous and influential innovations in campaign communications. Analysts are wise to continue to monitor and vigilantly assess the uses and impact of technological innovations on political campaigns.

REFERENCES

E.politics.com. 2006. "What We Can Learn from Online Politics from the 2006 Election." November 6 (accessed June 29, 2007, at www.epolitics.com).

Huckfeldt, R., and J. Sprague. 1995. *Citizens, Politics and Social Communication: Information and Influence in an Election Campaign.* New York: Cambridge University Press.

Jarvis, J. 2007. "The Guardian Column: The YouTube Campaign." *Buzzmachine.* January 29 (accessed February 15, 2008, at http://www.buzzmachine.com/guardian-column-the-youtube-campaign).

Kerbel, M. 2005. "The Media: The Challenge and Promise of Internet Politics." In *The Elections of 2004*, ed. Michael Nelson. Washington, DC: CQ Press.

Luo, M. 2007. "Democrats Lead in Raising Money Online." *New York Times.* July13 (accessed March 10, 2008, at http://query.nytimes.com/gst/fullpage.html?res=980 DE4D71E3EF930A25754C0A9619C8B63&sec=&spon=&pagewanted=1).

MarketingCharts.com. 2007. "Romney Leads in TV Ads, Obama Dominates Online." July 10 (accessed March 10, 2008, at http://www.marketingcharts.com/television/romney-leads-in-tv-ads-obama-dominates-online-921).

Marre, K. 2008. "Clinton Raising $1 Million Per Day This Month." *The Hill.* February 14 (accessed March 10, 2008, at http://thehill.com/campaign-2008/mcauliffe-clinton-raising-1-million-per-day-this-month-2008–02–14.html).

MacAskill, E. 2007. "U.S. Election 2008: Hillary and the Democrats Choose Web as the New Deal: Party Hopefuls Signal their White House Intentions with Videos on Internet." *The Guardian.* January 22, 17.

Melber, A. 2008. "Obama Downloads $7.9 Million From MoveOn and Web Donors." *The Nation.* February 7 (accessed online March 10, 2008, at http://www.thenation.com/blogs/campaignmatters?bid=45&pid=281732).

Newman, A. 2007. "A Theme Song for Clinton." *New York Times.* June 4 (accessed March 10, 2008, at http://www.nytimes.com/2007/06/04/technology/04song.html?scp=1 &sq=A+Theme+Song+for+Clinton&st=nyt).

Nucleus Research and KnowledgeStorm. 2007. The Votes Are In: Traditional Media Trumps Internet for 2008: Press Release (accessed March 10, 2008, at http://nucleusresearch.com/news/press-releases/the-votes-are-in-traditional-media-trumps-internet-for-2008).

Pew Research Center for People and the Press. 2008. "Internet's Broader Role in Campaign 2008." Report issued January 11 (accessed March 25, 2008, at http://people-press.org/report/384/internets-broader-role-in-campaign-2008).

Schatz, A. 2007. "Long Race Forces Ad Ingenuity." *Wall Street Journal*. June 19.

Schulman, D. 2007. "Meet the New Bosses." *Mother Jones*. June 20 (accessed March 10, 2008, at http://www.motherjones.com/news/feature/2007/07/meet_the_new_bosses.html).

Seelye, K. 2007. "New Presidential Debate Site? Clearly YouTube." *NYTimes.com*. June 13 (accessed March 10, 2008, at http://www.nytimes.com/2007/06/13/us/politics/13cnd-youtube.html?_r=1&oref=slogin).

Sender, J. 2007. "Viral Video in Politics: Case Studies on Creating CompellingVideo." *New Politics Institute*. January 9 (accessed March 10, 2008, at http://www.new politics.net/node/236?full_report=1).

Sifry, D. 2007. "The State of the Live Web, April 2007." *Sifry.com*. April 5 (accessed March 10, 2008, at http://www.sifry.com/alerts/archives/000493.html).

Sifry, M. 2008. "Obama, the Internet, and the Decline of Big Money and Big Media." *Techpresident*. February 6 (accessed March 10, 2008, at http://www.techpresident.com/blog/entry/21320/obama_the_internet_and_the_decline_of_big_money_and_big_media).

Stelter, B. 2007 "Colbert's Facebook Flock." *The Caucus*. October 25 (accessed March 10, 2008, at http://thecaucus.blogs.nytimes.com/2007/10/25/colberts-facebook-flock).

Techpresident.com. 2008a. "Weekly traffic share via Hitwise." February 12 (accessed March 10, 2008, at http://www.techpresident.com/scrape_plot/hitwise).

_____. 2008b. "YouTube Stats: Presidential Candidates on YouTube Powered by Tubemogel." February 15 (accessed March 10, 2008, at http://www.techpresident.com/youtube).

TheHotlineBlog. 2007. "On the Download: Million Dollar Web Campaigns." *National Journal*. July 30 (accessed March 10, 2008 at http://hotlineblog.nationaljournal.com/archives/2007/07/on_the_download_32.html).

ThinkProgress.org. 2008. "No Questions on Global Warming Asked at CNN's Coal Industry-Sponsored Presidential Debates." *ThinkProgress*. January 22 (accessed March 10, 2008, at http://thinkprogress.org/2008/01/22/coal-cnn).

YouTube.com. 2008. "YouChoose'08: Candidate Videos." YouTube (accessed March 10, 2008, at http://www.youtube.com/youchoose).

Candidate Web Sites

In recent election cycles, campaign Web sites for federal candidates in the United States have become ubiquitous. Online presence in the form of Web sites has also expanded considerably for candidates seeking statewide and municipal offices. The selections in part 1 of this volume advance a series of systematic analyses of candidate Web sites. The authors devote considerable attention to candidate Web sites, as these are the dominant form of direct, online communications from candidates to voters. Analyses of the content and features on candidate Web sites offer glimpses into candidate strategy as well as into a campaign's outlook about voters. Strategic reasons for incorporating–or not incorporating–certain features (like interactivity, for example) or content elements on candidate Web sites often can be revealed through analyses of the sort advanced by the authors. Moreover, as indicators of campaign quality, Web site design and content can be as telling as examinations of other forms of direct candidate communications that have been studied extensively, including television advertisements, speeches, and press releases. It is also useful to study the factors associated with various types and levels of Web site content.

Candidate Web sites are also important for another reason. Many of the innovations that campaigns are capitalizing on are accessed through or otherwise connected to the main candidate Web site. Candidate Web sites in contemporary and future campaigns are likely to be the main gateway to candidates and their organizations. To the extent that campaigns wish to direct supporters and traffic to other areas–fund-raising, mobilization, and organizing, for example–they will do so from the entry point of the main site. As such, candidate Web sites facilitate many of the developments discussed in this book.

From a practical perspective, campaign operatives will find the authors' observations about candidate Web sites useful for guidance about the implementation of Web site content and design.

2

The Technological Development of Candidate Web Sites

How and Why Candidates Use Web Innovations

JAMES N. DRUCKMAN
MARTIN J. KIFER
MICHAEL PARKIN

The Internet has become a vital resource in American political campaigns. It provides candidates with unmediated and inexpensive access to voters while also offering new technological options for communication and information presentation. Candidates now have the opportunity to create Web sites with features such as multiple media, personalized information, and even two-way communication. While these innovations seem promising, the decision to use them is far from automatic. Candidates must carefully weigh practical and political considerations before incorporating new technologies into their Web sites, because each innovation has advantages and drawbacks.

In this chapter, we investigate how and why political candidates use a host of emerging Web technologies. Prior research focuses on a single campaign and either offers a rich description of the technologies used on a small group of sites (for example, King 1999; Cornfield 2004; Bimber and Davis 2003) or focuses on a specific feature found across a wider sample of online campaigns (for example, Dulio, Goff, and Thurber 1999; Schneider and Foot 2002).[1] We take a more comprehensive approach by exploring multiple technological features found across a large and representative sample of congressional campaign Web sites over two elections. Specifically, we analyze 444 U.S. House and Senate candidate Web sites from the 2002 and 2004 campaigns. We focus on the extent to which candidates have moved beyond the "electronic brochure" format by incorporating various presentation (such as video and audio) and interactive features (such as personalized information and two-way communication).[2] This provides insight into how candidates approach technology and balance the various costs and benefits associated with each innovation.

We then examine the conditions that motivate candidates to use emerging technologies by supplementing our Web data with detailed information about candidates, races, and constituencies. We investigate how the decision to use certain features is affected by things like available resources (such as campaign funds), increased ease of using technologies (such as developments over time), demand effects (such as voter constituency), and strategic dynamics (such as race competitiveness). Considering both practical and political motivations provides a clearer picture of when candidates will use certain technologies and when they will avoid them.[3]

We start in the next section with an overview of campaigning on the Web. We then discuss how and why candidates might use Web technology before describing our data collection and reporting the results of our analysis. We end with a discussion that highlights the board implications of our findings.

Campaigning on the Web

In less than a decade, it has become virtually mandatory for candidates to have a campaign Web site. In 1998, only 35 percent of major-party House candidates and 72 percent of major-party Senate candidates posted campaign Web sites (Kamarck 1999, 100). By 2004, these numbers had jumped to 81 percent and 92 percent respectively (Goldsmith 2004; also see Foot and Schneider 2006, 7–11), leading some to suggest that "The question is no longer whether candidates for major office will have a Web site, but what the Web site will look like and how it will be used" (Williams, Aylesworth, and Chapman 2002, 43; also see Williams 2003).

Campaign Web sites have attracted an increasing number of users, and there is some evidence to suggest that they influence voters and, thus, election outcomes. Williams (2003, 4) calculates that individual Senate candidate Web sites, for example, received between 1,000 and 800,000 visits in 2000, while just two years later the number of hits ranged from 6,854 to 1,615,819.[4] Multiplying these visitation statistics with the number of candidate Web sites that now exist, and noting that Web site visitors tend to be quite politically active (for example, Norris 2004), one gets the sense that online campaigns may have notable political influence that is sure to grow. Moreover, candidate Web sites undoubtedly affect many more voters indirectly through activists who disseminate information (see Foot and Schneider 2006, 86 and 129–155; Gordon 2006) and, perhaps most importantly, journalists who frequently visit these sites to gather material (see Ireland and Nash 2001, 14–15; Schneider and Foot 2002).

The Web's growing prominence in American political campaigns affects candidates who must decide how to use this relatively new medium and the emerging technologies it offers. It is important to understand how candidates make these decisions because the technologies they select will ultimately affect how voters and journalists receive and process campaign information.[5] Indeed, online campaigns provide an intriguing venue for analyzing the interaction between candidates and observers. In the next section, we draw on campaign and information processing research to explain some of the reasons that candidates might have for using or avoiding technologies given their presumed effect on Web site visitors.

Web Site Technology

To gauge the extent to which candidate Web sites utilize emerging technology, we examine whether they incorporate features that would be impossible to include in a single, static paper brochure. This approach has been used by others (for example, Kamarck 1999; Foot, Schneider, Xenos, and Dougherty 2003), although we clarify the "electronic brochure" standard by investigating whether candidates are using particular presentation and interactive features. The specific presentation features include multimedia content and display options, while the interactive features include personalization functions, external links, and two-way communication. In constructing their Web sites, candidates make strategic choices about each of these dimensions based, in large part, on each innovation's perceived costs and benefits.

The Internet offers a platform to bring together multiple forms of media that help to present information vibrantly. Audio clips, for example, enable candidates to personalize and highlight certain information. Similarly, candidates who opt to include dynamic visuals, such as videos, likely do so in order to draw the audience's attention to the display (Graber 2001) and possibly to accentuate perceptions of the candidate's personal qualities (Keeter 1987; Druckman 2003). Multimedia features can make a candidate's Web site more engaging, but they also require some technological skill and available resources, albeit not much. Moreover, audio and video have the potential drawback of distracting visitors from important information found in the text. In this way, moving beyond an "electronic brochure" may work against ensuring that key messages are clearly received.

Candidates also must decide how much information to provide and how often to update information. The Internet is virtually limitless in terms of providing information, and a frequently updated Web site allows candidates to get their message across and keep visitors interested so that they might return. In fact, Davis (1999, 116) notes, "A Web site that never (or only infrequently) changes will be visited once or twice and then abandoned. Voters will not return unless they believe that something new has happened" (also see Cornfield 2004, 26–27; Bimber and Davis 2003, 127–130). However, providing too much information can clutter the Web site and make it hard to navigate, while candidates must also consider the effort and expense associated with updating multiple pages of information (see, for example, Cornfield 2004, 25).

Interactivity

The Internet provides for interactivity, which enables users to actively engage the campaign and/or other users online. Stewart, Pavlou, and Ward (2002, 368) state that "perhaps the most interesting and novel attribute of the new media is their capability for interactivity, which is becoming increasingly more pronounced with the infusion of more-advanced communication media" (also see Tedesco 2004). Interactive features can engage users by granting them control, which stimulates attention and learning (see, for example, Southwell and Lee 2004, 645), although the attention may not be focused on the exact information the candidate prefers (Eveland and Dunwoody 2002).

Personalization is a form of interactivity in which users can personalize their engagement with the campaign through the Web site. Users may be given the opportunity to take a quiz, provide information, or move information around to suit their personal preferences. Candidate Web sites can also engage users through targeted marketing. Specifically, the Web site can solicit personal information from the user (for example, zip code, political leanings, attitudinal measures) and then send crafted messages designed for specific segments of the population. For example, if a user enters that he or she views education as the most important campaign issue, then the Web site could automatically produce messages about education (see Cornfield 2004, 42; Stewart, Pavlou, and Ward 2002, 368–369). All of these personalization features allow users to customize their interaction with the candidate's Web site. While personalization often enhances the persuasiveness of the candidate's message (O'Keefe 2002, 245–246), it can also create segments of incompletely informed voters who learn less about other aspects of the candidate's message (Chadwick 2006, 8). Personalization features can also be challenging to incorporate, as the technology is relatively new. Ultimately, personalization goes well beyond an "electronic brochure" by actively engaging users, but it may also lead to a less coherent understanding of the candidate's overall goals and intentions (Stromer-Galley 2000).

The trade-off between information control and interactive engagement arises to an even greater extent when it comes to providing external links. Users who enjoy freedom to explore will likely be more engaged with the site, although links also allow for more selectivity and limit the control over what specific information the audience accesses (see Tewksbury and

Althaus 2000, 458; Foot, Schneider, Dougherty, Xenos, and Larsen 2003). Of course, this also depends on exactly where the links lead. For example, links to voter registration Web sites and news articles that the campaign carefully selects are relatively safe in that the content is predictable and visitors are likely to return to the candidate's site (Foot and Schneider 2006, 59). However, links to a political party or presidential candidate are riskier because the campaign has no control over the information presented there and it may not be entirely consistent with the candidate's message (see Davis 1999, 101). External links are easy to incorporate, but candidates will have to think carefully about each individual link and its potential effect on Web site visitors.

Web interactivity involves not only content but also the possibility of communication between the Web site and its users, and/or between users themselves (what Bucy 2004 and Kaye and Johnson 2006, 149, call interpersonal interactivity). Communication through features such as message boards, forums, and live chats can certainly stimulate attention and enhance the likelihood of forming "online communities," which, as Howard Dean's 2004 presidential campaign showed, can have numerous benefits (see Trippi 2004; Tedesco 2004, 515; on persuasion and interactivity, see Stromer-Galley 2000; Stewart, Pavlou, and Ward 2002; O'Keefe 2002, 257). However, these features, again, allow for less control over the flow of information, require strong logistical capabilities, and may, in fact, be more technologically interesting than politically useful (see Davis 1999, 115).

New presentation and interactive technologies continue to develop, and many of them seem to have exciting political applications that enable candidates to move beyond the static "electronic brochure" format. However, each new innovation has trade-offs that the candidate must weigh. In some cases, the innovation may still be rather complicated so that only certain candidates can think about using it. In other cases, the tension is between retaining control over the message that visitors receive and the desire to develop an engaging Web site that stimulates interest and support. All of these are important considerations for any campaign, although, as we will discuss in the next section, there are factors that likely motivate candidates one way or the other.

Explaining Technological Choices

There are various possible determinants of the technological choices that candidates make for their Web sites. Indeed, candidates must consider both practical and political issues in making these decisions. For example, candidates need to think about the technical ease of using certain technologies as well as their cost, demand, and the political price they may exact. In this section, we elaborate on these considerations and discuss how they might affect choices to use emerging technologies.

Technology generally becomes easier to use with time. Improvements and advancements allow candidates to at least consider incorporating features that may have once been too complex. Therefore, time itself may be a determinant of using particular tools that were once considered complicated, like multimedia, personalization features, and two-way communication. For those elements that have always been quite simple (for example, external links, display options), time ought not to be much of a factor (see, for example, Foot and Schneider 2006, 158).

A number of candidate-level variables also might affect decisions about technology. To begin with, well-funded candidates may be more likely to use certain technologies—particularly complicated ones—because they can afford to pay for developing a sophisticated Web site. Conversely, candidates with limited campaign funds may wish to spend their money on things other than Web site technology (Bimber and Davis 2003, 27; Herrnson, Stokes-Brown, and Hindman 2007, 32). The candidate's party and gender may also influence technology decisions, although expectations for each are not entirely obvious. It may be the case that one party is more technologically savvy than the other (Puopolo 2001. 2034; Ireland and Nash 1999)[6] and that gender matters in the sense that it generates different approaches to campaigning (on gender, see, for example, Kahn 1996; Gulati and Treul 2003; Puopolo 2001, 2039). Incumbency status may also affect these decisions in that challengers may have a stronger inclination to use technology as a way of gaining ground on established incumbents (see, for example, Fenno 1996; Herrnson 2004; Herrnson Stokes-Brown, and Hindman 2007, 33 and 35).

Differences in the office level being contested may factor into the extent to which candidate Web sites go beyond the "electronic brochure" standard. Compared to House candidates, Senate candidates typically have larger constituencies and staffs that could, all else being equal, incline them toward more technologically sophisticated sites (see, for example, Dulio, Goff, and Thurber 1999; Bimber and Davis 2003, 26–27; Herrnson 2004). In fact, a larger staff may be particularly helpful with some of the more intricate features while a more diverse constituency may encourage Senate candidates to pay greater attention to personalization features.

At the district level, demand effects may influence candidates' decisions about technology. Income and education could be particularly important, as wealthy and well-educated districts tend to have more access to the Internet and thus greater familiarity with certain technologies (see Bimber and Davis 2003, 104–107; Foot and Schneider 2006, 171).[7] Candidates from districts with presumably less Internet acumen may not feel obligated to have complex sites or may, in fact, try to present simple sites to ensure their message reaches the intended audience (see Herrnson, Stoke-Brown, and Hindman 2007, 33). Partisanship in the district (such as percentage of Republicans/Democrats) is an obvious political consideration that might affect decisions about technology in that Republicans tend to be slightly more active online (Pew 2000).[8]

In terms of strategic political considerations, race competitiveness could have an important role to play in decisions about Web site technology. As races tighten, candidates must think more about the consequences of their decisions and try to stimulate voters while retaining control over their message. Technologies that do not severely compromise message control (for example, multimedia, display options) should be most commonly used in tight races where candidates have an incentive to employ features that make their Web sites more vibrant and engaging. Conversely, technologies that sacrifice message control (for example, personalization, external links, two-way communication) ought to be negatively associated with race competitiveness because candidates in tight races need to ensure that their message is clearly articulated and understood. For candidates in close races, message clarity may trump the extra stimulation that these features provide (see Foot and Schneider 2006, 172). Ultimately, race competitiveness may be a key factor in determining which technologies candidates use and which they avoid.

Data

To test these expectations about how and when candidates use Web technology, we examine data from an extensive content analysis of congressional candidate Web sites from the 2002 and 2004 campaigns. In each year, we identified every major-party Senate candidate Web site and took a random sample of major-party House candidate Web sites, stratified by region. A team of trained content analyzers then coded the sites, rendering a total sample of 444 candidate Web sites—59 Senate and 116 House Web sites for 2002, and 67 Senate and 202 House Web sites for 2004.[9] Coders analyzed the entirety of each individual Web site and identified a series of political and technological indicators.[10] We then supplemented these Web data with information about the candidates, races, and districts.

We use data from the Web sites to capture the key presentation and interactive dimensions previously discussed. To measure presentation features, we created a "multimedia" variable that indicates whether the candidate's Web site included a video and/or audio file. We also measured display features, in particular, whether the site had more than one page ("pages") and if there was information on the site that appeared to be updated ("new info"). Our "personalization" measure indicates whether the site included any of the following options to personalize the visitor's interaction with the site: to take a quiz; personalize information for targeted marketing;[11] arrange information; add quantitative data; and/or add qualitative information. Our second interactive feature measures the use of external "links" to one of the following: the candidate's political party; a presidential campaign Web site (2004 only); a news outlet (2004 only); a registration Web site; and/or any other external site. We focus specifically on the "party link" in parts of our analysis as the particular target of this link may be quite consequential and it was measured over both campaigns. Finally, we measure the use of "two-way communication" features as the existence of a live chat function, a candidate chat function, and/or a forum (that is, message board).[12]

To get a sense of what motivates candidates to use these features, we add to our Web data with various measures for each candidate. Measures for "2004" (year), "Senate" (office level), "Democrat" (candidate's party), and "Female" (candidate gender) are all straightforward dichotomous (0/1) variables taken from *The Almanac of American Politics* (Barone and Cohen 2003, 2005; Barone, Cohen, and Cook 2001) where necessary. "Incumbency" is measured with dummy variables indicating whether or not the candidate is a "challenger," "open seat candidate," or "incumbent" (we exclude the challenger category in our multivariate analyses). At the district level, we measure "district partisanship" based on the percentage of votes in the district (or state) cast for George W. Bush in 2004 as reported in *The Almanac of American Politics*. The district-level measures for "income" and "education" come from the 2000 Census. "District income" is the average household income (in tens of thousands of dollars) in the district (or state) and "district education" is the percentage of people in the district (or state) with at least a high school education. We measured each candidate's available resources with data from the Federal Election Commission on the amount of money each raised in millions of dollars. Finally, we used data *from The Almanac of American Politics* to create a measure of race competitiveness. We took the difference in the vote totals from the winner and loser and then, following convention (Jacobson 1992, 33; Foot and Schneider 2006 173), broke the races into thirds: "highly competitive," "mildly competitive," and "noncompetitive."[13]

Table 2.1 provides descriptive information about these measures. Our sample includes 175 candidate Web sites from 2002 (39.4 percent) and 269 from 2004 (60.6 percent). A little over 28 percent of the sites were from Senate candidates, 46.4 percent came from Democrats, and 15.1 percent were from female candidates. In terms of candidate status, 43.8 percent of our sample were incumbents, 41.3 percent were challengers, and 14.9 percent were candidates involved in open-seat races. The district-level percentage

TABLE 2.1

Descriptive Data

Variable	Number of candidates	
Year	444	2002 = 39.4% 2004 = 60.6%
Office	444	House = 71.6% Senate = 28.4%
Party	444	Democrat = 46.4% Republican = 53.6% Third party = 0.2%[a]
Incumbency status	443	Incumbent = 43.8% Challenger = 41.3% Open seat = 14.9%
Gender	444	Male = 84.9% Female = 15.1%
Average district partisanship (% for Bush in 2004)	444	53.57% (10.80%)[b]
Average district income	444	$54,053.90 ($11,678.07)
Average district education (% with more than high school)	444	81.43% (5.98%)
Average funds raised (millions of dollars)	426	$2.03 ($2.87)
Average race competitiveness (margin of victory)	444	29.42% (19.66%)

[a]The data set includes Bernard "Bernie" Sanders (Independent-VT), who was the incumbent member of the House of Representatives for Vermont's at-large seat, making him a "major party candidate" for his district.

[b]Standard deviations in parentheses.

of Bush voters in 2004 ranged from 13 percent to 86 percent with an average score of 53.6 percent. Average district-level income ranged from $34,962 to $109,760 with a mean of $54,054, while the percentage of the population in each district (or state) with at least a high school education ranged from 50.4 percent to 92.5 percent with a mean of 81.4 percent. Finally, the average candidate in our sample raised a little over $2 million (2.03 million), while the average margin of victory was 29.4 points.

The Prevalence of Web Technology

To what extent have candidates moved beyond the "electronic brochure" standard by using emerging Web technologies? Table 2.2 reports the percentage of congressional candidate Web sites in our sample that utilized individual technological features. The results are broken into year and office level to provide further insight into possible trends.

Table 2.2 shows that, in terms of multimedia features, 43.7 percent of candidate Web sites went beyond static presentations (text, pictures, or graphics) to include dynamic content such as audio and/or video.[14] While nearly all candidate Web sites include pictures (97.3 percent) or graphics (87.2 percent) (data not in table), less than half of the candidates in our sample made their sites more stimulating and vibrant with video and/or audio files. This is somewhat surprising given the relative ease of using these features; however, the marginally significant increase between years (39 percent in 2002 to 47.6 percent in 2004; $z = 1.79$, $p = .0728$) and the robust difference between office levels (36.8 percent for House and 63.5 percent for Senate) suggests that usability and resources may be a factor in deciding whether to use multimedia technology.[15] Moreover, the fact that well-funded Senate candidates are more likely to have ready-made audio and video clips for other venues might help explain why they use this technology more than their House counterparts.

In terms of display options, we find that virtually all candidates have taken advantage of the Internet's limitless potential to provide information over multiple pages. In fact, 92.6 percent of all candidates in 2002 had multiple pages and by 2004 there was only one candidate (for the House) who offered a single-page Web site that would be virtually identical to a paper brochure. We also find that in 2004 (we did not code this in 2002) the majority of candidates (80.2 percent) made the effort to update information on their sites. The fact that Senate candidates (92.5 percent) were significantly more likely to do this than House candidates (76.1 percent) suggests that available resources may play a role in the decision to use this capability.

The results in table 2.2 also show that, on average, one-quarter of congressional candidates incorporated some sort of personalized interaction feature (for example, quiz, moving content, targeted marketing) on their Web sites. However, there are significant differences over time and across office level. Combining House and Senate candidates, we find that whereas only 18.3 percent of them used personalization features in 2002, 29.4 percent used them in 2004—a sign that these features are getting more popular with time. Also, 32.5 percent of Senate candidates across the two campaigns (2002 and 2004) used these features compared to 22.0 percent at the House

TABLE 2.2

Percentage of Sites with Dynamic Features

	2002		2004		
Feature	*House*	*Senate*	*House*	*Senate*	*Average*
Multimedia	30.2	57.6	40.4	69.2	43.7
Pages	92.2	93.2	99.5	100.0	96.8
New info	—	—	76.1	92.5	80.2
Personalization	19.0	16.9	23.8	46.3	25.0
Links	66.4	62.7	77.2	79.1	72.7
Two-way communication	9.5	3.4	9.4	13.4	9.2
Number of sites	116	59	202	67	444

level. Overall, the relatively low adoption rate could be primary evidence that most candidates want to shape the possible range of experiences that individuals have on the site and preserve the integrity of information they provide, in the context it was intended. However, the differences over time and across office levels could suggest that the use of personalized interaction features is being influenced by the increasing ease with which they can be used and the resources and objectives of Senate candidates who may want to offer a more customized experience to visitors from their larger and more diverse constituencies.

A clearer dynamic that offers users more choice and thus the candidate less control over what users see is the availability of external links. Our results show that 72.7 percent of candidates provided external links. Moreover, there has been a significant increase across congressional candidate Web sites from 2002 (65.1 percent for House and Senate candidates combined) to 2004 (77.7 percent for both House and Senate candidates). Differences, however, between House (73.3 percent) and Senate (71.4 percent) candidates are statistically insignificant ($z = .40$, $p = .69$). While the general evidence suggests that candidates are fairly comfortable with providing external links, further analysis indicates key differences based on where the links lead. Across 2002 and 2004, 44.2 percent of our House and Senate candidates provided links to relatively safe voter registration Web sites. Candidates in 2004 were equally likely (45.4 percent) to provide links to news sources, including links to specific articles or reports about the candidate. However, when it comes to the riskier links to party and presidential candidate sites, congressional candidates are much more hesitant. In 2004, only

15.2 percent of campaign Web sites linked to a presidential candidate site, while 27.6 percent linked to their party's Web site in 2002 and 2004. This suggests that candidates take a calculated approach toward external links by providing "safe" links more frequently than potentially "risky" links.

Our results also show that congressional candidates have yet to fully utilize the Internet's potential for two-way communication. In the aggregate, only 9.2 percent of candidate Web sites had at least one two-way communication feature (for example, live chat, forum, candidate chat). Although there was virtually no difference between House (9.4 percent on average between 2002 and 2004) and Senate (8.7 percent on average between 2002 and 2004; z = .233, p = .816), there was a slight, albeit statistically marginal, increase from 2002 (7.4 percent on average for House and Senate candidates) to 2004 (10.4 percent for House and Senate candidates: z = 1.10, p = .27). Still, around 90 percent of all candidates have avoided any use of two-communication features on their Web sites. By not utilizing the Web's potential for two-way communication, candidates retain control over the messages found on their Web sites, although they miss an opportunity to engage visitors in dialogue about the candidate and the campaign. Admittedly, two-way communication technology may have been difficult to implement in 2002, but by 2004 it would have been relatively easy for candidates to provide some sort of forum for two-way communication and/or discussion (such as forum or message board). The fact that this technology is still relatively underutilized suggests that the desire to control the message may be quite important for candidates.

There are certainly signs that, by and large, congressional candidates are moving beyond the static "electronic brochure" standard, albeit with some hesitation. In terms of presenting information, a strong majority of Senate candidates and a growing segment of House candidates are incorporating multimedia features that make their sites more vibrant and engaging. Virtually all candidate sites have multiple pages and a very large proportion keep their sites fresh with updated information—something that would be impossible with a brochure. In terms of interactivity, there has been somewhat less progress, with only a quarter of candidate Web sites utilizing personalized interaction features and less than 10 percent of sites offering venues for two-way communication. As for external links, candidates seem more willing to provide links to sources that may potentially help them (for example, voter registration, news stories about the candidate) than to Web sites where the candidate relinquishes control over the message such as party, presidential candidate). This overall pattern of results suggests that candidates are indeed quite calculating when deciding about Web technology and tend to prefer features that make their sites more compelling without sufficient costs or potential for message distortion.

Explaining the Use of Web Technology

We have alluded to some of the factors (such as year and office level) that may affect the way candidates use Web technology. However, we now conduct a more robust test of the considerations that motivate candidates to embrace or avoid particular innovations. To do this, we use logistic regression analysis (see table 2.3 for detailed results) and, for ease of interpretation, calculate and graph the changes in the relative odds of using the different features for each one-unit change in the significant independent variables.[16] We have excluded "pages" from this analysis because of a lack of variation on that measure (96.8 percent of candidate Web sites had more than one page). In addition, we report the results for "party link" instead of all external links because the preceding analysis shows important differences between links based on where they go on the World Wide Web.

Figure 2.1 shows that using multimedia to present information—namely, with audio and/or video—is a function of both practical feasibility (for example, time, available resources) and political motivations (for example, race competitiveness). The fact that multimedia use increased substantially from 2002 to 2004 reflects the growing availability of this technology, while its positive association with funds raised further suggests that feasibility issues are at play. The odds of a candidate using multimedia features increased by 74.9 percent over the two years and by 28.3 percent for every additional million dollars raised. The results also show that incumbents are 50.2 percent less likely than challengers (the excluded base) to use audio and/or video. We also find multimedia use is positively associated with district-level education, which is a demand feature that presumably reflects the need to appeal to a more sophisticated electorate that is likely to be online. In terms of purely political motivations, we find that the odds of using multimedia increase by 42.5 percent for every one-unit increase in race competitiveness (for example, from uncompetitive to moderately competitive races) which is a clear indication that, as races get closer, candidates look to utilize technologies that can make their sites more vibrant without exacting large resources or message distortion costs.

To understand how candidates think about displaying information, we analyzed the factors associated with updating candidate Web sites in 2004 (updating was not measured in 2002). Figure 2.2 shows that both practical feasibility and political motivations are again at work. Specifically, the decision to keep a candidate's Web site fresh and dynamic is driven by office level, incumbency status, and race competitiveness. The fact that Senate candidates are almost two-and-a-half times more likely to update than House candidates suggests that large staffs can better handle this time-consuming chore and that Senate candidates may feel a stronger need to provide current

TABLE 2.3
Determinants of Web Technology Use

	Multimedia	New info	Personalization	Party link	Two-way communication
2004	.559**		.765***	-.039	.303
	(.228)		(.255)	(.235)	(.374)
Senate	.264	1.211*	.480	-.166	-.722
	(.312)	(.706)	(.320)	(.341)	(.546)
Democrat	.338	.429	.691***	.329	.928***
	(.217)	(.351)	(.236)	(.230)	(.361)
Open seat	-.358	-.722	.279	.456	.696
	(.357)	(.689)	(.375)	(.393)	(.503)
Incumbent	-.698***	-.951**	-.175	.556**	-.633
	(.254)	(.403)	(.270)	(.267)	(.415)
Female	-.130	.960	-.144	.613**	-.968
	(.307)	(.652)	(.340)	(.309)	(.641)

District partisanship	−.004 (.011)	.011 (.016)	.002 (.012)	.009 (.011)	.001 (.017)
District income	−.125 (.119)	.071 (.187)	−.184 (.139)	−.017 (.117)	−.040 (.190)
District education	.046** (.023)	.007 (.036)	.009 (.025)	.050* (.026)	.005 (.037)
Funds raised	.249*** (.074)	.094 (.139)	.057 (.053)	−.079 (.070)	.158** (.071)
Race competitiveness	.354** (.157)	.446* (.252)	−.258 (.168)	−.434*** (.164)	−.562** (.248)
Constant	−4.450** (1.752)	−1.010 (2.540)	−1.487 (1.898)	−4.949** (1.942)	−1.958 (2.682)
Log likelihood	−503.763	−221.256	−449.357	−471.397	−241.543
N	420	256	426	424	426

Note: Entries are logit coefficients with standard errors in parentheses.

***p < .01, **p < .05, *p < .10 for two-tailed tests.

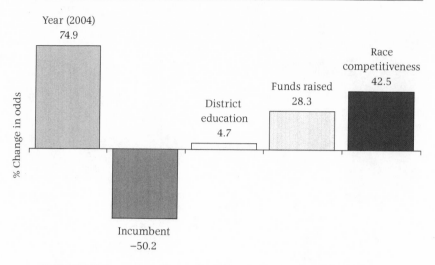

FIGURE 2.1 Percentage Change in Odds of Using Multimedia Features

information to their larger and more heterogeneous constituencies. The fact that incumbents are 61.3 percent less likely to update their sites than challengers speaks to the idea that incumbents typically feel more secure and less pressured to gain repeat visitors. While other candidate characteristics and demand effects are insignificant predictors, we again find that race competitiveness plays an expected role in the decision to update information (odds of updating increase by 56.2 percent for every one-unit increase in race competitiveness). As races get tighter, candidates are more inclined to enhance their Web sites with features such as updated information that make their sites more interesting without jeopardizing message clarity.

Overall, in terms of presenting information on their Web sites, we find that candidates are influenced by both practical and political considerations. Feasibility issues (for example, ease of using technology, staff size, and financial resources) are naturally important, although we also find consistent political incentives to provide vibrant and fresh information that come from incumbency status and race competitiveness. Ultimately, the inclusion of presentation features that go beyond the "electronic brochure" standard seems to be a function of both practicality and strategic motivations.

What determines the extent to which candidates use interactive technologies on their Web sites? In terms of offering personalized interactive features, we find that feasibility is a major consideration, although race competitiveness seems to play a role as well. Our results show that personalized interaction features grew more popular over time—the odds increased by 114.8 percent between 2002 and 2004. This clearly indicates that candidates warmed up to this technology as it improved and became easier to use. We also find some marginally significant evidence that Senate candidates used features like quizzes, moving information, and targeted marketing more than House candidates (p =.133), presumably because their larger staffs were better equipped to incorporate this technology and the fact that there might be a greater incentive to offer personalization features to a more diverse constituency. The fact that Democratic candidates used this technology significantly more than Republicans is somewhat difficult to explain given that Republican strategists have gained a reputation for effective targeted marketing (perhaps it stems from the Democrats' minority status). It is also important to note that we find a negative, albeit marginally significant (p =.124), relationship between race competitiveness and personalized interaction features, which suggests that as races tighten, candidates are 22.7 percent less likely to offer technologies that could interfere with the campaign's message. It seems that candidates in close races would have an incentive to avoid features that allow visitors to personalize their interaction with the site—these candidates need, more than others, to ensure that visitors get a clear and uniform understanding of their positions and campaign themes even if that means that the site is less engaging.

External links are another feature that can stimulate attention but also have potential political drawbacks. To get a sense of what motivates candidates to use or avoid external links, we focused on the determinants of providing a link to the candidate's political party Web site, because it provides a clear example of the tension that external links cause.[17] Figure 2.4 shows that the decision to provide a "party link" is driven by candidate

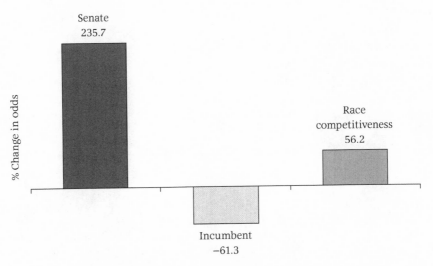

FIGURE 2.2 Percentage Change in Odds of Using New Information Features

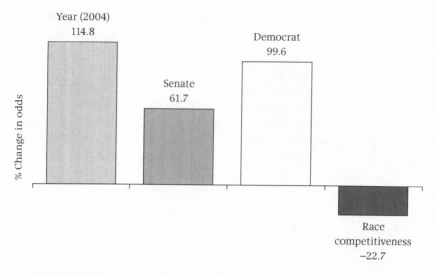

FIGURE 2.3 Percentage Change in Odds of Using Personalization Features

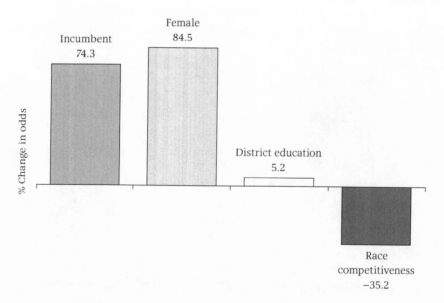

FIGURE 2.4 Percentage Change in Odds of Using Party Link

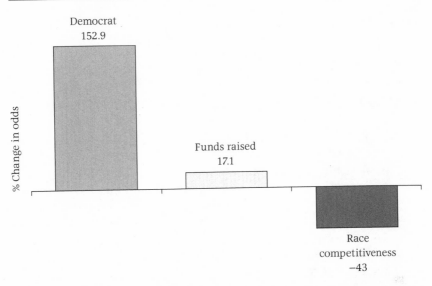

FIGURE 2.5 Percentage Change in Odds of Using Two-Way Communications Features

status and gender, race competitiveness, and district-level education. Party links are provided fairly uniformly across elections, office levels, and party affiliations, although the odds that an incumbent will use them are 74.3 percent higher than they are for challengers. Moreover, female candidates are 84.5 percent more likely than male candidates to link to the party's Web site, which speaks to their possible need to define themselves clearly to the electorate. While district partisanship and average income are insignificant, we find that district-level education is positively associated with party links, which is consistent with a growing sentiment that more sophisticated constituents tend to be stronger partisans (see Wilson 2006). Again, however, we find that as races tighten, candidates shy away from features that jeopardize their control over the information that visitors will receive (the odds decrease by 35.2 percent for each level of race competitiveness). Candidates in tight races have a greater need to ensure that visitors stay on their sites and are not distracted by visiting a party Web site, where the candidate has no control over what the visitor will encounter.

Finally, our analysis of the reasons candidates might use or avoid two-way communication features again highlights the importance of political considerations when deciding about Web technology. Figure 2.5 shows that the use of two-way communication features like chats and message boards is driven by party affiliation, funds raised, and race competitiveness. The fact that Democrats are more likely to offer two-way communication features may be the result of Howard Dean's success with these technologies in the 2004 presidential election. (It also may relate to their minority party status, since they may attract users likely to criticize the majority Republican Party; see Druckman, Kifer, and Parkin 2007). In terms of funds raised, the odds of using two-way communication increase by 17.1 percent for every million dollars raised, which suggests that resources play a role in determining whether this technology is used. We also find, once again, that race competitiveness is an important factor in determining the use of technology. In this case, the odds of using two-way communication drop by 43 percent for every one-level increase in race competitiveness, which confirms the hesitancy that candidates in tight races have about relinquishing control over their Web site's central message, even if it means that the site will be less engaging.

The pattern of results reported in figures 2.1 through 2.5 is quite clear in that decisions about using Web technology have both practical and political components. Feasibility is a necessary precondition for using technology, and the results show that the use of particular features tends to increase with enhanced feasibility whether by improved technology over time (2004), having larger office staffs (Senate), or more available resources (funds raised). In terms of demand effects from the district, we find that the partisanship and average income in the district never matter, although higher levels of education tend to be associated with more sophisticated Web sites. While demand effects generally play a secondary role in decisions about technology, strategic political considerations are consistently consequential. Incumbents typically created less dynamic Web sites than challengers, and, for each technology, race competitiveness was either a significant or nearly significant predictor. In fact, race competitiveness was positively associated with using presentation technologies that exacted few political costs while being negatively associated with using interactive technologies that jeopardized control over the campaign's message. Clearly, being able to include a technology is not enough; candidates must also have political motivations for going beyond the "electronic brochure" standard.

Discussion

The emergence of the Internet has provided political candidates with a new way to campaign, and technological innovations continually provide opportunities for candidates to connect with Web site visitors. While each new feature has its own potential benefits, it also has its own unique drawbacks that candidates must consider before using. By analyzing both presentation and interactive features on a large and representative sample of congressional campaign Web sites, we have shown that candidates have generally moved beyond an "electronic brochure" standard, although they have had some trepidation in doing so. Moreover, our results show that their hesitancy in using these technologies is not only based on practical considerations of feasibility but also on critical political considerations that force candidates to weigh the strategic benefits and costs of each feature.

These findings provide insight into the nature of contemporary campaigns. In fact, when it comes to studying campaign behavior, candidate Web sites are ideal because, unlike debates or ads, they are used by nearly all candidates and offer an unmediated composite of the campaign, thus giving a complete view of the campaign's overall approach. In other words, evidence from candidate Web sites provides a broad and generalizable picture of how candidates campaign.

Our results confirm, first of all, that available resources are a critical determinant of campaign strategy. Even with Internet technology where things are relatively inexpensive, candidates who have raised substantial amounts of money and/or have larger staffs (as in the Senate) are better able to utilize enhanced technology and thus present campaign information in a more compelling and possibly more persuasive manner (see Parkin 2007). This speaks to the cumulative advantage that well-funded candidates enjoy, even when it comes to the Internet. Without sufficient funds, candidates may not be able to use the Web to its full potential and may miss the opportunity to engage visitors with dynamic presentations of information. There is, however, an uplifting aspect of our results in that time is positively associated with technology use. This suggests that the effect that resources have on the ability to create captivating Web sites may diminish in future elections, thereby leveling the playing field. However, for the time being, it seems that, as with other forms of campaigning, resources matter.

Our results also underscore the importance of message control as part of running a successful campaign. Political scientists have long understood that candidates have an incentive to present and protect a specific message that they feel will be most effective in gaining the public's support (see, for example, Abbe, Goodliffe, Herrnson, and Patterson 2003). This study shows that candidates with large leads or deficiencies in the polls tend to be less protective of their message—their Web sites include more communication features that have the potential to present information that is "off message." In fact, candidates who feel that they have little to lose often seem to embrace the idea of online deliberation and discussion as part of a healthy campaign. They also appear to be comfortable with visitors focusing on a specific area (such as policy or event) or visiting external links that might interest and/or inform them. Evidence of this comes not only from congressional races but also from renegade presidential primary candidates who feel they have more to gain than to lose by using the Web to engage voters in political dialogue (see, for example, Trippi 2004).

We have found, however, that when races tighten so too does control over the message. As evidenced by their Web sites, candidates in close races guard their message carefully by presenting information in a clear manner that gives little (if any) room for distortion through interaction or dialogue. These candidates want the public to clearly understand the campaign's crafted message and certainly do not want to risk having the media or Web site visitors become distracted by conversations being held on the site by people chatting in some type of online forum. Moreover, these candidates attempt to keep voters focused on "the message" by offering few novelties and/or links to other sites. This behavior also applies to frontrunners at other office levels who feel that opening their Web site could jeopardize their lead (see, for example, Faler 2003). Our results clearly show the tendency for campaigns to become more circumspect as races tighten.

All of this has important implications for those who visit candidate Web sites. Public interest in a candidate increases when races are close. Journalists want to research the candidate, activists want to lend support, and average voters want to learn more about the contenders. Unfortunately, this is precisely when candidates exercise the most control over their message, denying visitors what they seek. Candidates are less likely to use technological innovations that will allow visitors to explore and discuss. Instead, interactive features give way to greater presentation technologies (such as videos) that offer voters a more regimented and limited experience as the campaign attempts to control the basis for evaluation and accountability. In this way, competition and deliberation seem to be at odds—competition leads candidates to use the Web restrictively, thereby hampering its potential to provide voters with a venue for meaningful dialogue and consideration. In other words, candidates avoid key technologies just when they could be most useful to voters, which highlights the friction between the untamed world of online politics and the controlled objectives of a political campaign.

The inverse relationship between competitiveness and interactivity also speaks to important questions pertaining to accountability in politics. Increased competition is often seen as a key mechanism for ensuring democratic accountability—officeholders need to respond to issues raised by their competitors and the media (see, for example, Schattschneider 1960). Yet one of the hopes of the Internet was that it would enhance the impact of citizens—as opposed to elite politicians and the media—in determining the basis of democratic accountability. As Coleman (2004, 1) explains, "Twentieth-century mass media have been described as producing a 'one-way conversation' (Postman 1986). Instead of dialogical deliberation, political communication has tended to be monological . . . a non-interactive political discourse." He continues, "The prospect of using the inherent interactivity of the Internet to enhance democracy has been raised by a number of scholars." However, the idea that competition and opportunities for interactivity may be at odds with one another raises the question of whether there exists a more general tension between these different bases of accountability. By controlling the campaign agenda, candidates restrict citizens from determining the issues on which they will ultimately be held accountable.

Conclusion

Research on how and why candidates use Web technology will undoubtedly continue. However, the results reported here make it clear that there is a need to understand the adoption of Web technology as much more than a simple case of viability and comfort with innovations; it is, in fact, also very much a serious political question in which strategic campaign considerations play a large role. Moreover, these strategic decisions provide insight into campaigns more generally and raise important questions about the relationship between candidates and voters in the American democracy.

NOTES

An earlier version of this chapter was published in *Social Science Computer Review* (2007) 25:425–442. Reprinted by permission.

1. However, see Foot and Schneider (2006) and Herrnson, Stoke-Brown, and Hindman (2007).

2. The concept of an "electronic brochure" has been used in other studies, including Kamarck (1999), Foot, Schneider, Xenos, and Dougherty (2003), and Herrnson, Stokes-Brown, and Hindman (2007).

3. Although there are some similarities, our approach is sufficiently different from that of Foot and Schneider (2006, 157–186). Most notably, we conceptualize technological features more specifically and focus our analyses on them, which differs from Foot and Schneider's broader examination of "informing, involving, connecting, and mobilizing" practices. Moreover, we examine the motivations for using distinct technological features rather than broad categories of features such as "informing" or "involving" practices.

4. Williams's numbers include both major-party and third-party Senate candidates.

5. For example, Lupia and Philpot (2005) show that visitors are most affected by Web sites that present information in a way that is consistent with the visitors' tastes.

6. Puopolo (2001, 2038) finds that "Republicans win the title of 'Most Web Savvy.'"

7. Foot and Schneider (2006, 171) suggest that "to the extent that political campaigns gauge their Web campaigning strategy on the basis of their target electorate's use of the internet, both family income and level of education serve as reasonable proxies for these factors."

8. Pew (2000) reports that in 2000 "more Republicans than Democrats went online for election news (37 percent of Republican online users vs. 34 percent of

Democrats)." Pew also finds that "Republicans hold a clear advantage in online activism over Democrats, measured in terms of interactive participation. More GOP consumers of online election news reported sending or receiving e-mail supporting or opposing a candidate (29 percent to 20 percent among Democrats); Republicans were also more likely to participate in online polls (39 percent to 31 percent) and more likely to contribute money through candidate Web sites (6 percent to 3 percent)."

9. Details about the entire coding project are available from the authors. In addition to introducing new elements from the literature on political campaigns and information processing, we build on Paul and Fiebich's (2002) "elements of digital storytelling." Our framework differs from other content analyses (including Xenos and Foot 2005; Bimber and Davis 2003; Gulati and Treul 2003) in that it is more systematic, includes multiple years and office levels, and examines the entire candidate Web site rather than just the front page.

10. To assess the reliability of the coding, we randomly sampled approximately 30 percent of the Web sites and had one of two reliability coders code these sites. Specific reliability statistics are available from the authors; in general, we found high levels of reliability, nearly always exceeding the .80 threshold (see Riffe, Lacy, and Fico 1998, 131; Neuendorf 2002, 143).

11. Our specific coding instructions for "personal" were: "On any part of the site that you examined, could you personalize the information, such that you would receive information that may differ from what another web visitor would receive (even if this would lead you to some other page; you don't need to examine this other page, but note its presence)? For example, you might enter your zip code and receive voting information, or something else specific to you (or people like you) such as information about an issue you care about. (Note this does not apply to information for general groups such as senior citizens.) The codes are: 0 = no personalized information at all; 1 = personalized information."

12. Our Web coding covered a host of other variables, including some technological measures such as one-way communication (e-mail subscriptions, voter contact) and structural features (blinking, scrolling, graphic movement). However, we focus only on those technological features, with sufficient variances, that indicate the extent to which candidates are moving beyond the "electronic brochure" standard. Also, we do not include blogs as part of two-way communication because they had yet to really develop this capability by 2004.

13. We do not use a continuous measure for race competitiveness because we do not expect slight differences to be meaningful. Dividing the measure into thirds follows convention (Jacobson 1992, 33) and facilitates interpretation. Highly competitive races have an average margin of victory of 10.6 percent (with a maximum of 20 percent), while mildly competitive races are between 21 percent and 35 percent (average is 29.1 percent) and noncompetitive races have margins of victory larger than 36 percent (average is 52.4 percent).

14. Six cases were excluded from this part of the analysis because coders were not using computers with audio capabilities and thus could not accurately measure the existence of audio features.

15. Unless otherwise noted, all reported differences are statistically significant at the $p < .05$ level or better in two-tailed difference of proportion tests.

16. We calculate the percentage change in odds with the formula: $100 * (Exp(B)-1)$.

17. Our logistic regression for "external links" more generally found positive and significant associations with year ($p = .004$) and Democratic candidates ($p = .017$), while none of the other factors reached statistical significance. These somewhat inconclusive findings are likely the result of the differences between external links in terms of where they take the visitor.

REFERENCES

Abbe, O., J. Goodliffe, P. Herrnson, and K. Patterson. 2003. "Agenda Setting in Congressional Elections: The Impact of Issues and Campaigns on Voting Behavior." *Political Research Quarterly* 56 (4): 419–430.

Barone, M., and R. Cohen. 2003. *The Almanac of American Politics: 2004.* Washington, DC: National Journal Group.

Barone, M., and R. Cohen. 2005. *The Almanac of American Politics: 2006.* Washington, DC: National Journal Group.

Barone, M., R. Cohen, and C. Cook, Jr. 2001. *The Almanac of American Politics: 2002.* Washington, DC: National Journal Group.

Bimber, B., and R. Davis. 2003. *Campaigning Online: The Internet in U.S. Elections.* New York: Oxford University Press.

Bucy, E. 2004. "Interactivity in Society: Locating an Elusive Concept." *The Information Society* 20 (5): 373–383.

Chadwick, A. 2006. *Internet Politics: States, Citizens, and New Communication Technologies.* New York: Oxford University Press.

Coleman, S. 2004 "Connecting Parliament to the Public via the Internet: Two Case Studies of Online Consultations." *Information, Communication and Society* 7:1–22.

Cornfield, M. 2004. *Politics Moves Online: Campaigning and the Internet.* New York: The Century Foundation Press.

Davis, R. 1999. *The Web of Politics: The Internet's Impact on the American Political System.* New York: Oxford University Press.

Druckman, J. 2003. "The Power of Television Images: The First Kennedy-Nixon Debate Revisited." *The Journal of Politics* 65:559–571.

Druckman, J., M. Kifer, and M. Parkin. 2007. "Going Negative in a New Media Age: Congressional Campaign Websites, 2002–2006." Paper presented at the annual meeting of the Midwest Political Science Association, Chicago, IL.

Dulio, D., D. Goff, and J. Thurber. 1999. "Untangled Web: Internet Use During the 1998 Election. *PS: Political Science and Politics* 32 (1): 53–59.

Eveland, W. and S. Dunwoody. 2002. "An Investigation of Elaboration and Selective Scanning as Mediators of Learning from the Web and Print." *Journal of Broadcasting & Electronic Media* 46: 34–53.

Faler, B. 2003. "Add 'Blog' to the Campaign Lexicon." *Washington Post.* November 15, sec. A, p.4.

Fenno, R. Jr. 1996. *Senators on the Campaign Trail: The Politics of Representation.* Norman: University of Oklahoma Press.

Foot, K., and S. Schneider. 2006. *Web Campaigning.* Cambridge: MIT Press.

Foot, K., S. Schneider, M. Dougherty, M. Xenos, and E. Larsen. 2003. "Analyzing Linking Practices: Candidates Sites in the 2002 U.S. Electoral Web Sphere." *Journal of Computer Mediated Communication* 8 (4) (accessed June 22, 2007, http://jcmc.indiana.edu/vol8/issue4/foot.html).

Foot, K., S. Schneider, M. Xenos, and M. Dougherty. 2003. Opportunities for Civic Engagement on Campaign Sites (accessed June 22, 2007, http://politicalweb.info/reports/information.html).

Goldsmith, S. 2004. "Major-party Candidates Work on the Web, While Many Challengers Stay Offline" (accessed December 2004 at (http://uwnews.washington.edu/ni/public/print2.asp).

Gordon, R. 2006. "Internet Rewrites Political Playbook: Tech Savvy Campaigns Go Online to Find Votes, Volunteers, Funds." *San Francisco Chronicle*, p. A1.

Graber, D. 2001. *Processing Politics: Learning from Television in the Internet Age.* Chicago: University of Chicago Press.

Gulati, G., and S. Treul. 2003. "Divided by Gender: Congressional Elections and Presentation of Self on the Internet." Paper presented at the annual meeting of the American Political Science Association, Philadelphia.

Herrnson, P. 2004. *Congressional Elections: Campaigning at Home and in Washington.* Washington, D.C.: CQ Press.

Herrnson, P., A. Stokes-Brown, and M. Hindman. 2007. "Campaign Politics and the Digital Divide: Constituency Characteristics, Strategic Considerations, and Candidate Internet Use in State Legislative Elections." *Political Research Quarterly* 60 (1): 31–42.

Ireland, E., and Nash, P. 2001. *Winning Campaigns Online: Strategies for Candidates and Causes, Second Edition.* Bethesda, MD: Science Writers Press.

Jacobson, G. 1992. *The Politics of Congressional Elections.* 3rd ed. New York: Harper Collins.

Kahn, K. 1996. *The Political Consequences of Being a Woman.* New York: Columbia University Press.

Kamarck, E. 1999. "Campaigning on the Internet in the Elections of 1998." In *Democracy.com: Governance in a Networked World*, ed. E. Kamarck and J. Nye Jr. 99–123. Hollis, NH: Hollis Publishing.

Kaye, B., and T. Johnson. 2006. "The Age of Reasons: Motives for Using Different Components of the Internet for Political Information." In *The Internet Election: Perspectives on the Web in Campaign 2004*, ed. A. Williams and J. Tedesco. Lanham: Rowman and Littlefield.

Keeter, S. 1987. "The Illusion of Intimacy: Television and the Role of Candidate Personal Qualities in Voter Choice." *Public Opinion Quarterly* 513: 344–358.

King, D. 1999. "Catching Voters in the Web." In *Democracy.com: Governance in a Networked World*, ed. E. Kamarck and J. Nye Jr., 125–131. Hollis, NH: Hollis Publishing.

Lupia, A., and T. Philpot. 2005. "Views from Inside the Net: How Websites Affect Young Adults' Political Interest." *Journal of Politics* 67 (4): 1112–1142.

Neuendorf, K. 2002. *The Content Analysis Guidebook.* Thousand Oaks, CA: Sage.

Norris, P. 2004. "Who Surfs?: New Technology, Old Voters, and Virtual Democracy in U.S. Elections 1992–2000." In. *Democracy.com?* ed. E. Kamarck. Washington, DC: Brookings Institute.

O'Keefe, D. 2002. *Persuasion: Theory and Research.* 2nd ed. Thousand Oaks, CA: Sage.

Parkin, M. 2007. "Campaigns in Cyberspace and the Impact of Presentation Technology on Website Visitors." Paper presented at the annual meeting of the Midwest Political Science Association, Chicago.

Paul, N., and C. Fiebich. 2002. "The Elements of Digital Storytelling" (accessed June 22, 2007, at http://www.inms.umn.edu/elements/index.php).

Pew. 2000. Internet Election News Audience Seeks Convenience, Familiar Names (accessed February 3, 2007, at http://people-press.org/reports/print.php3?PageID=137).

Postman, N. 1986. *Amusing Ourselves to Death: Public Discourse in the Age of Show Business.* New York: Penguin Books.

Puopolo, S. 2001. "The Web and U.S. Senatorial Campaigns 2000." *American Behavioral Scientist* 44 (12): 2030–2047.

Riffe, D., S. Lacy, and F. Fico. 1998. *Analyzing Media Messages: Using Quantitative Content Analysis in Research.* Mawah, NJ: Erlbaum.

Schattschneider, E. 1960. *The Semisovereign People: A Realist's View of Democracy in America.* New York: Holt, Rinehart and Winston.

Schneider, S. and K. Foot. 2002. "Online Structure for Political Action: Exploring Presidential Web Sites from the 2000 American Election." *Javnost* 9 (2): 43–60.

Southwell, B., and M. Lee. 2004. "A Pitfall of New Media? User Controls Exacerbate Editing Effects on Memory." *Journalism & Mass Communication Quarterly* 81 (3): 643–656.

Stewart, D., P. Pavlou, and S. Ward. 2002. "Media Influences on Marketing Communications." In *Media Effects: Advances in Theory and Research*, ed. J. Bryant and D. Zillmann. Mahwah, NJ: Erlbaum.

Stromer-Galley, J. 2000. "Online Interaction and Why Candidates Avoid It." *Journal of Communication* 50 (4): 111–132.

Tedesco, J. 2004. "Changing the Channel: Use of the Internet for Communicating About Politics." In *Handbook of Political Communication Research*, ed. L. Kaid, 507–532. Mahwah, NJ: Erlbaum.

Tewksbury, D., and S. Althaus. 2000. "Differences in Knowledge Acquisition Among Readers of the Paper and Online Versions of a National Newspaper." *Journalism & Mass Communication Quarterly* 77:457–479.

Trippi, J. 2004. *The Revolution Will Not be Televised: Democracy, the Internet, and the Overthrow of Everything.* New York: HarperCollins.

Williams, C., A. Aylesworth, and K. Chapman. 2002. "The 2000 e-Campaign for U.S. Senate." *Journal of Political Marketing.* 1 (4): 39–64.

Williams, C. 2003. "An Assessment of Candidate Web Site Performance and Effectiveness." Paper presented at the annual meeting of the Midwest Political Science Association, Chicago, IL.

Wilson, J. 2006. "Divided We Stand." *Wall Street Journal Online* (accessed September 28, 2007, at http://www.opinionjournal.com/federation/feature/?id=110007966).

Xenos, M., and K. Foot. 2005. "Politics as Usual, or Politics Unusual? Position-Taking and Dialogue on Campaign Websites in the 2002 U.S. Elections." *Journal of Communication* 55 (1): 169–185.

3

Closing Gaps, Moving Hurdles

Candidate Web Site Communication in the 2006 Campaigns for Congress

GIRISH J. "JEFF" GULATI

CHRISTINE B. WILLIAMS

In the 2006 midterm elections, even more campaigns and interest groups had an online presence than in 2004, and their activities had matured relative to previous years (Rainie and Horrigan 2007). Moreover, citizens seeking information about U.S. Senate races increased fivefold over the 2002 midterm election level and doubled for U.S. House races. Although mainstream media continued to dominate the content that citizens viewed online, 20 percent reported going directly to a candidate's Web site to learn about the campaign (Rainie and Horrigan 2007). Television remained the medium of choice, but the Internet's financial role continued to enlarge. Estimates put the total for online fund-raising at $100 million and online campaign advertising at $40 million (Cornfield and Rainie 2006).

Candidate Web sites are now a fixture of the electoral landscape. Early academic studies of Web sites as a campaign medium were descriptive, focusing initially on a particular election year, a single campaign, or level of office (Bimber and Davis 2003; D'Alessio 1997; Dulio, Goff, and Thurber 1999; Foot and Schneider 2002; Klotz 1997; Puopolo 2001; Williams, Aylesworth, and Chapman 2002). A number of recent studies have compared Web sites across levels of office (Greer and LaPointe 2004; Herrnson, Stokes-Brown, and Hindman forthcoming), examined similarities and differences among various political systems (Gibson et al. 2003; Norris 2001; Van Dijk 2005; Ward, Gibson, and Lusoli 2006), and provided in-depth analysis of specific Web site features and campaign functions (Conners 2005; Druckman, Kifer, and Parkin 2006; Endres and Warnick 2004; Xenos and Foot 2005;). Finally, several studies have begun to offer historical perspectives on campaign Web site design and use (Chadwick 2006; Foot and Schneider 2006), the role and function of Web sites, and their electoral and political impact (Bimber and Davis 2003; Gibson and McAllister 2006).

Our knowledge of candidate and party campaign Web sites, drawn from research on recent elections, shows several trends. First, all actors have increased their web presence and certain content and functionality or tools have become standard features on these sites. For example, nearly all web sites include information about their producer: candidate biographies, campaign contacts, speeches, and the like (Benoit and Benoit 2005; Williams and Gulati 2006). By 2000, secure servers for credit card transactions had became available, such that most campaigns now raise money online. They typically also collect information from visitors who wish to receive campaign emails or volunteer to work for the campaign (Benoit and Benoit 2005; Conners 2005). Informational content (replication and transmission of content produced offline, or "brochureware") remains dominant; two-way communication and interactive formats (aimed at relationship building or engagement, and mobilization) are less common (Bimber and Davis 2003; Gulati 2003; Kamarck 2002; Klotz 2007; Williams, et al. 2002).

Second, there are significant differences in the quality of content and technological sophistication of campaign Web sites. These differences have been associated with producer, constituency, and election characteristics. For example, challengers often have a greater Web presence, a different and sometimes more significant issue focus than incumbents (Druckman, Kifer, and Parkin 2006; Xenos and Foot 2005). Similarly, major parties and their candidates have more developed sites than minor ones or independents (Gibson, et al. 2003; Greer and LaPointe 2004; Gulati 2003; Jankowski and van Os 2004). Other studies have found that younger candidates and whites have a greater Web presence, as well as higher quality and sophistication than their counterparts (Herrnson, Stokes-Brown, and Hindman forthcoming), and that female candidates put greater emphasis on issues and interactive content (Druckman, Kifer, and Parkin 2006; Puopolo 2001). Most studies have shown that the candidate's financial wherewithal is an important differentiator. Constituency characteristics that matter to Web site development have included lower percentages of minority voters and senior citizens, and higher percentages of college-educated, high-income and urban or suburban dwellers, which all correlate with high Internet usage (Herrnson Stokes-Brown, and Hindman forthcoming; Williams and Gulati 2006). Various election characteristics, such as higher levels of office (Greer and LaPointe 2004; Herrnson, Stokes-Brown, and Hindman forthcoming), electoral competition (Gulati 2003; Xenos and Foot 2005), and electoral systems and political culture (Gibson et al. 2003; Herrnson Stokes-Brown, and Hindman forthcoming; Jankowski and van Os 2004;

Lusoli 2005; Lusoli, Gibson, and Ward 2007; Ward, Gibson, and Lusoli 2006) also have predicted greater Web presence, content quality, and technological sophistication.

A comparative assessment of Web sites is complicated by the evolution of technologies and their strategic applications by campaigns over time. To aid in this task, researchers have proposed various developmental orderings of content and functionality (tools or activities). Most treatments distinguish between passive informational content and those features or tools that facilitate user manipulation of, or interaction with, the content, other users and/or the campaign enterprise (Gibson and Ward 2000; Lusoli 2005). The lowest level or stage is the establishment of a Web presence and posting of informational content that has been reproduced from other offline media sources, archived, and transmitted to Web site viewers. The highest level or stage affords Web site users some degree of coproduction of content (from personalization to blog entries or online chats and virtual town meetings), two-way communication, and ability to follow on offline or online activity. Foot and Schneider's (2006) hierarchy of campaign Web site practice is among the most thorough and empirically substantiated to date. They find that the informational level is foundational to all others, while involving and contacting are independent practices, but foundational to the highest level, mobilizing.[1]

Finally, comparative assessment of campaign Web sites requires analysts to identify and distinguish among the various producer and user perspectives. Government entities, political parties, candidates, and news media organizations are among those who produce Web sites containing election-related content, but they do so for very different reasons. While the consumers of their contents are presumed to be citizens, they also include some uniquely differentiated subgroups such as campaign staffers or journalists. Moreover, members of the general public who visit a campaign Web site have varying degrees of interest in or support for its producer, as well as different demographic profiles and other qualities that a campaign might wish to (micro) target. Lusoli (2005) makes a useful basic distinction between the public and political dimensions of the Websphere. Contact information, voter registration information, privacy policies, and e-news bulletins are illustrative of the public electoral space. In contrast, the political electoral space is action oriented and includes candidate endorsements, election materials for distribution, and opportunities for donating and volunteering. Some of these are standard, low-level informational features (posting an endorsement); those that facilitate interactions with other actors (distribution lists or materials) represent high-level mobilization efforts.

Research Questions

This study concerns itself with four research questions. First, how do congressional candidates' 2006 campaign Web sites differ from previous years? We expect to see diffusion of the innovation continuing, both in terms of the proportion of candidates having a Web presence and in the quality of content and technological sophistication those Web sites exhibit. Laggards should catch up with leaders, but new innovations will continue to raise the bar.

Second, how do U.S. House candidates' campaign Web sites differ from those of Senate candidates? Consistent with other studies, we expect the greatest advances at the highest levels of office. The Senate represents a higher-stakes election that generally attracts more attention, greater financial resources, and better-known political consultants. Reelection is less certain than in the House; incumbent senators are less likely to run unopposed and more likely to face stronger challengers (Jacobson 2004). Moreover, the difficulties attached to reaching a more geographically dispersed electorate make the efficiencies of online campaigning more attractive.

Third, what other candidate attributes are associated with higher and lower levels of Web-site quality and sophistication? Among these, previous research suggests that major party candidates will outperform those of minor party and independent status, but the gap may be closing. While incumbents generally have more resources, earlier studies found that they were less inclined to engage in online campaigning. Have expectations about Web sites become so widespread in the media and public at large that all candidates now need a respectable presence? One of the most consistent differentiators has been the candidate's financial resources, but it remains to be determined whether this remains true for all types of content and levels of sophistication.

Finally, what electoral and constituency factors explain differences in content quality and technological sophistication of candidates' campaign Web sites? The competitiveness of the race seems to encourage Web site use and innovation. In addition, constituency characteristics associated with heavy Internet use (a younger, more affluent electorate) seem to generate higher expectations for Web sites and make them a more attractive means of reaching voters in densely populated electoral districts such as cities and suburbs.

We apply our assessments of Web site quality and sophistication to each of Foot and Schneider's (2006) three domains: information, involvement and engagement (connecting), and mobilization. We expect the evolutionary trajectory of each domain to differ by year, level of office, candidate, and electoral and constituency attributes. The baseline, informational level should show the most standardization across types of candidates and races, while the highest, mobilization level should be the most highly differentiated. Within the latter group, those features representing true, two way communication and coproduction of content will be relatively rare. As Stromer-Galley (2000) explains, political campaigns resist using human-interactive features because they undermine their ability to control the message and maintain ambiguity in their communications.

Data and Methods

To examine how congressional candidates campaigned on the World Wide Web in 2006 and to gain insights into how online campaigning has evolved, we conducted a content analysis of the campaign Web site of every U.S. Senate and House candidate who had a presence on the Web in 2006. House races provide a large sample of candidates, allowing us to use multivariate analysis to study different subgroups and form generalizations about Internet campaigning. Senate sites have evolved faster than House sites, thus allowing us to examine some of the more innovative and sophisticated items featured in the most recent election as well as to preview what we might see in the 2008 presidential election.

In 2006, there were 129 candidates running for 33 Senate contests.[2] Thirty-two of the candidates were Democrats and 32 were Republicans. Among third-party candidates, 14 ran as Libertarians, 9 ran as Greens, and 21 ran under the banner of a variety of smaller parties. Joseph Lieberman (ID-CT), Bernie Sanders (I-VT), and 19 other candidates ran as independents. Approximately 88 percent (N=114) of the Senate candidates listed a Web address for the 2006 campaign. A few of these candidates never developed a site during the campaign or simply redirected visitors to a national or state party site. Excluding these candidates, we had 109 Senate sites for our content analysis.

For the 435 House races, there were for 428 Democratic candidates, 388 Republicans, 110 Libertarians, 41 Greens, 70 candidates from smaller third parties, and 65 independents. Of these 1,102 candidates, 81 percent (N=894) listed a Web address. After excluding the undeveloped and nonpersonal sites, we had 865 House sites available for content analysis.

The recent literature on Internet campaigning (Gulati 2003; Kamarck 2002; Williams and Gulati 2006, Williams, Aylesworth, and Chapman 2002) has examined four major areas of content, features, and tools on candidates' campaign Web sites: (1) informational content; (2) involvement and engagement, (3) mobilization; and (4) interactivity. In order to make valid comparisons with past elections and better assess how the Web sites are evolving as a campaign tool, we coded for the presence or absence of twenty-one forms of content that fall within these four areas and, in most cases, used the exact same wording and coding protocol (see appendix 3.1).

After extensive pretesting, the content analysis of the 979 Senate and House candidates' Web sites were conducted throughout October 2006.[3] Four research assistants and one of the authors of this chapter supervised a staff of fifteen coders for the content analysis. Each supervisor was responsible for training and monitoring the work of four staff members. After the analysis was completed, approximately 10 percent of the sites were randomly selected for reliability analysis. The average agreement across all twenty-one questions was 93.5 percent.[4]

We begin by describing our findings for the U.S. Senate, followed by the House of Representatives. Where possible, we compare our results to results from studies of earlier campaigns (Williams and Gulati 2006).

Analysis and Findings

Web Presence

A record percentage of candidates for the U.S. Senate campaigned over the World Wide Web in 2006. As can be seen in Figure 3.1, 85 percent of the Senate candidates had their own personal Web sites in 2006. In 2004, only 74 percent of Senate candidates were online. As figure 3.1 also shows, this was the third consecutive election cycle where about three-fourths of the candidates were online. Senate candidates' Web presence started to level off six years ago, then reached a new and slightly higher plateau in this last election cycle.

It also was a record-setting year for House online campaigns, as 79 percent of the candidates posted their own Web site in 2006. But unlike online campaigns in the Senate, each successive election cycle has been accompanied by a steady increase in the percentage of candidates present on the Web. Figure 3.1 also shows that 55 percent of House candidates campaigned on the Web in 2000, increasing to 61 percent in 2002 and 74 percent in 2004. Thus in House races, Web site presence continues to increase, albeit more gradually in 2006. If Web site adoption has an upper limit, the House could reach a plateau equal to or somewhat lower than the Senate's in another election cycle or two. Adoption rates will likely slow until holdout candidates who are long-time incumbents retire. Upper limits recognize that some candidates, by choice or circumstance, do not or cannot mount a serious campaign effort through the Internet or any medium of mass communication.

For the second consecutive cycle, more than 90 percent of the major-party Senate candidates campaigned online (see table 3.1). Among Democrats (and the two independents who caucus as Democrats, Mr. Lieberman

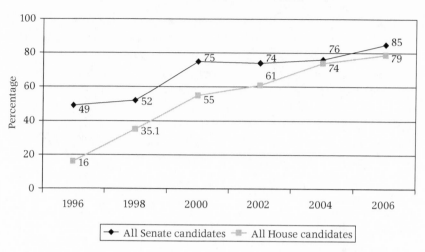

FIGURE 3.1 Congressional Campaigns on the World Wide Web, 1996–2006

and Mr. Sanders), 97 percent had a Web site in 2006, with only incumbent Senator Ben Nelson (D-NE) absent from the Web. Last year, 94 percent of Republicans had a campaign Web site. Incumbent Senators Trent Lott (R-MS) and Craig Thomas (R-WY) were the only Republicans who did not campaign online in 2006. For the second consecutive election cycle, however, every major-party challenger and candidate for an open seat had a presence on the Web.

Independents and third-party candidates for the Senate saw a significant increase in Web presence between 2004 and 2006. Whereas only 54 percent of minor-party candidates had a Web presence in 2004, 77 percent had a Web presence in 2006. The Libertarians led the way with 93 percent of their candidates present on the Web, followed by the Greens with 89 percent. Although there is a gap of 18 percent between major- and minor-party candidates, this is the smallest difference between the two groups since the inception of Web campaigning and is consistent with other reports (Klotz 2004; Panagopoulos 2005).

In House races, Democrats were the most likely to campaign online (88 percent), followed by Republicans (84 percent), Greens (63 percent), and Libertarians (58 percent). Only 57 percent of independents and 53 percent of the smaller third-party candidates campaigned on the Web. As a group, 86 percent of major-party candidates had their own Web sites in 2006, while only 57 percent of minor-party candidates had their own sites. Thus, the wide gap we observed in Senate campaigns prior to 2006 still persists in House campaigns.

A multivariate logistic regression analysis of Web presence for House candidates confirms that major-party candidates are more likely to campaign online, even after taking electoral and constituency factors into account.[5] But as can be seen in table 3.2, the differences between the Greens and Libertarians and the Democrats and Republicans are not significant at the .05 level. What is significant is that unlike their Senate counterparts, House incumbents were less likely to campaign online than either their challengers or candidates for open seats. Since Senate rules prohibit senators from updating their office Web sites during the sixty days before the election but House rules make no such prohibition, House incumbents may have less need to invest in a separate Web site. Moreover, because House reelection rates exceed those for the Senate, representatives have less need to engage in campaign activities across the board.

Another important factor in explaining Web presence is money. House candidates with more financial resources are more likely to campaign online than candidates with fewer resources. While it is understandable that more money is needed to produce and present sophisticated content in the most accessible way, it costs very little to launch a Web site. Today, a candidate can set up a profile for free on such popular Web sites such as Blogspot and MySpace. The observed relationship between money and Web presence may indicate that many of the candidates without Web sites are simply not serious candidates. Not only do they seem to be investing little time in fundraising, but they also do not seem to be very interested in promoting their own candidacy.

TABLE 3.1

2006 Congressional Presence on the World Wide Web by Party

	Senate		House	
	%	N	%	N
Democrats	97	32	88	428
Republicans	94	32	84	388
Libertarians	93	14	58	110
Greens	89	9	63	41
Other third parties	67	21	53	70
Independents	62	21	57	65
All	84.5	129	78.5	1102

TABLE 3.2

Multivariate Logit Analysis of 2006 House Campaigns' Web Site Presence

Independent variables	B	Standard error	Wald	Sig.
Party (Democrats = reference category)				
Republicans	−0.200	0.220	0.823	0.364
Libertarians	−0.661	0.360	3.369	0.066
Greens	−0.729	0.449	2.633	0.105
Others	−1.128	0.349	10.444	0.001
Incumbency status (open-seat candidates = reference category)				
Incumbents	−1.885	0.429	19.359	0.000
Challengers	0.041	0.363	0.013	0.910
Competitive seat	0.335	0.338	0.983	0.321
Contributions received (ln)	0.198	0.026	57.737	0.000
Percentage with college degrees	0.017	0.011	2.457	0.117
Percentage over age 64	−0.026	0.030	0.762	0.383
Percentage white	0.013	0.005	5.331	0.021
Percentage urban	0.002	0.006	0.114	0.735
Constant	−0.280	0.571	0.241	0.623
N	1,102			
Percent correctly predicted	79.4			
−2 log likelihood	928.446			
Chi-square	218.931			
Pseudo R^2	0.278			

Informational Content

Since the first online campaigns, the most fully developed characteristic of candidates' Web sites has been the availability of campaign information. Its prevalence is explained by the fact that Web sites represent a cost-effective means of communicating at any time of the day the most up-to-date information about candidates and their campaigns to the public and the media. Candidates can use a variety of media formats on the Web site to provide details about their personal qualities, background and record of accomplishments unfiltered and without concerns for space limitations (Bimber and

Davis 2003; Ireland and Nash 2001). The absence of space limitations allows candidates to elaborate fully, in a variety of ways, and to archive that content on the site, making it easy for voters, journalists, and other observers to acquire a more comprehensive view of the candidate and the campaign. This content usually is generated by the campaign itself but also can originate from a national party organization, the media, and campaign supporters whose content is either posted on the site or made available through a link to the external source.

As the first column of data in table 3.3 shows, 98 percent of the Senate Web sites that we analyzed had information about the candidates' issues positions, either directly on the home page or on a separate page dedicated specifically to issues. The percentage of candidates posting information about issues has risen steadily over the past few years and represents an encouraging trend. In 2000, 57 percent of the campaigns included this information on their Web sites, rising to about 75 percent in 2002 and 93 percent in 2004. Although candidates often are criticized for avoiding a discussion of the issues (Jacobson 2004; Mayhew 1974), it seems that when given the opportunity for unfiltered communication with the electorate, most Senate candidates are now more eager to reveal their stands on the issues and details of their policy proposals. As substantive news coverage of campaigns continues to decline, and horse race coverage in particular increases (Gulati, Just, and Crigler 2004), this is a welcome development.

Almost all of the campaigns posted their e-mail address (89 percent) and the candidate's biography (87 percent) on the Web site. In addition, 73 percent of the campaigns either posted or linked to news about the campaign. Major-party candidates were more likely than minor-party candidates, however, to include bios and news. As the second column of data in table 3.3 shows, 96 percent of Democratic and Republican candidates included a bio page and 96 percent included campaign news, either on the site or through external links. In contrast, the third column in the same table shows that only 78 percent of independents and third-party candidates included a bio and only 53 percent included news about the campaign.

Among the House candidates who campaigned online, the results mirror the Senate findings. As table 3.4 shows, 89 percent posted biographical information either on their home page or on a separate page, and 87 percent of the House candidates provided the campaign's e-mail address on the site. Fewer House than Senate candidates posted information about their issue positions (77 percent) and news about their campaigns (62 percent). For these categories of content, House campaign Web sites were less informative than Senate campaign Web sites.

In most cases, there was a significant gap between major- and minor-party candidates in how informative their Web sites were, and the gap was

TABLE 3.3

Political Content on 2006 Senate Campaign Web Sites by Party

	All candidates %	Major-party candidates %	Minor-party candidates %
Position papers/issue positions	98	100	97
E-mail address provided	89	90	87
Candidate biography	87	**96**	**78**
Campaign news	73	**96**	**53**
Audio or video clips	66	**92**	**31**

Note: Bold entries indicate that the difference (X^2) between major- and minor-party candidates is statistically significant at the .05 level.

fairly substantial. Whereas 95 percent of Democrats and Republicans posted their biographies, only 67 percent of minor-party candidates did so. In addition, major-party candidates were significantly more likely to post campaign news than minor-party candidates. However, there was no difference in the propensity of major- and minor-party candidates to express their issue positions and provide their e-mail addresses on their Web sites.

The Senate and House differences based on party status suggest that a high priority for minor-party candidates is to raise issues and promote issue stances that are important to them, which may not otherwise be reported in the news media. Their efforts in this regard duplicate those of major-party candidates. On the other hand, minor-party candidates may be disinclined to post bios because doing so would call attention to their untraditional or sparse political credentials. The relative paucity of campaign news may be because minor party candidates may hold fewer campaign events and have lower activity levels to report than major-party candidates.

One form of content that has demonstrated considerable growth from the past election cycles was the use of streaming and downloadable audio and video. This could include either professionally produced campaign advertisements and videos or "homemade" clips of campaign events. It also may include a welcome message from the candidate. Only a third of the Senate campaigns included audio or video on their Web sites in 2000. By 2004, slightly more than half had done so. In 2006, 66 percent of Senate candidates had some form of video available on their Web sites. The gap between major- and minor-party candidates was widest for this form of content compared to all others.

TABLE 3.4

Political Content on 2006 House Campaign Web Sites by Party

	All candidates %	Major-party candidates %	Minor-party candidates %
Candidate biography	89	**95**	**67**
E-mail address provided	87	88	83
Position papers/issue positions	77	77	80
Campaign news	62	**68**	**39**
Audio or video clips	40	**44**	**25**

Note: Bold entries indicate that the difference (X^2) between major- and minor-party candidates is statistically significant at the .05 level.

In contrast, as can be seen in table 3.4, only 40 percent of House candidates provided visitors with audio or video clips. Moreover, Republicans and Democrats were nearly twice as likely as independents and third-party candidates to post audio or video items.

The gap in integrating more sophisticated multimedia tools suggests that the candidates who are better financed and running more professional campaigns stand to benefit more from the Internet, despite the gap in Web presence having nearly disappeared. Video content should become even more prevalent in future Web campaigns as more Americans access the Internet through a broadband connection and come to expect content to be delivered in this format. As video becomes easier to produce and store, more minor-party candidates may catch up in taking advantage of this tool. However, as one sophistication gap closes, advancing technological innovation may open another.

Involvement and Engagement

Another important function of Web sites is to reinforce supporters' commitment to the campaign by helping them understand their stake in the campaign or at least feel that their involvement in the campaign matters. Features and content that facilitate contact and associations with the campaign and other supporters already involved are distinguishable from informational content in that the latter tends to be one-directional, from the candidate to the Web user (Foot and Schneider 2006). These features are interactive in only a limited sense, however, because they do not establish genuine two-way communication or respond to a visitor's input or request.

TABLE 3.5

**Engagement and Involvement Features on 2006
Senate Campaign Web Sites by Party**

	All candidates %	Major-party candidates %	Minor-party candidates %
Donations by credit card	74	**94**	**47**
Online volunteer form	64	**90**	**27**
E-newsletter sign-up	53	**77**	**18**
Facebook Election Pulse profile	40	**50**	**17**
Blog	39	45	31
Voting information	31	**44**	**13**
Candidate's schedule	29	34	22
RSS updates	18	21	13
Online poll	8	10	5

Note: Bold entries indicate that the difference (X^2) between major- and minor-party candidates is statistically significant at the .05 level.

A common way for campaigns to help their supporters feel they are involved in some way is to facilitate their making a financial contribution online. One of the most significant innovations of the 2000 presidential campaigns was the use of the Internet as a fund-raising tool (Bimber and Davis 2003). In 2004, both President Bush and Senator Kerry raised a large portion of their funds over the Internet, and most small donors made their contributions online (Graf et al. 2006; Rainie, Cornfield, and Horrigan 2005). As table 3.5 indicates, we found that 74 percent of the Web sites had a feature that allowed supporters to donate money to the campaign with their credit card, a slight increase from two years ago.

The second most prevalent feature used to engage supporters was a volunteer form that allowed supporters to provide their contact information and then submit the form to the campaign electronically. A majority of the Senate Web sites (53 percent) also included a way for supporters to sign up online for the campaign's e-newsletter or other forms of electronic updates.[6] Only 31 percent of the Web sites included information about how to vote absentee or general information about registering to vote and polling locations, which was similar to what was found two years earlier. A more recent innovation for alerting supporters about new or updated content on the Web site is through a news feed, such as RSS. Only 18 percent of the campaign Web sites included this feature in 2006.

Three-fourths of House candidates provided their supporters with a means to donate online by using a credit card (see table 3.6). The second most prevalent feature used to facilitate associations between supporters was the electronic volunteer sign-up form, which was found on 69 percent of the House campaign Web sites. A majority (52 percent) of the Web sites included a way for supporters to subscribe to the campaign's e-newsletter or to receive e-mail update of the campaign. In addition, 35 percent of the major-party House campaigns posted the candidate's schedule on the site and 34 percent included voter registration and voting information. For these five features we found no significant differences between House and Senate candidates, as can be seen by comparing the first columns of data in tables 3.5 and 3.6.

Two other more recent innovations for connecting like-minded people over the Internet are campaign Web logs (blogs) and social networking sites. While in earlier campaigns, supporters, opponents, and observers debated the merits of a candidate or issue on user-created newsnet discussion boards and chat rooms, today's campaigns have started their own blogs and created

TABLE 3.6

Engagement and Involvement Features on 2006
House Campaign Web Sites by Party

	All candidates %	Major-party candidates %	Minor-party candidates %
Donations by credit card	75	**83**	**38**
Online volunteer form	69	**81**	**17**
E-newsletter sign-up	52	**59**	**19**
Voting information	34	**37**	**23**
Candidate's schedule	29	**35**	**20**
Blog	23	23	21
Facebook Election Pulse profile	15	**18**	**5**
RSS updates	8	8	8
Online poll	5	5	5

Note: Bold entries indicate that the difference (X^2) between major- and minor-party candidates is statistically significant at the .05 level.

profiles on Facebook and MySpace. Although blogs received considerable hype in 2004, social networking sites (including You Tube) were the Web tools that caught the eye of the media in 2006. Among 2006 Senate candidates, 40 percent expanded on the profile created specifically for them by Facebook in their Election Pulse campaign and 39 percent started a campaign blog.

We found that candidates for the House were about half as likely as their Senate counterparts to adopt more recent innovations in online campaigning. Specifically, less than one-fourth of the House campaigns had a blog and only 15 percent had developed their Facebook profile.[7] In addition, only 8 percent of the candidates included an RSS option on their Web sites and only 5 percent included an opportunity for a visitor to participate in an online poll. These data confirm that Senate rather than House campaigns constitute the early adopters for Web site innovations. They have greater scale, financial, and consulting resources, and competitive incentives to support this technological experimentation.

Two services that citizens would like more campaigns to provide but have received little attention from the candidates themselves are posting of the candidate's itinerary and opportunities to participate in online polls. Only 29 percent of the candidates posted their schedules online and only 8 percent included an online poll. Although roughly the same percentage of campaigns included an online poll in 2004 and 2006, significantly fewer campaigns posted their candidate's schedule in 2006.

There were substantial differences between the major- and minor-party Senate candidates in the number of features they included to engage their supporters. As can be seen by comparing the second and third columns of data in table 3.5, major-party candidates were more likely to process credit card contributions online, allow online volunteer and newsletter sign-ups, and provide information about voting than minor-party candidates. In some sense this indicates progress for minor-party candidates, since they lagged behind in many more features in 2004.

In the online House campaigns, there also were substantial differences between the major- and minor-party candidates' use of their Web sites to engage their supporters and encourage their involvement. Comparing the second and third columns of table 3.6 shows that Democrats and Republicans were more likely to use their sites to offer online volunteer forms, e-newsletter subscriptions and voting information, process credit card transactions, and post their schedule. They also were more likely to expand on their Facebook profile. Major- and minor-party candidates displayed virtually no difference in hosting a campaign blog, offering RSS, and conducting an online poll. These latter innovations occur at much lower incidence levels than for the Senate, which suggests that the major- minor- party digital divide we observed there and for many other features does not materialize until an innovation reaches a threshold takeoff point.

Mobilization

While reinforcing supporters' commitment to the candidate is essential for any campaign to remain competitive, transforming those committed supporters into activists or advocates for the campaign is what may be needed to carry the candidate to victory. Assembling a group of engaged volunteers can be an important way to build community within a campaign, but these volunteers also can be used to spread the candidate's message and persuade others to vote for the candidate and possibly even to work for the campaign. For that reason, we also include the feature of an electronic volunteer sign-up as a mobilization tool. In most cases, this feature allows supporters not only to provide their contact information but also to indicate the specific activities that they would be willing to do.[8]

As table 3.7 reports, the online volunteer sign-up form is the most prevalent mobilization tool found on candidates' Web sites. Only two other mobilization tools—downloadable campaign materials and tell-a-friend—are found on more than one-third of the Web sites. The ability to obtain information about acquiring campaign merchandize and materials, either for purchase or from the campaign to distribute, was found on 27 percent of the sites. The ability to express a desire to host an event and to be directed to the e-mail address of the local newspaper for purposes of writing a letter to the editor was found on 17 percent of the campaign sites. Along with the tell-a-friend feature, these were three relatively new tools widely used on the Web in 2006. Minor-party candidates lagged behind significantly in each of these new tools. Downloadable materials (for example, flyers and brochures in PDF format) produced the only nonsignificant difference between major- and minor-party candidates.

Turning to the House campaigns, an online volunteer form was the only online tool among those used for transforming supporters into advocates that we found on more than one-fifth of the Web sites. As table 3.8 reports, only 18 percent of the House candidates had campaign materials that could be downloaded from the site, and only 15 percent provided information about acquiring campaign merchandize and materials. Few House candidates provided an electronic means for scheduling a campaign event or house party (16 percent), forwarding the campaign's Web address to a friend (12 percent), or a direct link to the local newspapers' Web page for submitting letters to the editor. And only 4 percent had some content available in a foreign language. House candidates lagged behind their Senate counterparts in all but two mobilization tools, volunteer and event-scheduling forms.

TABLE 3.7

Mobilization Tools on 2006 Senate Campaign Web Sites by Party

	All candidates %	Major-party candidates %	Minor-party candidates %
Online volunteer form	64	**90**	**27**
Downloadable materials	36	40	29
Tell a friend	34	**48**	**13**
Campaign materials and merchandise	27	**38**	**13**
Event form	17	**23**	**9**
Letter to the editor	17	**27**	**2**
Foreign-language content	13	**18**	**7**

Note: Bold entries indicate that the difference (X^2) between major- and minor-party candidates is statistically significant at the .05 level.

TABLE 3.8

Mobilization Tools on 2006 House Campaign Web Sites by Party

	All candidates %	Major-party candidates %	Minor-party candidates %
Online volunteer form	69	81	17
Downloadable materials	18	18	16
Event form	16	19	2
Campaign materials and merchandise	15	16	10
Tell a friend	12	14	4
Letter to the editor	8	10	3
Foreign-language content	4	4	3

Note: Bold entries indicate that the difference (X^2) between major- and minor-party candidates is statistically significant at the .05 level.

Interactivity

Just two Senate candidates—James Webb (D-VA) and Rae Vogeler (G-WI)—included the capability to conduct live chats, a technology that has existed for some time. These chats allow visitors to interact with the campaign in real time, approximating true two-way communication by simulating the feel of a town hall meeting. Clearly, fully integrating live chats into a campaign demands much of a candidate's time and, unlike a moderated blog, makes it difficult for the candidate to control the nature and tone of the conversation (Stromer-Galley 2000). Until user expectations and demand increases and resistance from established providers diminishes, it is unlikely that this innovation will be actualized and diffused. Only nine House candidates, including incumbent David Wu (D-OR) and new member Zach Space (D-OH), included the capability to conduct live chats.

Multivariate Analysis

To identify more precisely which Senate candidates were more likely to include the various forms of informational content, engagement features, and mobilization tools on their campaign Web sites, and the reasons for the variation, we constructed three additive indices from seventeen of the twenty items discussed.[9] We then regressed these indices on party affiliation, incumbency status, electoral vulnerability, campaign resources, and four indicators of citizen-demand for the Internet.[10]

As can be seen in the first column of table 3.9, the most informative Senate candidates were those with the most resources and those from states that are more urban and have fewer minorities. All of the partisan difference that we observed in the bivariate analysis disappeared once other variables were taken into account. It is not surprising that money is highly significant in explaining content since it can be quite expensive to produce professional quality video and archive it on the a Web site. Thus, Democrats and Republicans are more informative than minor-party candidates because they have more resources for producing and delivering content. In addition, viewers need a broadband connection for video clips to be accessible, a service that is more prevalent among white households and less available in rural areas.

Money also has a significant impact on the extent to which candidates use their Web sites to engage their supporters. Most of these services require an experienced staff person to manage the flow of information coming into and out of the campaign. For example, it may be relatively easy to provide a feature where supporters enter their e-mail address to receive updates or an e-newsletter. It is a more time-consuming matter, however, to organize all the addresses into a database and then actually to produce the newsletter for distribution. But as can be seen in the second column of table 3.10, the major-party candidates and the Greens were more likely to engage supporters, regardless of their financial situation. Also, challengers were more likely to use their Web sites to connect supporters with others in the campaign. Thus, while resources are important for engaging supporters on the Web, candidates who already are engaging their supporters offline may find that replicating those services online can be done fairly easily.

The third column of table 3.9 displays the results of the multivariate analysis of mobilization. In this case, money does not have a significant impact. Rather, Senate candidates in the most competitive races are the most likely to use the Web for transforming supporters into advocates. Where the outcome is not in doubt, there may be little need for campaigns to invest time in these tools. At the same time, these tools are relatively inexpensive to maintain and thus do not require a large budget to implement.

What is surprising in these results is that Republicans were significantly less likely than Democrats to use the Web for mobilizing voters. It was the Republicans who put great emphasis on house parties and personal contact to turn out their vote in 2002 and 2004, and they used the Web to facilitate those forms of mobilization. Factors that might explain why 2006 was different could include the nature of a midterm election or the parties' changed competitive positions. Possibly the Republican Party organization was not equipped to mobilize voters for congressional (state and district) offices in the way it had been for the presidential election of 2004. Or, Web site mobilization was not seen as an effective means to overcome negative perceptions of congressional candidates linked by party affiliation to a now unpopular Republican administration On the other hand, it may be that Democrats (and Greens) simply outdid the Republicans in this election. Another possibility is that the two major parties are beginning to use the Web very differently in their mobilization strategies, with Republicans abandoning the Web and Democrats integrating it much deeper into their overall campaign strategy.

Using the same additive index and model, we replicated our multivariate analysis for the features on the House sites. As was the case for Senate sites, the partisan difference that we observed in the bivariate analysis disappeared once other variables were taken into account. As can be seen in the first column of table 3.10, the most informative House candidates were those with the most resources. While none of the constituency variables mattered, two other electoral factors did matter: candidates challenging incumbents and those running in the most competitive races were more informative. Thus, in races for the House, candidates who began in a disadvantaged position, regardless of party, not only had the most incentive to use their Web sites for presenting themselves to the public but they took advantage of the opportunity. And they were even more likely to pursue the opportunity in cases where the outcome of the race was in doubt.

TABLE 3.9

Multivariate Analysis of Informational Content, Engagement Features, and Mobilization Tools on 2006 Senate Web Sites

Independent variables	Content	Engagement	Mobilization
Party (Democrats = reference category)			
Republicans	**−0.011**	**−0.076**	**−0.201*****
	0.045	0.052	0.050
Libertarians	**−0.155**	**−0.306*****	**−0.321*****
	0.099	0.113	0.109
Greens	**0.150**	**0.017**	**−0.095**
	0.098	0.112	0.108
Others	**−0.083**	**−0.365*****	**−0.301*****
	0.095	0.108	0.104
Incumbency status (open-seat candidates = reference category)			
Incumbents	**−0.022**	**0.144**	**0.050**
	0.058	0.067	0.064
Challengers	**−0.050**	**0.009****	**0.089**
	0.069	0.079	0.076
Competitive seat	**−0.014**	**0.021**	**0.079**
	0.039	0.045	0.043
Contributions received (ln)	**0.029****	**0.026***	**0.011**
	0.012	0.013	0.013
Percentage with college degrees	**−0.003**	**−0.001**	**−0.005**
	0.005	0.006	0.005
Percentage over age 64	**0.004**	**0.000**	**−0.001**
	0.010	0.012	0.011
Percentage white	**0.003****	**−0.002**	**0.001**
	0.001	0.002	0.002
Percentage urban	**0.004****	**−0.002**	**0.002**
	0.002	0.002	0.002
Intercept	**0.640*****	**0.477***	**0.472***
	0.216	0.247	0.237
N	109	109	109
Adjusted R^2	0.402	0.532	0.417

Note: OLS. Bold entries are unstandardized regression coefficients; standard errors are in italics.

$*p < .10$ $**p < .05$ $***p < .01$

TABLE 3.10

Multivariate Analysis of Informational Content, Engagement Features, and Mobilization Tools on 2006 House Web Sites

Independent variables	Content	Engagement	Mobilization
Party (Democrats = reference category)			
Republicans	**−0.030**	**−0.081*****	**−0.042*****
	0.023	*0.019*	*0.012*
Libertarians	**−0.002**	**−0.193*****	**−0.070****
	0.052	*0.042*	*0.028*
Greens	**0.024**	**−0.098***	**−0.082****
	0.066	*0.053*	*0.035*
Others	**−0.029**	**−0.211*****	**−0.088*****
	0.046	*0.037*	*0.025*
Incumbency status (open-seat candidates = reference category)			
Incumbents	**−0.054**	**0.094*****	**0.035***
	0.039	*0.031*	*0.021*
Challengers	**−0.098*****	**0.019**	**−0.010**
	0.037	*0.030*	*0.020*
Competitive seat	**−0.064***	**0.013**	**0.030***
	0.033	*0.026*	*0.018*
Contributions received (ln)	**0.024*****	**0.023*****	**0.012*****
	0.003	*0.003*	*0.002*
Percentage with college degrees	**0.0004**	**0.001**	**0.001**
	0.001	*0.001*	*0.001*
Percentage over age 64	**0.004**	**−0.003**	**−0.004****
	0.003	*0.003*	*0.002*
Percentage white	**0.0005**	**0.0005**	**0.0003**
	0.001	*0.001*	*0.000*
Percentage urban	**0.001**	**0.0004**	**0.001**
	0.001	*0.001*	*0.000*
Intercept	**0.265*****	**0.283*****	**0.158*****
	0.072	*0.058*	*0.039*
N	865	865	865
Adjusted R^2	0.109	0.287	0.244

Note: OLS. Bold entries are unstandardized regression coefficients; standard errors are in italics.

*$p < .10$ **$p < .05$ ***$p < .01$

Money, party affiliation, and incumbency status also were important factors explaining the extent to which House candidates used their Web sites to engage their supporters. But in contrast to what we observed in the analysis of the Senate sites, House Democratic candidates were the most likely to use the Web for connecting supporters with the campaign. In addition, challengers were the most likely to use their Web sites for engaging supporters, while incumbents were the least likely to do so. Again, because incumbents also have an office Web site, they may not see the need to invest the time to manage these services, unless they already have covered most of their other campaign activities and then still have plenty of excess funds available for other activities.

The third column of table 3.10 displays the results of the multivariate analysis of mobilization, which are generally similar to the results observed for engagement. Democratic candidates were the most likely to use the Web for mobilizing their supporters, while Republicans did not behave any differently than the minor-party candidates. Again this gap between Democrats and Republicans is surprising given the emphasis on mobilization that Republican consultants and strategists employed as recently as the 2004 presidential election. Incumbents also were less likely to use the Web for mobilizing their supporters, but the gap between challengers and open-seat candidates was not significant. In contrast to what we observed for the Senate, both money and competitiveness were significant in explaining mobilization. While candidates see mobilization tools as necessary for winning a campaign in both Senate and House races, it is a standard set of features in online campaigning only for those House campaigns with the most financial resources. Finally, in contrast to Senate sites, one constituency factor was significant in explaining the number of mobilization tools on House sites. Candidates running in districts with more senior citizens were less likely to employ online mobilization tools than candidates in districts with fewer senior citizens. It may be that in a smaller constituency, older voters expect candidates to use more face-to-face methods of encouraging advocacy for the campaign and candidates thus redirect fewer resources to online campaigning.

Conclusions and Discussion

By 2006, increases in Web presence had slowed and appeared at or near a plateau. Third-party and independent candidates had closed the gap with major-party candidates in Senate races, but not in the House races. Absent a serious challenge, incumbents and poorly financed candidates for the House tend to forego posting a campaign Web site.

In terms of informational content, House candidates, particularly independents or those from third parties, were not as likely as those running for the Senate to post information about their issue positions. Biographies and campaign news were less prevalent, and the difference between major- and minor-party candidates was pronounced, but a majority of each group included these informational features. These findings confirm our expectation that baseline informational Web content has become standardized. On the other hand, technologically sophisticated audio and video content showed the largest gap between the two levels of office, and among the major-party candidates and third-party and independent candidates. Only for major-party Senate campaigns did audio and video content achieve saturation level.

House and Senate candidates were equally likely to involve and engage visitors by providing the means to donate online or request an e-newsletter. Online volunteer sign-up was the most prevalent mobilization tool for both levels of office, but the percentages dwindled for other means of sharing or distributing Web content to others. Only about one-third of the campaigns posted the candidate's schedule or voter registration information. Third-party and independent candidates lagged behind on all involvement and mobilization features. These findings illustrate the greater emphasis campaigns place on political activities relative to public ones (Lusoli 2005). Finally, although small percentages of congressional candidates took advantage of the newest innovations and interactive features in 2006, Senate races lead the way.

Multivariate regression analyses provided additional insights into which candidate, electoral, and constituency factors explained differences in Web site content and sophistication. Results varied for House and Senate campaigns, as well as across the three content domains. Financial resources underwrite the highest levels of informational and engagement content, although we also found that the Web sites of Democrats, Greens, and challengers demonstrated more interest in relationship building. This seems to reflect both a difference in party philosophy (the former two cases) and a greater need to establish a connection with voters (the latter two cases). Democrats also hold an edge in mobilization content, but the competitiveness of the race emerges as an additional factor. Volunteers are an important resource that can tip the balance, mattering as much in close House races as money, which can be harder to raise than for the higher-visibility Senate seats.

The 2006 midterm elections witnessed three trends that offer a preview of what to expect in 2008. First, lower offices, third parties, and less well financed candidates can and do close the gap with higher-status peers on baseline Web site features and functionality. Moreover, their increasing use of campaign Web sites to lay out issue positions suggests that the World Wide Web affords them better coverage than these candidates would garner in mainstream media outlets. The converse also holds: higher-office seekers affiliated with either major party and financially well endowed will be the first and most likely to deploy cutting edge Web site features and technology. Disadvantaged candidates face a moving target as the innovation bar is raised each election cycle. Finally, we find more evidence that Web-site features and functionality by which citizens coproduce content and interact in two-way communication with the campaign and each other are not being adopted widely or quickly. That will require removing the disincentives of high investment of time and low control over message and increasing the demand for such services from political activists and other key constituencies.

One of the major innovations of the 2006 midterm elections emerged not on campaign Web sites but on social network sites such as Facebook, MySpace, and You Tube. Facebook profiles typically included informational content such as photographs, statements on policy positions, and qualifications for office. These became, in effect, mini campaign Web sites that Facebook members could find by searching for the candidate by name, party, or geographic location. The feature involved and engaged members because they could register support for the candidate, post comments on the candidate's "wall," and invite their friends to become supporters. Facebook then displayed the number of supporters for each candidate and calculated the percentage of "votes" that candidate had in their race.[11] The site facilitated mobilization by including a link to Rock the Vote, which provides voter registration and other election information targeted at young people.

The interesting question is whether these social network sites can be appropriated for political purposes as a campaign resource targeted to specific new populations.[12] Other innovations such as blogs and mobile technologies have not lived up to expectations for their election role, and Meetup seems more useful in bringing together people who are geographically dispersed for pursuit of national level office, as Howard Dean and Wesley Clark did in the 2004 presidential nomination contest. At this point, social network sites would not appear to be substitutes for campaign Web sites: they serve a different primary purpose and audience whose reasons for visiting lie elsewhere. Like Meetup, they may serve to identify supporters to each other across spatial boundaries and create a community of interest that can pursue its political objectives through traditional offline activities (Sander 2005). For the candidates, these social networking sites offer low-cost exposure to a demographic that may be of particular interest or to a volunteer recruitment pool. In contrast to campaign Web sites, any other benefit would seem to derive from their potential for long-term relationship building. For the campaigns, however, the interesting question becomes whether their official Web sites will acknowledge and promote their social networking profiles or, if they want to take mobilization to the next level, integrate social networking tools into their own campaign strategy.

APPENDIX 3.1. CODING PROTOCOL

1. Candidate ID #.
2. Candidate name.
3. Candidate's biography (on home page or separate section).
4. Candidate/campaign news (on home page or separate section).
5. Issue statements or section (not including discussion of issues in biographical statement; ok if issues clearly identified on home page).
6. Campaign videos (professionally made videos, such as campaign ads and welcome messages; video coverage of campaign, speeches, events, interviews; and home-made videos, similar to the material found on YouTube).
7. Downloadable campaign materials (the only example seems to be a PDF version of a flier or brochure).
8. RSS (XML and other similar feeders, such as My Yahoo or My MSN).
9. Online volunteer sign-up forms.
10. E-newsletter subscription.
11. Information about obtaining or ordering campaign merchandise (does not include check-offs in "volunteer" section; includes campaign materials such as signs, banners, stickers and buttons, and merchandise such as t-shirts and coffee mugs).
12. Donations by credit card (make sure you can pay by credit card, not just fill out information and print out the form w/payment; does not include check-offs in "volunteer section").
13. Voter registration information (this includes knowing where to vote, how and where to register, information on absentee ballot, early voting).
14. Foreign-language version or content (this may appear on a filter page, prior to home page).
15. Campaign schedule (Where will the candidate be? Make sure there is actual content here, about the candidate's future whereabouts. One site simply listed November 7, Election Day, as the only campaign event.).
16. Can e-mail campaign (this includes traditional e-mail link or a form that pops up to write your message).
17. Online poll or survey (usually about voters' opinions).
18. Candidate/campaign blog.
19. Online chat (real time chat, could be 24/7 or scheduled chats).
20. Webcam (for example, 24/7 coverage of campaign office or of specific event).
21. Event form (does not include schedule of events; includes allowing a supporter to RSVP or sign up for a reminder, invite the candidate to an event, organize a new event, host a house party)
22. Tell a friend (Is there a way to pass on information to a friend?).

23. Letter-to-the-editor link/form (this provides supporters with a link to a newspaper's online letter-to-the-editor form. We are not counting campaign-written letters that are forwarded to the newspaper.

24. Initials of coder:

NOTES

An earlier version of this chapter was published in *Social Science Computer Review* (2007) 25: 443–465. Reprinted by permission.

1. According to Foot and Schneider (2006), "informing" refers to the creation of Web site features that present information; "involving" refers to those that facilitate affiliation (relationship building) between the site's producer and visitors; "connecting" involves creating a bridge between site users and a third actor; and "mobilizing" allows users to involve others in the goals and objectives of the campaign, generally by employing online tools in the service of offline activities.

2. Our list of candidates initially was derived from candidates listed on Politics1.com, Project Vote Smart, and C-SPAN.org. Once the elections were complete, we removed any candidates that were not included on the "Offical List of Nominees for the 110th Congress," obtained from the House of Representatives Office of the Clerk. The only candidates we excluded from our final data file that were on the official list were write-in candidates, who were not included on any official election results.

3. To see how the Web sites appeared when they were coded, go to www.archive.org and enter the site's complete URL into the WayBackMachine search.

4. Since we also recorded the initials of all coders, we were able to check if any coders made too many errors. We identified one such coder and removed all of that coder's work from the analysis. Corrections were made in any case where mistakes were found.

5. The lack of variance on the dependent variable Web presence is not conducive to performing multivariate logistic regression analysis for our Senate data. Running the same model as the House resulted in no significant results.

6. For both of these features, we did not have the resources to follow up on whether visitors received a response from the campaign after they expressed an interest in volunteering or receiving the e-newsletter. In 2008, taking a sample of the Web sites and tracking responses from the campaign would provide additional insight into how campaigns use the Web and specifically how they are using it to engage supporters.

7. Facebook is a self-enrolling online community whose members, prior to 2006, consisted primarily of students, faculty, and staff at U.S. colleges and universities. To allow its members to connect with candidates, Facebook created entries for all U.S. congressional and gubernatorial candidates in September and then allowed the candidates or their campaign staff to personalize their profiles with everything from photographs to qualifications for office. Because this feature was not part of the candidate's official campaign Web site, we did not seek to identify the presence or absence of a Facebook profile as part of our content analysis. Rather we went directly to Facebook's Election Pulse (http://www.facebook.com/election_pulse.php) and identified which candidates had personalized their profiles by the end of October.

GIRISH J. GULATI AND CHRISTINE B. WILLIAMS

8. The standard volunteer form allows a supporter to indicate his or her interest in the following activities: scheduler, organize meetings, researcher, schedule events, fund-raiser, accompany candidate to events, press secretary, sign holder on street, fairs, in front of meetings, volunteer coordinator, distribute pamphlets, phone caller, write thank you letters, media list organizer, computer expert, Internet expert, and other.

9. Issues, e-mail address, biography, news, and audio/video clips make up the Content Index. Credit card donations, online volunteer form, e-newsletter sign-up, blog, voting information, and candidate's schedule make up the Engagement Index. Downloadable materials, tell-a-friend, campaign materials, event form, letter-to-the-editor, foreign language content, online volunteer form, and voting information make up the Mobilization Scale.

   The items for each scale were selected on the basis of face validity and subjected to a factor analysis to confirm that all the items loaded on a single factor. Those that did not load high were excluded from the index. Items that loaded high on multiple indices were included in each.

10. Vote results were obtained from CNN (http://www.cnn.com/ELECTION/2006/). When results for minor-party candidates were not available, we obtained the data directly from the state agency responsible for compiling voting records and results. Campaign finance data were obtained from the Federal Election Commission. Our four indicators for citizen demand are the median household income in the state, the percentage of residents over age twenty-four with a college degree, the percentage of residents above age sixty-four, and the percentage of residents classified as white. These data are from the 2000 Census and were obtained from the U.S Bureau of the Census.

11. Barack Obama (D-IL), not a candidate for reelection in 2006, had the highest number of supporters, with 21, 897, followed by Senate candidates Hillary Clinton (D-NY) with 15, 444 and Bob Casey (D-PA) with 10,062

12. Eons.com is a social network site aimed at baby boomers; CafeMom.com is one of several aimed at mothers. And the Facebook and MySpace demographic is spreading out: today, less than half are between the ages of eighteen and twenty-four (*Boston Globe*, March 7, 2007, pp. A1 and A14).

Benoit, P., and W. Benoit. 2005. "Criteria for Evaluating Political Campaign Webpages." *Southern Communication Journal* 70 (3): 230–247.

Bimber, B., and R. Davis. 2003. *Campaigning Online: The Internet in U.S. Elections.* New York: Oxford University Press.

Chadwick, A. 2006. *Internet Politics: States, Citizens, and New Communications Technologies.* New York: Oxford University Press.

Conners, J. 2005. "Meetup, Blogs and Online Involvement: U.S. Senate Campaign Web Sites of 2004." Paper presented at the annual meeting of the American Political Science Association, Washington, DC.

Cornfield, M., and L. Rainie. 2006. "The Web Era Isn't as New as You Think." *Washington Post*, p. B 3. November 5.

D'Alessio, D. 1997. "Use of the World Wide Web in the 1996 U.S. Election." *Electoral Studies* 16 (4): 489–500.

Druckman, J., M. Kifer, and M. Parkin. 2006. "Campaigns in a New Media Age: How Candidates Use the World Wide Web." Paper presented at the annual meeting of the Midwest Political Science Association, Chicago.

Dulio, D. A., D. Goff, and J. Thurber. 1999. "Untangled Web: Internet Use During the 1998 Election." *PS: Political Science and Politics* 32 (1): 53–59.

Endres, D., and B. Warnick. 2004. "Text-Based Interactivity in Candidate Campaign Web Sites: A Case Study From the 2002 Elections." *Western Journal of Communication* 68 (3): 322–342.

Foot, K., and S. Schneider. 2002. "Online Action in Campaign 2000: An Exploratory Analysis of the U.S. Political Web Sphere." *Journal of Broadcasting and Electronic Media* 46:222–244.

Foot, K., and S. Schneider. 2006. *Web Campaigning*. Cambridge, MA: MIT Press.

Gibson, R., and I. McAllister. 2006. "Does Cyber-Campaigning Win Votes? Online Communication in the 2004 Australian Election." *Journal of Elections, Public Opinion, and Parties* 16 (3): 243–263.

Gibson, R., and S. Ward. 2000. "A Proposed Methodology for Studying the Function and Effectiveness of Party and Candidate Web Sites." *Social Science Computer Review* 18 (3): 301–319.

Gibson, R., M. Margolis, D. Resnick, and S. Ward. 2003. "Election Campaigning on the WWW in the USA and UK: A Comparative Analysis." *Party Politics* 9 (1): 47–75.

Graf, J., G. Reeher, M. Mablin, and C. Panagopoulos. 2006. *Small Donors and Online Giving: A Study of Donors to the 2004 Presidential Campaigns*. Washington DC: Institute of Politics, Democracy & the Internet.

Greer, J., and M. LaPointe. 2004. "Cyber-Campaigning Grows Up: A Comparative Content Analysis of Web Sites for US Senate and Gubernatorial Races." In *Electronic Democracy, Mobilisation, Organisation, and Participation via New ICTs*, ed. Rachel Kay Gibson, Andrea Rommele, and Stephen J. Ward, 116–132. London: Routledge.

Gulati, G. 2003. "Campaigning for Congress on the World Wide Web and the Implications for Strong Democracy." Paper presented at the annual meeting of the American Political Science Association, Philadelphia.

Gulati, G., M. Just, and A. Crigler. 2004. "News Coverage of Political Campaigns." In *The Handbook of Political Communication Research*, ed. L. Kaid, 237–256. New York: Erlbaum.

Herrnson, P., A. Stokes-Brown, and M Hindman (forthcoming). "Campaign Politics and the Digital Divide: Constituency Characteristics, Strategic Considerations, and Candidate Internet Use in State Legislative Elections." *Political Research Quarterly*.

Ireland, E., and P. Nash. 2001. *Winning Campaigns Online: Strategies for Candidates and Causes: Second Edition*. Bethesda, MD: Science Writers Press.

Jacobson, G. 2004. *The Politics of Congressional Elections*. 6th ed. New York: Addison-Wesley.

Jankowski, N., and R. van Os. 2004. "The 2004 European Parliament Election and the Internet: Contribution to a European Public Sphere?" Paper presented at the annual meeting of Internet Communication in Intelligent Societies, Hong Kong.

Kamarck, E. 2002. "Political Campaigning on the Internet: Business as Usual?" In *Governance.com: Democracy in the Information Age*, ed. E. Kamarck and J. Nye Jr., 81–103. Washington, DC: Brookings Institution.

Klotz, R. 1997. "Positive Spin: Senate Campaigning on the Web." *PS: Political Science and Politics* 30 (3): 482–486.

———. 2004. *The Politics of Internet Communication*. New York: Rowman and Littlefield.

———. 2007. "Internet Campaigning for Grassroots and Astroturf Support." *Social Science Computer Review* 25 (1): 3–12.

Lusoli, W. 2005. "Politics Makes Strange Bedfellows." *Harvard International Journal of Press/Politics* 10 (4): 71–97.

Lusoli, W., R. Gibson, and S. Ward. 2007. "Italian Elections Online: Ten Years On." In *The 2006 Italian Elections*, ed. J. Newell. Manchester, UK: Manchester University Press.

Mayhew, D. 1974. *Congress: The Electoral Connection*. New Haven, CT: Yale University Press.

Norris, P. 2001. *Digital Divide: Civic Engagement, Information Poverty, and the Internet Worldwide*. New York: Cambridge University Press.

Panagopoulos, C. 2005. "Minor Parties and the Internet." Paper presented at the annual meeting of the Midwest Political Science Association, Chicago.

Puopolo, S. 2001. "The Web and U.S. Senatorial Campaigns 2000." *American Behavioral Scientist* 44 (12): 2030–2047.

Rainie, L., M. Cornfield, and J. Horrigan. 2005. *The Internet and Campaign 2004*. Washington, DC: Pew Internet and American Life Project (accessed March 25, 2005, at http://www.pewinternet.org/pdfs/PIP_2004_Campaign.pdf).

Rainie, L., and J. Horrigan. 2007. *Election 2006 Online*. Washington, DC: Pew Internet and American Life Project (accessed March 25, 2007, at http://www.pewinternet.org/pdfs/PIP_Politics_2006.pdf).

Sander, T. 2005. "e-Associations? Using Technology to Connect Citizens: The Case of Meetup.com." Paper presented at the annual meeting of the American Political Science Association, Washington, DC.

Stromer-Galley, J. 2000. "On-line Interaction and Why Candidates Avoid It." *Journal of Communication* 50 (4): 111–132.

Van Dijk, J. 2005. *The Deepening Divide: Inequality in the Informational Society*. Thousand Oaks, CA: Sage Publications.

Ward, S., Gibson, R., and W. Lusoli. 2006. "The Same the World Over? Candidate Campaigning Online in the UK and Australia." Paper presented at the Elections, Parties and Opinion Polls Conference, Nottingham, UK.

Williams, C., A. Aylesworth, and K. Chapman. 2002. "The 2002 e-Campaign for U.S. Senate." *Journal of Political Marketing* 1 (4): 39–63.

Williams, C., and G. Gulati. 2006. "The Evolution of Online Campaigning in Congressional Elections, 2000–2004." Paper presented at the annual meeting of the American Political Science Association, Philadelphia.

Xenos, M., and K. Foot. 2005. "Politics as Usual or Politics Unusual? Position-Taking and Dialogue on Campaign Web Sites in the 2002 U.S. Elections." *Journal of Communication* 55 (1): 169–185.

4

Trickle-Down Technology?

The Use of Computing and Network Technology in State Legislative Campaigns

CHAPMAN RACKAWAY

Technological advances increase the sophistication and improve the quality of numerous processes in the United States today. Businesses use technology, especially telecommunications technology, to improve the quality of their marketing efforts. Teachers use technology in the classroom to improve student learning outcomes. At the federal level at least, we know that the same is true of legislative campaigns. Technology advances the cause of federal-level campaigners, but does it have the same effect at the state level?

Scholars have shown that there is a lag effect in adopting new campaign techniques: candidates at the state level are slower to employ new campaign methods than their federal counterparts (Lynch and Rozell 2002). The last two presidential elections have seen an increase in popular media attention to the use of technology in the campaigns of the two nominees (Theimer 2003). The institutionalization of technology use in lower-level campaigns, though, has not been nearly as well explored.

How much has technology drilled down from federal campaigns to their state legislative counterparts? Are candidates and the members of their campaigns committed to using technology? Do legislative professionalism, fund-raising, party involvement, and professional management relate to a campaign's propensity to use technology?

Has Campaign Technology "Trickled Down" to the State-Level Candidate?

Observers point to 2006 as the breakthrough year for technology in campaign politics. presidential races have used Web technology for some time, but they are the cutting edge of technological use because of their professionalism and large fund-raising base. Lower-level campaigns find it much more difficult to devote the money and personnel to technology that are required to use it properly. However, for campaign technology to matter, it must be used at multiple levels of politics. Reich and Solomon point to 2006 as the year that campaigns across the board institutionalized the greater use of technology, but they focus on federal-level elections. The question remains whether technology has drilled down to state-level races as well, which would suggest that technology is truly embedded in campaigns throughout the American political realm (Reich and Solomon 2007).

Reich and Solomon also provide a guide for technology by categorizing the campaign uses of technology. Three particular areas stand out: building community; watching (and listening) as it all unfolds; and mobilizing the masses. Reich and Solomon make the case that technology allows for much more frequent and direct campaign communication to create a stable base of volunteers and use them as well as communicate campaign messages to an undecided audience.

Other research suggests a significant incentive for campaigns to adopt the technological tools that presidential candidates have been using for a decade. A 2006 survey showed that voters expect campaigns to use the Internet for campaign outreach. Eighty-seven percent of respondents to the survey expect political candidates to have a Web site; 70 percent expect the campaigns to use e-mail for direct voter communication; two-thirds expect candidates to use the Internet for fund raising, post video commercials on their Web sites, and run online ad campaigns; half expect campaigns to have blogs and podcasts (*Survey Says*, 2006).

Virtual Nuts and Bolts: Technological Components of the Current Campaign

No academic literature relates directly to the use of technology in campaigns. We can, however, determine eighteen different technological elements in the popular press that campaigns can use to satisfy the Reich and Solomon categories of communication, community building, and supporter mobilization. To the Reich and Solomon categories, we must add one more vital element: identification. In order to communicate with voters, a campaign must find them. Having a database of voters in the district in which a candidate is running is essential in using computing technology effectively (Blaemire 2001; Blaemire 2002).

For identifying voters, we can specify a single important campaign element: the use of a voter file or database. Campaigns can develop their own voter database using publicly available data from county clerks, secretaries of state, state political parties, or other sources. Some campaigns have access to voter files available over the Internet made available through parties or vendors, which allow them to query the database for specific information without creating or maintaining the database internally (Blaemire 2004).

One important new development in the use of those databases emerged in the form of 2004's most significant advance: "microtargeting." Microtargeting is the use of individual-level data for the purpose of focusing campaign messages on specific voters (Weigel 2006; Cornfeld 2007). Political parties and national campaigns have collected massive voter databases, merging magazine subscription and interest group membership rosters with state-produced voter lists.

In 2004, the Bush campaign used their microtargeting database to particular advantage among snowmobile owners in Michigan. By subsetting out snowmobile-enthusiast magazine subscribers, the Bush campaign could send a very specific message criticizing opponent John Kerry's environmental policy proposals and how they would affect snowmobilers (Gilgoff 2006). Microtargeting, connected with direct mail media, allow for increasing campaign sophistication and the narrow communication of campaign messages to potentially more responsive audiences.

The microtargeting data can be used not just to send mail to voters but also to pinpoint their homes for face-to-face contact. Some campaigns will use Global Information Systems (GIS) software, also called mapping software, to combine individual-level identification data with maps to guide door-to-door canvassers (Weigel 2006). Campaigns can tailor their face-to-face messages to specific neighborhoods or households when using the voter file and GIS software in tandem. Since research has shown that face-to-face interaction has the highest potential to drive turnout, being able to do door-to-door campaigning more efficiently and effectively would greatly benefit a campaign (Green 2004).

There is more software available than just GIS mapping, though. A number of vendors have created all-inclusive campaign management software that will database voters as well as volunteers, manage donations and track expenditures, allow budgeting and calendar management, and perform mail and e-mail merges. Some software even includes communication technology known as "team tools" that let staff and volunteers in the campaign communicate among themselves and help organize campaign activities. Campaigns have been using such software for a decade, but again that knowledge comes from federal-level campaigns only (Gimpel 2003).

For communication, the basic strategy involves activating a campaign Web site. Both of the major party nominees in 2000 used and aggressively promoted their Web sites, and in 2004 the candidates incorporated other tools to encourage regular traffic to those Web sites. As Web usage has expanded among the populace, campaigns have followed those voters online.

Campaign Web sites can be amazingly easy to establish. A single year of basic Web hosting, plus a domain name, costs less than sixty dollars. However, sophisticated Web sites require graphics, design, time to update, and some knowledge of HTML or other programming code. Campaigns at the state level may or may not see a value in putting so much time and effort into a Web site.

Within the Web site, there are more specific elements that point to the sophistication of Web use. A campaign may, for example, simply choose to put a Web page up that is an electronic version of a brochure: static and unchanging. The advantage of a Web site over traditional broadcast or print media is that it can change almost constantly and provide a variety of content choices. Weblogs, or blogs, can take the place of a campaign diary that keeps encouraging people to come to the Web site for new content daily, or more often, depending on the faithfulness of the poster. Blogs also allow viewer interaction in the form of comments that registered users can leave on the postings (Dotson 2007).

Another Web technology that presidential candidates have embraced is the microsite. Voters may not be interested in going to the candidate's primary Web site, but they may go to a site set up for a specific purpose. A microsite is a small Web site, separate from an organization or campaign's default Web site, with a separate domain name (or URL); it delivers more focused content about a specific platform item, issue, or concept. Microsites can be designed more effectively to be indexed by search engines, or become a hub for fund-raising or outreach programs ("Political Microsites," 2007). Howard Dean's 2004 campaign used microsites for specific constituency groups such as "Libertarians for Dean" and "Students for Dean." Messages can be targeted most specifically on microsites and have been shown to be very effective mobilization tools (Trippi 2004).

Blogs simply scratch the surface of what can be put on a Web site. Web-only video, known as viral video, can be uploaded to YouTube and posted on the Web site for viewers to see. One of the most popular pieces of viral video in a campaign was the short film *White House West*, which starred comedian Will Ferrell impersonating President George W. Bush for the liberal activist group Americans Coming Together. *White House West* was never broadcast on television but did appear on countless computer desktops, carrying a campaign message against President Bush while he was running for reelection in 2004 (Sender 2007).

Campaigns do not just put short films online; they also produce ads that are never to air on television but short enough to do so. The George W. Bush reelection campaign of 2004 started the practice of posting Web-only video on its Web site with the ad "Unprincipled," which attacked John Kerry's war record. One observer called the introduction of Web-only advertising "the single biggest innovation of the 2004 presidential campaign" (Manatt

2004). If technology does truly trickle down from the presidential level into the state campaigns, then 2006 should have shows at least some signs of Web-only video.

Three more possible Web elements remain, though, and they are some of the newest developments in Web technology. Podcasts are downloadable audio files that campaigns can record and post to their Web site, while RSS (Really Simply Syndication) feeds allow voters to use a Web browser plug-in to get a summary of new additions to the Web site with clickable hyperlinks to selectively investigate new items of interest on the campaign Web site. Additionally, campaigns can use e-postcards, electronic buttons, or other downloadable content for voter-to-voter communication that allow enthusiastic supporters to take the campaign message out to their own friends. Software can be written in-house or purchased from vendors to enable such interactive tools as well (Blanchfield 2006a).

For communication with and mobilization of those voters, Internet technology can also be extremely effective. Campaigns can use e-mail databases to communicate not only internally about electoral matters but also send messages to supporters. E-mail is not the only way to communicate with the public, too. Some campaigns in the United States and elsewhere in the world message their voters using SMS or text messaging on their cellular phones (Blanchfield 2006b).

The final area where campaigns are making use of technology is in their fund-raising efforts. Excepting the self-financed campaign, every candidate at every level needs to raise some kind of money. Traditional methods of direct mail and phone calls are being augmented or even replaced in some cases with Internet fund-raising. Technology allows separate databasing of donors and through e-commerce solutions campaigns can take donations online (Blaemire 2001; Donatelli 2005).

In sum, the following elements constitute a fairly complete list of campaign technologies a candidate's organization may decide to use. Each category is listed with its individual components:

1. Voter Identification and Location:
    a. Voter file or database
    b. GIS/mapping software
    c. Campaign software
    d. Team Tools
2. Communication Technologies
    a. Web site
    b. Blogs
    c. Viral video
    d. Web-only advertising

     e. Podcasts

     f. E-postcards/buttons/outreach

     g. RSS feeds

     h. Microsites/grassroots mobilization and outreach sites

     i. Other downloadable materials

  3. Direct Communication

     a. E-mail for voter contact

     b. E-mail for internal campaign communication

     c. Text/SMS messaging

  4. Fundraising

     a. Donor databases

     b. Online fund-raising

A campaign will use none of the above, a small collection of them, or perhaps the entirety of the techniques. All have been used at the presidential campaign level, but the question at hand relates to the use of those techniques at lower-level campaigns. As previous research shows, presidential and congressional campaigns develop techniques such as direct mail or fund-raising, and after a lag time state campaigns adopt those same techniques (Salmore and Salmore 1993; Lynch and Rozell 2002). Does technology use by a campaign follow this trend of "congressionalization"?

Lynch and Rozell's analysis calls Salmore and Salmore's results into question. The authors focused their efforts on the Virginia state legislative races for 1995. While there were many elements of increased professionalism in that year's campaigns, they were not well diffused throughout the body of candidates for office. One advantage that Lynch and Rozell show is that specific states will have distinct political cultures, and, as a result, different approaches to the use of campaign techniques, whether they be professional consultants or the employment of technology.

Lynch and Rozell chose a single state to study, which makes generalizing their results problematic. Indeed, with its professional legislature and proximity to Washington, DC (where the majority of campaign professionals can be hired, particularly for off-year elections), Virginia represents a unique case that provides little insight into other states. To truly tell if a lag effect exists, we must survey more than one state and ensure that the states in question are sufficiently different to compare.

In order to gauge the expansion of technology into state campaigns, we must have a mechanism to audit the state of technology use by state-level campaigns. As part of a larger research project in which I am engaged, the Changing State Legislative Campaign Project, I have probed two sets of state legislative candidates in the 2006 electoral cycle regarding their campaigns' use of technology.

online. Kansas's Secretary of State and Governmental Ethics Commission Web sites provided candidate names and addresses in addition to vote totals and campaign finance reports. North Carolina's State Board of Elections provided the same information.

Data and Method

To assess the state of technology use in those campaigns, I developed a survey originally created by Paul Herrnson and Owen Abbe of the University of Maryland. Professor Herrnson graciously provided me with a copy of his original instrument, which I adapted and added to for this project. Herrnson's survey was originally published in 2003 based on a 2000 survey of state legislative candidates in 1997 and 1998 (Herrnson 2003).

Abbe and Herrnson's work is instructive because of their parallel findings about campaign professionalism. At the state level, the candidates who hired political professionals were ones who were well funded (either self-financed or traditionally fund-raised). Not all campaigns used professional assistance, meaning there was a "professionalism gap" among state-level campaigns. We would expect campaigns that have professional staffing to be more likely to understand sophisticated campaign techniques and therefore more likely to use technology for campaign duties. Since Internet technology was only in use at the presidential level at the time of Abbe and Herrnson's work, there were no technology questions in the instrument. I have therefore added questions on the use of and satisfaction with each of the eighteen technological elements in a campaign.

After adapting Herrnson's survey, I collected the names, mailing addresses, and e-mail addresses of all candidates for the Kansas and North Carolina houses of representatives from their respective state elections officials. Both states provided databases with names and mailing addresses, but North Carolina did not include e-mail addresses in its database. The absence of available e-mail addresses precipitated a two-pronged approach to my study.

I conducted the survey through a combined traditional mail delivery and online entry. The initial mailing included a paper copy of the survey and a postage-prepaid return envelope along with a URL for the online survey instrument. For Kansas candidates, I e-mailed the candidates with a live-link URL to complete the survey online. Only six candidates chose to complete the online survey, however, as the vast majority completed their survey on paper.

A total of 378 candidates sought election to the legislatures of the two states in 2006, with 200 office-seekers in Kansas and 178 in North Carolina. Combining the online with paper mailed returns yielded 132 responses, for

Cases for Study

The Changing State Legislative Campaign Project selected two states for an in-depth survey of campaign professionalism: party involvement, and technology use. I chose the states of Kansas and North Carolina as the test subjects for the project.

Kansas and North Carolina are well-suited choices for analysis because of the contrasts between them. Kansas has a nonprofessional legislature in a midwestern state with a strong history of citizen politics. North Carolina has a professional legislature and is located in the South, with a history of more professionalized politics. Both states elect their entire slate of state representatives in even-numbered years. Midwestern/Plains states like Kansas are distant enough from Washington, DC, that they have little to no access to for-hire consultants from within the Beltway and little to no consultant base within the state. North Carolina, being closer to the DC area, would be more likely to have professionals who in turn would suggest an increased technological presence.

Kansas's legislature has 125 members, while North Carolina's has 120; there are a roughly equal number of districts despite very different populations. The states differ in partisan legislative control, as well. Kansas has a dominant 77–48 Republican majority, while North Carolina Democrats enjoy a 68–52 seat advantage in their House. North Carolina's 2005 population was listed by the Census Bureau at almost nine million, while Kansas's was 2.7 million. North Carolina differs from Kansas in having term limits. Kansas shows longer legislative careers and thus less familiarity with the technological advancements in today's campaigns.

The concentration of voters in North Carolina's districts may tell us that candidates need to be more creative in their efforts to reach voters than their counterparts in Kansas. The more voters in a district, the lower likelihood that a given candidate can reach all of the people he or she would like to meet face-to-face. With cultural, partisan, and structural differences, Kansas and North Carolina make good comparative cases around which to build a study.

One other cautionary note involves the differences between election processes in the two states. While North Carolina elects both its house and senate every two years, Kansas elects its entire state senate only in presidential years. Therefore, in 2006 there was no election to the Kansas senate. Since there is no comparison between Kansas and North Carolina's senate campaigns, I purposefully excluded the North Carolina senate data from this study.

Finally, data availability helped drive the choice of Kansas and North Carolina. For both states, necessary and relevant information could be found

TABLE 4.1

Basic Descriptive Sample Statistics

Democrat	70
Republican	62
Kansas	74
North Carolina	58

a 34.92 percent response rate. While disappointingly small, the return rate was enough to produce valid findings. Table 4.1 reports the basic frequencies for characteristics of the candidates who completed the survey. Democrats are slightly overrepresented, with 70 respondents compared with 62 Republicans. The differences are small, so they do not affect the results. Kansans returned their surveys at a better rate than North Carolinian candidates, with 74 Kansas returns to 58 from North Carolina. Overall, there should be no concerns about the representativeness of the data based on these results.

Once survey data was returned and entered, the two state disclosure offices provided total votes per candidate, as well as campaign finance data. I collected total contribution data for each campaign, in addition to more specific source-sector contribution data available through the Institute for Money in State Politics at www.followthemoney.org. Business, labor union, and political party committee contributions are all available through the Institute Web site, as is data on in-state contributions versus out-of-state contributions. Theoretically, a campaign with more out-of-state contributions would be more sophisticated and thus more likely to use technology on a wider scale.

With the addition of the voting and campaign finance data to the survey database, all of the necessary information was collected. Three questions are to be addressed in the remainder of this research: (1) How much of each of the eighteen forms of technology does a campaign use? (2) What factors, if any, drive the use of technology in a campaign? (3) Does technology impact the success of a campaign?

To test those three questions, I will use a variety of methods. To answer the first question regarding progress of technology, simply frequencies will suffice. For the second question, which assumes a binary dependent variable (did the campaign use that technology or not?), logistic regression is appropriate. Finally, the third question probes how vote totals change according to the use of technology, and with a theoretically unlimited number of votes available, standard OLS regression is the proper method of analysis.

Results: Technology Use

The answers to the first question of this project are remarkably similar to Abbe and Herrnson's findings, as well as those of Lynch and Rozell, that state legislative races do indeed lag behind their federal counterparts. State-level campaigns may be catching up to their "bigger siblings" in Congress and the presidency, but they are still at least two steps behind.

Table 4.2 reports the frequencies of use for each of the eighteen campaign technologies. A few important points stand out, most particularly that a majority of respondents use only four elements of the technology. Voter databases, perhaps the most basic and necessary of all technologies, are, unsurprisingly, used nearly universally. Nearly ninety percent of all state-level campaigns use a voter database of some kind, so that technology has reached

TABLE 4.2
Technology Use in Campaigns

Technology	Used	Percentage	Did not use	Percentage
Voter file or database	116	87.9	16	12.1
GIS/mapping software	54	41.9	78	59.1
Campaign software	38	28.8	94	71.2
Team tools	36	27.3	96	72.7
Web Site	88	66.7	44	33.3
Blogs	38	28.8	94	71.2
Viral video	24	18.2	108	81.8
Web-only advertising	32	24.2	100	75.8
Podcasts	26	19.7	106	80.3
E-postcards/buttons/outreach	42	31.8	94	68.2
RSS feeds	26	19.7	106	80.3
Microsites/grassroots mobilization/outreach sites	40	30.3	96	69.7
Other downloadable materials	26	19.7	106	80.3
E-mail for voter contact	82	62.1	54	37.9
E-mail for internal campaign communication	84	63.6	52	36.4
Text/SMS messaging	30	22.7	102	77.3
Donor databases	94	71.2	38	28.8
Online fund-raising	38	28.8	94	71.2

TABLE 4.3

State-Specific Distribution of Campaign Technology

Technology	KS	NC	N
Voter file or database	89.2%	86.3%	116
GIS/mapping software	43.2	37.9	54
Campaign software	32.4	24.1	38
Team tools	29.7	24.1	36
Web Site	64.9	69.0	88
Blogs	31.4	25.8	38
Viral video	18.9	17.2	24
Web-only advertising	24.3	24.1	32
Podcasts	21.6	17.2	26
E-postcards/buttons/outreach	29.7	34.5	42
RSS feeds	21.6	17.2	26
Microsites/grassroots mobilization/outreach sites	29.7	31.0	40
Other downloadable materials	24.3	13.8	26
E-mail for voter contact	67.6	55.2	82
E-mail for internal campaign communication	64.9	62.1	84
Text/SMS messaging	27.0	17.2	30
Donor databases	75.7	65.9	94
Online fund-raising	21.6	37.9	38

down to state campaigns. Donor databases are also used by almost two-third of all campaigns. Clearly data is important to these campaigns, but data management is not. Just 28.8 percent of campaigns used campaign management software, although more than 40 percent used GIS software. Mapping seems to be an intriguing value, and might have to do with Kansas's strong door-to-door tradition. Kansas voters value face-to-face contact, and mapping software helps make that door-to-door more productive and feasible.

The majority of respondent campaigns also use Web sites and e-mail communication, but none of the component technologies that would suggest sophistication on a greater scale. Just 28 percent of respondents had some kind of blog or daily diary component to their Web site, while less than a quarter had any kind of video on their site. Fewer than 20 percent of respondents used podcasts or RSS feeds in their campaign communication, and just over 30 percent used other downloadable or voter-to-voter mechanisms, such as e-postcards.

TABLE 4.4

Party-Specific Distribution of Campaign Technology

Technology	D	R	N
Voter file or database	85.7%	90.3%	116
GIS/mapping software	45.7	35.5	54
Campaign software	31.4	25.8	38
Team Tools	25.6	25.8	36
Website	71.4	61.3	88
Blogs	31.4	25.8	38
Viral video	17.1	19.4	24
Web-only advertising	25.7	22.6	32
Podcasts	17.1	22.6	26
E-postcards/buttons/outreach	34.3	29.0	42
RSS feeds	17.1	22.6	26
Microsites/grassroots mobilization/outreach sites	28.6	32.3	40
Other downloadable materials	17.1	22.6	26
E-mail for voter contact	62.9	61.3	82
E-mail for internal campaign communication	65.7	61.3	84
Text/SMS messaging	25.7	19.4	30
Donor databases	68.6	74.2	94
Online fund-raising	28.6	29.0	38

A "two-track" attitude toward technology appears in table 4.2. The elements that most campaigns integrate are either basic (e-mail use, campaign Web site creation, use of existing mobilization sites such as Meetup.com) or can be provided to all candidates through the state party organization (voter and donor files). Campaigns embrace technology that is easy for them to use or adapt to, but they do not embrace the higher-functionality elements that require more monetary investment or labor (e-postcards, viral video, team tools). The spread of campaign technology is advancing in state legislative campaigns, but that spread is not universal. Candidates who embrace technology use it selectively, and certainly not all candidates use the technology. The question remains whether any differences exist between candidates in the two states, the two parties, and incumbents and challengers.

Kansas is slightly more technologically sophisticated than North Carolina, though not by very much. With the notable exception of online fund-raising, among all respondents who did use any of the eighteen techno-logical components, Kansan candidates engaged in the majority of technology use. North Carolinians were more aggressive online fund-raisers, despite not using technology as much in any other way. The greater professionalism of North Carolina's campaigns likely puts a premium on fund-raising, and thus we get a glimpse into the mind of the Kansas and North Carolina candidates. Both see technology as a means to an end: North Carolina candidates appears to see technology mostly as a cash cow, while Kansans regard technology as a means to engage in traditional retail politics.

Party affiliation appears to make a difference in the use of technology. If money were the driving factor behind technology use, we would expect money-advantaged Republicans to use technology more aggressively, since they tend to raise more money. Democrats, though, tend to have technology

TABLE 4.5

Seat Status Distribution of Campaign Technology

Technology	Challenger	Incumbent	N
Voter file or database	82.4%	93.8%	116
GIS/mapping software	41.2	40.6	54
Campaign software	32.4	25.0	38
Team tools	29.4	25.0	36
Web Site	70.6	62.5	88
Blogs	35.3	21.9	38
Viral video	23.5	12.5	24
Web-only advertising	26.5	21.9	32
Podcasts	23.5	16.6	26
E-postcards/buttons/outreach	29.4	34.4	42
RSS feeds	23.5	16.6	26
Microsites/grassroots mobilization/outreach sites	29.4	31.3	40
Other downloadable materials	20.6	18.8	26
E-mail for voter contact	65.7	59.4	82
E-mail for internal campaign communication	58.8	68.8	84
Text/SMS messaging	29.4	15.6	30
Donor databases	64.7	78.1	94
Online fund-raising	29.4	28.1	38

better diffused throughout their cohort of candidates. While Republicans are more likely to use voter and donor databases, they do so only by a small margin. More sophisticated technology, such as viral video, campaign management software, podcasting, and e-postcards, are used by a greater percentage of Democrats than Republicans. So while Republicans might use technology in greater numbers, Democrats are more sophisticated in their technology usage.

Mostly due to campaign experience, incumbency, should drive greater technology use than that of challenger candidates. Challengers, though, show a greater tendency toward technology use than incumbents in almost all areas. In the use of voter files, e-postcards, microsite usage, internal e-mail, and donor databases, incumbents do lead. In all other areas, challengers use technologies slightly more. The most important point is that the difference between incumbent and challenger technology use is very slight. Challengers may see technology use as an opportunity to overcome the myriad advantages incumbent candidates have in campaigns, leading to their embrace of campaign technology.

Results: Determinants of Technology Use

Results have given us some conclusive insights into the state of technology use, but we must also ask the question about causation. Challenger status, party affiliation, and state do show differences in technology use, but the small differences in many areas of use may not be the result of a causal relationship. Do party, state, status, and other factors in fact influence technology use?

Besides state and party, there are four plausible explanations for the propensity to use a campaign technology. Fund-raising encompasses two of those factors. Aggregate spending totals for the campaign committee should help explain technology use, as would out-of-state fund-raising. Out-of-state fund-raising tends to come from political action committees and other sophisticated groups that target their donations. A campaign would have to employ sophisticated techniques to be taken seriously by out-of-state groups.

One obvious concern with the use of fund-raising as a causal factor for technology use is endogeneity. Fund-raising ability is often related to campaign experience, or campaign professionalism, and thus might show a spurious relationship. In fact, the use of a campaign spending variable may be influenced by self-financed campaigns or heavily loan-subsidized efforts. However, campaign spending should be related to technology use, as using those tools should increase the cost of a campaign significantly. Also, previous works, notably Abbe and Herrnson's (2003), use campaign spending as a variable. Following their lead, I conducted a nonrecursive two-stage least squares test between campaign technology use and spending, with the result suggesting that the relationship is not endogenous.

Another factor is the candidate's length of time in office. I do not use age here. Candidates who are more experienced tend to be more familiar and comfortable with the style of campaigning they know, and therefore likely to be more technology-averse. To test the influence of campaign experience, I asked respondents to list the year they first ran for political office.

The last factor is campaign professionalism, probed for in the survey I administered to the subjects. The question is a simple yes/no prompt asking if the candidate hired a professional campaign manager. A professionally managed campaign should be much more likely to adopt new technologies into their practices.

With those five variables in place, I ran logistic regressions with each of the eighteen technology variables set as the dependent variable in each analysis, the results of which are reported in table 4.6. The results of the regression are contrary to the idea of greater technological suffusion throughout state legislative campaigns. In only two cases do any variable become statistically significant: the use of voter files and direct-to-voter e-mail communication.

Voter files regress positively and significantly, with the two possible measures of professionalism and sophistication, namely out-of-state fund-raising and professional campaign management. Also as expected, the sign of the coefficient for length of political career is negative, suggesting that newer candidates are more willing to embrace technology. However, the aggregate amount raised does not meet standards of statistical significance. Most of the expected determinants were significant for the use of voter files, but that is where the expected results end.

In every single other factor, save one, no variables meet statistical significance. The use of e-mail for voter contact displays a statistically significant coefficient with aggregate fund-raising, but that is the only significant independent variable associated with e-mail. And not one other technological element produces a significant coefficient when regressed against our campaign factors.

Table 4.6 shows us that technology occupies a new space in terms of our understanding of campaigns. All of the traditional indicators of a campaign with great chance of success do not produce significant results against variables of technology use. If there is a determinant, or a series of them, for campaign technological sophistication, the literature has not yet produced it or them. We know what does not drive technological sophistication, though: fund-raising, campaign professionalism, overall campaign spending, legislative professionalism, or partisan differences.

TABLE 4.6
Determinant Factors of Technology Use

Technology	Party	State	Spending	Out-of-state	Career length	Professional	Constant
Voter file or database	0.650	1.198	0.000	0.000*	−0.001*	1.176*	0.738
GIS/mapping software	−0.302	0.149	0.000	0.000	−0.002	−0.113	4.558
Campaign software	−0.084	0.402	0.000	0.000	−0.003	−0.065	4.540
Team tools	0.058	0.414	0.000	0.000	−0.003	−0.050	3.900
Web Site	−0.650	−0.617	0.000	0.000	−0.001	0.407	3.507
Blogs	−0.441	0.387	0.000	0.000	−0.003	0.033	4.108
Viral video	−0.071	0.070	0.000	0.000	−0.003	−0.250	3.701
Web-only advertising	−0.386	−0.118	0.000	0.000	−0.003	−0.259	4.668
Podcasts	0.219	0.173	0.000	0.000	−0.002	−0.130	3.175

E-postcards/buttons/outreach	-0.168	-0.288	0.000	0.000	-0.002	0.030	4.279
RSS feeds	0.219	0.173	0.000	0.000	-0.002	-0.130	3.175
Microsites/grassroots/outreach sites	-0.178	-0.409	0.000	0.000	-0.002	-0.073	4.289
Other downloadable materials	0.306	0.767	0.000	0.000	-0.003	0.010	3.015
E-mail for voter contact	-0.008	0.885	0.000*	0.000	-0.001	-0.173	2.600
E-mail for internal campaign communication	-0.102	0.158	0.000	0.000	-0.002	-0.097	3.613
Text/SMS messaging	-0.302	0.800	0.000	0.000	-0.002	-0.045	3.234
Donor databases	0.132	0.096	0.000	0.000	-0.001	0.390	3.119
Online fund-raising	-0.102	-0.969	0.000	0.000	-0.003	0.177	4.601

Note: All reported statistics are logistic regression coefficients. * = Significant at .10 level.

Party may play a vital role in the use of voter files, however. Both of the parties in each state have made significant investments in voter databases over the last six years, and so every nominee will have access to the database. The party variable likely fails to achieve significance because there is no difference in the two parties' ability to provide voter files. Instead, the lack of significance in the party variable suggests an overall increase in sophistication for both Republicans and Democrats in the states studied.

Results: Effects of Technology Use

The third and final question to address here is the effectiveness of this technology. Perhaps the fact that none of the standard and expected campaign predictors show statistical relationships with the technological variables can be explained by the relatively limited use of this technology in campaigns. If the technologies used do not pay off in the form of improved vote totals, candidates will be more reluctant to use them. We must determine if using any of these technological methods has an impact on the candidate's eventual vote, which would suggest perceived value among candidates and thus a greater likelihood of adoption of those new technologies.

I performed an ordinary least squares regression analysis with the vote total as the dependent variable. The equation used total amount spent, first year of candidacy, campaign professionalism, and the technological element variables regressed against vote total. Campaigns might be loath to spend money and effort on technology that they believe will not help their bottom line, votes. Conversely, if technology use is significantly and positively related to vote totals, future campaigns might be more likely to adopt those tools and accelerate the "congressionalization" process as theorized by Lynch and Rozell.

Table 4.7 reports the results from the regression model. The results from table 4.6 show that fund-raising is the most important factor in earning votes among respondents to the survey. Apparently, technology does not change vote totals or even correlate with the spending habits of campaigns. None of the voter targeting methods achieves statistical significance in the model. Even the use of a voter file, which would easily separate a good campaign from a hopeless one, does not significantly affect the total vote.

One variable of Web communication, use of blogs, emerges as statistically significant. The presence of a Web site has no effect, and neither do any of the other more sophisticated uses of the Web. Online diaries on candidate sites do appear to have an impact. Theoretically, blogging makes sense as a statistically related variable. A campaign that uses a blog encourages regular traffic to its Web site. The regular traffic should drive name recognition higher and in turn increase the candidate's votes.

These results suggest that Web strategies that encourage regular visits to the Web site are very effective, though we would therefore expect RSS feeds also to be significant, which they are not. The explanation may be in the fact that blogs are easier to create than an RSS feed, and campaigns may simply lack the expertise to create those feeds. Candidates can use free blogging software or stand-alone Web sites, decreasing both the labor and monetary cost of blogging. RSS feeds require more programming, meaning time and/or labor. Subsequently, it is not surprising that blogs would be used more (and more effectively) than RSS feeds.

Turning to direct communication, the e-mails and text message variables seem to change little in the established pattern of insignificant technology use. E-mail, both for direct voter contact and internal campaign communication, does not satisfy statistical significance, despite the fact that both are used fairly widely. Despite popular claims that technology encourages two-way communication, the two-way communication methods available to candidates are not widely used or effective in achieving campaign goals.

The variable for use of a grassroots mobilization site shows evidence of a significant relationship with the vote. One important lesson from 2004 was the vitality of voter and volunteer mobilization efforts by candidates and parties alike. Campaigns like Howard Dean's presidential effort were built upon the power of the Internet to connect, communicate with, and mobilize a volunteer network. State level campaigns appear to have begun learning those lessons (Nelson 2005; Shea 2006).

The use of online fund-raising practices is perhaps the most significant finding reported in table 4.7. Using online fund-raising should in theory help raise more money for the campaign as well as being a sign of an aggressive campaign organization. Any technology that helps a campaign's ability to spend money is vital, but technology in and of itself does not bring more votes to a candidate. Online fund-raising involves a serious investment in Web design and technology, so it is likely that only a professional campaign would adopt the practice. As Howard Dean's presidential campaign in 2004 showed, online fund-raising can be very effective at enfranchising new voters while at the same time boosting overall income for the campaign (Trippi 2004). Dean's name has emerged twice in relation to the significant areas of technology use in campaigns, adding credence to the idea of a trickle-down, or "congressionalization," of state campaigns. Seeing the very visible Dean campaign tactics, lower-level campaigns decide to adopt them for their own efforts.

A cautionary note is necessary regarding online fund-raising. Spending by a campaign is highly important to increasing the vote, but technology in all its forms seems to have only limited impact on vote totals. If spending and technology use were indeed endogenous to the model, then we would

TABLE 4.7
Vote Total as Predicted by Campaign and Technology-Specific Variables

	B	Standard error	t	Significance
(Constant)	1037.969	5957.883	.174	.863
Use of voter file or database	372.562	2655.366	.140	.889
Use of campaign Web site	65.490	2311.667	.028	.978
Use of GIS or mapping software	−2175.841	2510.140	−.867	.392
Use of campaign management software	−4789.397	3666.185	−1.306	.199
Use of blogs or online diaries	9406.731	3187.332	2.951	.005**
Use of e-mail for voter contact	−205.861	2140.902	−.096	.924
Use of internal e-mail	−1136.019	2703.731	−.420	.677
Use of donor databases	3738.466	2228.954	1.677	.102
Use of text messaging	412.077	2682.656	.154	.879
Use of Web video	1066.682	5934.891	.180	.858
Use of Web-only advertising	−3351.832	3292.948	−1.018	.315
Use of grassroots mobilization Web sites	−5948.056	2712.718	−2.193	.035*
Use of online fund-raising	10383.047	3188.745	3.256	.002**
Use of podcasts	−11680.994	8129.099	−1.437	.159
Use of other downloadable content	5458.065	5186.834	1.052	.299
Use of e-postcards or voter-to-voter content	−3214.635	3067.902	−1.048	.302
Use of team tools	5871.244	4024.338	1.459	.153
Incumbent/challenger	2496.442	1578.294	1.582	.122
Total amount raised by candidate	.035	.027	1.312	.197
First run for public office	−.402	2.740	−.147	.884
Professional campaign management	−196.641	826.483	−.238	.813
State	9359.183	1697.499	5.514	.000**
Political party affiliation	−1404.584	1481.728	−.948	.349

Note: OLS. R-square: .738 * = Significant at .05 level. ** = Significant at .01 level.

expect to see the technology variables also achieve significance, yet they do not. Spending and technology use are not significantly related. The campaign that seeks new avenues of outreach would be wise to establish a Web site with an e-commerce solution and a blog, since those are the most salient forms of technology for a successful campaign.

Spending should be significantly related to technology use for the simple reason that technology costs money. We must think about the technology used by a campaign, though, to understand why the two are not related. Both parties in both states, for example, provide online access to their voter and donor files to candidates for free or a nominal fee ($50). If neither state had a free or low-cost database, the campaigns would either have to buy access from a private vendor or go without, and they likely would go without. Since there was little or no cost involved, campaigns were open to the technology. Web sites, which can be hosted for a year for less than fifty dollars, also do not represent a significant cost commitment on the part of the campaign. Neither does using Meetup.com or Craigslist for mobilization, as the sites do not charge for access.

Where cost for a campaign becomes significant is in the area of sophisticated technology, especially Web-embedded video and the like. Podcasting requires software and microphones, video requires an expensive camera, and posting either video or audio files on a Web site requires space and download bandwidth that would significantly increase the cost of a campaign site. Campaign software is an additional high-cost item, with low-end packages starting in the $500 range and increasing in both cost and functionality into the thousands of dollars.

Campaigns in 2006 seem to embrace the technology that is easy to integrate and less costly to the campaign. The two-track approach to technology, where a handful of technological entrepreneurs adopt new technologies into their campaign quickly, adds a new insight into our knowledge of campaign process in the states.

Concluding Observations

Campaigns are ever-evolving entities, and so is the technology that those campaigns employ. Students of technology refer to Moore's Law, which states the number of transistors on an integrated circuit for minimum component cost doubles every twenty-four months. Moore's Law suggests that computing technology develops at an exponential rate. The results today emphatically state that campaigns, particularly at the state level, are glacially slow compared to the advances in technology that they use.

Presidential campaigns adopt technological innovations very quickly, and those new developments expand into other federal races thereafter.

Congressional candidates adopt technology within one or two cycles after their presidential counterparts. State-level candidates, though, lag behind. State legislative races are operating at a campaign level roughly comparable to those of presidential candidates of 1996.

Regardless of the professionalism of one's state legislature, one's party, or the professionalism of a campaign, technology is not widely used for elections to those state houses. Voter files are commonplace, but video and interactive features are not. The technological paradigm has not yet shifted for state candidates, and the main reason seems to be money.

Spending relates strongly to technology use, both as a measure of the campaign's sophistication and the campaign's capacity to adopt new technologies. A professional campaign today hires, as one of its staffers, a full-time computing consultant whose job would include database management, Web design and/or administration, blog updating, and online fund-raising oversight. Technology requires both time and expertise, two factors that low-level campaigns lack.

The "trickle-down" or "congressionalization" effect may be inevitable, however, as it appears to be in other areas. The process will just develop quite slowly. Fund-raising and professionalism have already developed and partly institutionalized in state legislative campaigns, as will the use of technology. The finding that online fund-raising is so closely related to electoral success should encourage candidates to consider a larger online presence alone.

Caveats and Directions for Future Research

A pair of warnings must accompany these findings. First is the fact that all elections are time-bound. Exogenous factors such as a personal scandal or a statewide voter repudiation of the party in power may suppress the effectiveness of technology in one election and allow it to emerge in subsequent contests. Single-election-cycle studies have only one data point in time, meaning that while we have a good picture of the state of today's state-level campaign technology, that picture will change drastically over the next few elections. Second, while Kansas and North Carolina were carefully chosen for their representativeness of the variety of state legislative campaigns, they are only two states of fifty.

That later, expanded, study, is indeed the next step. The intent of the 2006 iteration of the Changing State Legislative Campaign Project was to serve as a pilot for later and larger studies, which at this writing I am preparing to perform for the 2008 election cycle. New technologies will also develop that must be included in those future studies. Future surveys for the project will include the number of staffers dedicated to technology administration in each campaign and subject questions regarding video produced by extra-campaign personnel, such as "fan videos" of the style currently being placed on sites like YouTube. Citizens are expressing their preferences through short video clips not sanctioned by or coordinated by the campaigns. Such grassroots efforts could be the campaign realization of the "Web 2.0" phenomenon of user-created content, and as such they will be important to track.

Finally, other causal factors may be driving the campaigns that do use technology. If aggregate fund-raising does not explain why some campaigns use technology and others do not, then some as-yet unexplained factor must. The great mystery to unlock in future studies is the cause of technology use in campaigns.

NOTE

An earlier version of this chapter was published in *Social Science Computer Review* (2007) 25: 466–483. Reprinted by permission.

My sincere thanks to Paul Herrnson, who gave me a copy of his original survey instrument to use in this manuscript. Also, my gratitude to Jason Stegmeier, who collected the campaign finance and voting data in addition to entering the survey data here. Without either of these gentlemen this work would not have been possible.

REFERENCES

Abbe, O. 2003. "Campaign Professionalism in State Legislative Elections." *State Politics and Policy Quarterly* 3 (3): 233–256.

Blaemire, R. 2001. "Database Management One Size Does Not Fit All." *Campaigns & Elections* 9 (22): 45–46.

———. 2002. "Voter Files: Yesterday, Today, and Tomorrow." *Campaigns & Elections* 5 (23): 58–60.

———. 2004. "Developing a Web-Based Voter File System." *Campaigns & Elections* 25 (5):58.

Blanchfield, T. 2006a. "Kick Apps on Your Web site." *Campaigns & Elections* 27 (10): 103.

———. 2006b. "The Texting Phenomenon: Countries Across the World: Use Text Messaging to Help With Campaigns." *Campaigns & Elections* 27 (6): 42.

Cornfeld, M. 2007. "Maximizing Microtargeting." *Campaigns & Elections* 28 (1): 54.

Donatelli, R. 2005. "Budget for Online Fund Raising: Advertise Now or Pay Later." *Campaigns & Elections* 26 (7): 39.

Dotson, C. 2007. "The Newest Member of the Staff." *Campaigns & Election* 28 (2): 55.

Gilgoff, D. 2006. "Everyone is a Special Interest: In Their Hunt for Voters, Microtargeters Study How You Live and What You Like." *U.S. News & World Report*. September 25.

Gimpel, J. 2003. "Computer Technology and Getting Out the Vote: New Targeting Tools." *Campaigns & Elections* 24 (8): 39–40.

Green, D. 2004. *Get Out the Vote! How to Increase Voter Turnout*. Washington, DC: Brookings Institution Press.

Lynch, G. and M. Rozell. 2002. "The 'Congressionalization' of State Legislative Races." *Social Science Journal* 39 (1): 43–51.

Manatt, D. 2004. "Web Video." *Campaigns & Elections* 25 (5): 36–37.

Nelson, M. 2005. *The Elections of 2004*. Washington, DC: CQ Press.

"Political Microsites Confirm a New World Order." 2007 (accessed February 27, 2007, at http://www.microsite.com/blog/archives/11).

Reich, B., and D. Solomon. 2007. "2006: Finally, Campaigns Plug In—For Real." *Campaigns & Elections*. 28 (2): 39–40.

Salmore, S., and B. Salmore 1993. "The Transformation of State Electoral Politics." In *The State of the States*, ed. C. E. Van Horn. Washington, DC: Congressional Quarterly Press.

Sender, J. 2007. *Viral Video in Politics*. San Francisco: New Politics Institute.

Shea, D. 2006. *Fountain of Youth: Strategies for Mobilizing Young Voters in America*. Lanham, MD: Rowman and Littlefield.

Survey Says: Campaigns Succeed on the Internet. 2006. San Diego, CA, E-Voter Institute: 2.

Theimer, S. 2003. "Presidential Hopefuls' Web Sites Show Internet's Growing Role in Campaigns." *Government Technology*. August 21.

Trippi, J. 2004. *The Revolution Will Not Be Televised: Democracy, the Internet, and the Overthrow of Everything*. New York: Regan Books.

Weigel, D. 2006. "The Political Bull's-Eye; Persuading the Right People With Microtargeting." *Campaigns & Elections* 27 (1): 20–24.

5

Do Campaign Web Sites Really Matter in Electoral Civic Engagement?

Empirical Evidence from the 2004 and 2006 Post-Election Internet Tracking Survey

HUN MYOUNG PARK

JAMES L. PERRY

Since the mid-1990s, the Internet and World Wide Web (WWW) have been changing society remarkably. Government has provided electronic information and services through portal sites. Political parties have used campaign Web sites for election campaigns. Almost all senators and representatives have their own Web sites to disseminate information and communicate with their constituents. Political use of the Internet, in particular campaign Web sites, becomes a common phenomenon. The interactive nature and massive information transfer capability of the Internet are implicitly assumed to produce a positive effect on politics and democracy. Do campaign Web sites really matters in electoral politics and civic engagement?

As the Internet permeates everyday life, scholars from many disciplines have investigated its impact on various aspects of society such as public service delivery, social capital, digital inequality (digital divide), and the like (Rheingold 1993; Bimber 2003; Selnow 1998; Norris 2001; DiMaggio et al. 2001; Katz and Rice 2002; Robbin, Courtright, and Davis 2004). Relatively little is known, however, about the relationship between Internet use (campaign Web site use) and civic engagement. Enthusiasts argue that the Internet will facilitate deliberative and participatory democracy (Rheingold 1993; Grossman 1995; Barber 1999). Studies of the political use of the Internet suggest that the Internet is less likely to mobilize citizens and more likely to reinforce their power status (Davis 1999; Norris 2001). Bimber (2001, 2003), Bimber and Davis (2003), and Delli Carpini and Keeter (2003) reported little evidence to support a significant relationship between the two. How do we reconcile the conflicting evidence about the impact of the Internet on civic engagement?

This chapter attempts to solve the puzzle. It begins by discussing diversity of civic engagement. The existing research on Internet use and civic engagement is then reviewed from three different perspectives. We next describe the 2004 Internet Tracking Survey of the Pew Internet and American Life Project and explain the propensity score matching method and the recursive bivariate probit model. The analysis presents the average effect and discrete change of campaign Web site use on individual electoral civic engagement. Finally, we discuss the findings and their implications for theories and methods in this field.

Diversity of Civic Engagement

Civic engagement refers to citizens' individual and collective involvement in public affairs. Civic engagement encompasses a variety of forms of political and nonpolitical activities. Common forms of civic engagement are voting; working in election campaigns for political parties; contributing to political causes and candidates; contacting public officials; attendance at public meetings, political rallies, protests, or speeches; signing petitions; serving local organizations; and writing articles for mass media (Verba, Schlozman, and Brady 1995; Putnam 2000; Ramakrishnan and Baldassare 2004). Some engagements are partisan-oriented and electoral, while others are nonelectoral. Some engagements are based on individual choices, whereas others involve collective actions. Some are deliberative and others are action-oriented.

There are many practical problems in defining and measuring civic engagement and political participation (Robbin, Courtright, and Davis 2004; Weissberg 2005). Weissberg (2005) argues that the conventional definition of political participation is conceptually vague and illusory, failing to capture its variety in the real world. He claims that existing literature tends to focus on political activities that are easy to measure and treats all activities equally. Jennings and Zeitner criticize survey methodology because it focuses on limited numbers of civic engagement indicators and provides insufficient evidence for generalization (2003, 313). Weissberg (2005) also points out that most researchers take the election-centered approach and analyzes a collection of individual "acts" rather than "activities" that they want to study ultimately.

Verba, Schlozman, and Brady differentiate political activities according to the capacity to convey information (or messages), strength of pressures, and required resources (1995, 43–78). Hence, incidents of individual civic engagement should be differentiated from one another. Financial contributions to a political party and candidate can send many strong messages to politicians, but they in turn require more resources, money, in particular. Serving local organizations and participating in protests may also convey strong messages to politicians and public officials; however, the required resources for these activities are not material resources like money, but time and skills that enthusiasts are willing to spare. Voting conveys a few weak messages. A person is given only one ballot regardless of wealth, occupation, and education, and the likelihood that his or her ballot makes a difference in outcomes is very low. The voting cost is relatively low. Voting is, from the view of Verba, Schlozman, and Brady (1995), sui genesis.

Relationship Between the Internet and Society

DiMaggio et al. (2001) review five research domains for the Internet and society: digital inequality, community and social capital, political participation, organizational impact, and cultural impact. More recently, Robbin, Courtright, and Davis (2004) provide a summary of research on the impact of information and communication technology (for example, e-government and e-democracy) on political life. Arguments in the research literature reflect three perspectives about the relationship between Internet use and society: optimism, pessimism, and skepticism (Arterton 1987; DiMaggio et al. 2001; Norris 2001; Katz and Rice 2002; Bimber 2003).

Internet enthusiasts have a utopian view that the Internet will get people more involved in public life, facilitate formation of social networks (social capital), and contribute to participatory and deliberative democracy (Rheingold 1993; Grossman 1995; Corrado 1996; Barber 1999; Ward, Gibson, and Nixon 2003). Cyber-optimists emphasize that information technology reduces the costs of information and communication and thus allows citizens to obtain and disseminate political information in an efficient and timely manner. This cost reduction, in particular, provides minority or marginalized groups of people with opportunities to have their voices heard in the public sphere (Rheingold 1993). The Internet and related technologies are viewed as a vehicle for mobilizing constituents, transforming and reinventing government, and revitalizing deliberative and "strong" democracy (Barber 1999).

The pessimists argue, however, that the Internet reinforces rather than transforms existing power relationships and patterns of political participation (Davis 1999; Norris 2001; Kavanaugh 2002). The Internet facilitates the civic engagement of people who are already informed and motivated; the Internet does not change the involvement level of people who are disenfranchised (Norris 2001; Kavanaugh 2002). The Internet is less likely to mobilize the disengaged and more likely to reinforce established political actors who can take greater advantage of using political information on the network, deepening the digital divide between the information haves and have-nots (Norris 2001).

Finally, the skeptics hold the cautious view that the Internet, despite its potential, does not necessarily facilitate or destroy civic engagement,

TABLE 5.1

Perspectives on the Relationship between the Internet and Society

	Key arguments	*Role of the Internet*
Optimism	Mobilization, transformation, participatory and deliberative democracy	Determinant (positive)
Pessimism	Reinforcement, displacement, digital inequality (digital divide), "engaging the engaged"	Determinant (negative)
Skepticism	Normalization, reflection (mirroring), supplement (complement), "politics as usual"	Reflected and socially shaped/constructed

but reflects "politics as usual" (Bimber 2003; Margolis and Resnick 2000; Kamarck 2002; Davis, Elin, and Reeher 2002; Uslaner 2004). Bimber (2001) argues that the Internet may reduce the costs of obtaining information and thus improve availability of information; however, the cost reduction and availability are not substantially related to voting and political engagement. Bimber (2001) reported a marginally significant relationship only between the Internet and financial contributions to parties and candidates. Based on analysis of the 2000 Missouri race, Bimber and Davis (2003) conclude that campaign Web sites have a weak effect on electoral politics such as voting. Delli Carpini and Keeter (2003) also found little evidence to support a significant relationship between the use of the Internet and civic engagement. More recently, Uslaner concludes that the Internet is not transforming but looks much like the world and that the Internet does not make up for the decline in civic engagement, nor does it facilitate social capital (2004, 239). This normalization thesis suggests that cyberspace is taking on the characteristics of ordinary life (Margolis and Resnick 2000). Table 5.1 summarizes the three perspectives on the relationship between the Internet and society.

Methodology Review

A variety of methods have been employed to examine the relationship between Internet use and civic engagement. Norris (2001) depends largely on descriptive methods, while Scott (2006) develops public involvement indices and then applies analysis of variance (ANOVA) to compare group means of the indices. Scott (2006) performs a content analysis to measure the extent that municipal government Web sites provide information and services to improve public involvement.[1]

Bimber (2001, 2003) simply employs the binary logit model to analyze the American National Election Studies data in 1998 and 2000. Bimber (2001) argues that failure of the "instrumental-quantitative conceptions of information" endorses more qualitative conceptions of information environment and political knowledge. However, the failure does not appear to come from an innate defect of the instrumental approach, but from irrelevant models and the lack of rich data. He mistakenly treats the expansion of political information through the Internet as "a form of natural experiment." Jennings and Zeitner (2003) conduct linear regression analysis using longitudinal survey data to find no significant association between the political use of the Internet and civic engagement.

Existing research employs univariate and descriptive methods to estimate the effects of Internet use but seldom carefully considers the key issues associated with modeling the relationship between Internet use and civic engagement. Internet use may be endogenous in some civic engagement and exogenous in others. Internet use and civic engagement may be jointly determined with some correlation.[2] Their relationship is often reciprocal in reality rather than unidirectional (Norris 2000, 2001; DiMaggio et al. 2001). In addition, the "missing data problem" resulting from self-selection is common in nationwide surveys because randomized experiments may be costly, unfeasible, and/or undesirable. If an individual receives the treatment, we cannot observe what the outcome would have been had he or she been assigned to the control group. This missing data problem makes it difficult to estimate the net impact of treatment using the traditional approaches.

However, little effort was made in past research to address endogeneity and missing data problem. Despite a direct causality that is often posited by enthusiasts, existing research has produced inconsistent results that raise many theoretical and methodological issues.

Data: 2004 Post-Election Internet Tracking Survey

The Pew Internet and American Life Project has provided data sets of nationwide surveys that examine the impact of the Internet on American society. In each survey, a nationally representative sample is drawn from adults living in continental U.S. households using the standard list-assisted random digit dialing (RDD) method. This study employs the 2004 Post-election Internet Tracking Survey that was conducted from November 4 to 22 of that year (Pew Internet and American Life Project 2004).[3] The final response rate was 30.6 percent. The data set used includes a total of 2,146 observations, excluding those (N=54) with missing values in age.

Six types of electoral civic engagement are considered (table 5.2). The first type is to send e-mails urging people to vote without reference to a

TABLE 5.2

Summary of Dependent Variables (N = 2,146)

	Engaged	Not engaged	Missing
E-mails urging to vote	155 (7.22)	1,062 (49.49)	929 (43.29)
Attendance at a rally	158 (7.36)	1,984 (92.45)	4 (0.19)
Solicitation (e-mails)	147 (6.85)	1,071 (49.91)	928 (43.24)
Solicitation (call or visit)	184 (8.57)	1,961 (91.38)	1 (0.05)
Financial contributions	314 (14.63)	1,826 (85.09)	6 (0.28)
Voting	1708 (79.59)	435 (20.27)	3 (0.14)

particular candidate. This engagement appears less partisan-oriented and more deliberative than attendance at a campaign rally, which is an action-oriented partisan engagement. Sending e-mails urging people to vote for a particular candidate is solicitation for votes. The fourth engagement is another solicitation by making telephone calls or visiting at homes. Financial contributions mean giving money to a political candidate. Despite its unique-ness, voting is also considered to compare with other electoral engagements. See the appendix to this chapter for details about questions selected.

Political knowledge and motivation are computed by averaging several binary variables of related questions. Family income is drawn by taking the midpoint of each income range. Online use intensity is computed from the

TABLE 5.3

Summary of Interval Independent Variables (N = 2,146)

	N	Mean	S.D.[a]	Minimum	Median	Maximum
Political knowledge	2,145	.249	.337	0	0	1
Political motivation	2,145	.346	.294	0	.333	1
Family income ($1,000)	1,733	52.360	34.076	5	45	115
Age	2,146	49.405	17.874	18	49	94
Internet experience	2,121	4.008	3.928	0	4	10
Online use intensity	1,303	12.090	9.074	0	11.5	30

[a]Standard deviation.

TABLE 5.4

Summary of Key Independent Variable Distribution

	Yes (1)	No (0)	Missing
Partisanship (partisan = 1)	1,389 (64.73)	652 (30.38)	105 (4.89)
Education (college = 1)	714 (33.27)	1,420 (66.17)	12 (0.56)
Gender (male = 1)	1,010 (47.06)	1,136 (52.94)	
Race (white = 1)	1,741 (81.13)	367 (17.10)	38 (1.77)
Broadband user	717 (33.41)	459 (21.39)	970 (45.20)
Use of campaign Web sites	299 (13.93)	1,003 (46.74)	844 (39.33)

Note: Percentage in parentheses. N = 2,146

two variables that measure frequencies of online use from home and work. A variable for weighting is provided in the November 2004 Internet Tracking Survey data set. Those who identify themselves as either Republican or Democrat are set to 1 for partisanship. College graduates are those who earned B.A., master's, and/or Ph.D. degrees. Broadband users have Internet connections of DSL-enabled phone line, cable TV modem, wireless (including satellite), T-1, fiber optic at home, or access to the Internet at work. Use of campaign Web sites is whether citizens have visited campaign Web sites to get news or information about the election. Tables 5.3 and 5.4 provide descriptive statistics of independent variables.

Methods

Many studies envision a unidirectional relationship between Internet use and society, but this relationship is a misspecification because of the nebulous causal relationship between them (Arterton 1987; Bimber 2001; DiMaggio et al. 2001). Internet use and civic engagement may be determined jointly. Their relationship may be reciprocal rather than unidirectional. In general, Internet use may be an endogenous variable for some civic engagement and exogenous for other types of engagement. Also, the "missing data problem" is pervasive in observational studies. A citizen is either an Internet user or nonuser, not both. Research that does not account for these issues will report biased and unreliable estimates of effects. This study employs propensity score matching (PSM) and the recursive bivariate probit model (RBPM) to deal with the missing data problem and endogeneity. The results are summarized in the following section.

Findings

Use of campaign Web sites positively influences electoral civic engagement, but its effect varies across individual engagements. Campaign Web site experience has a negligible impact on voting.

Sending E-mails Urging People to Vote

The propensity score matching (PSM) suggests that campaign Web site users are on average 17.4 percent (=.294-.121) more likely than nonusers to send e-mails urging people to vote without reference to a particular candidate (table 5.5).[4] The left plot of figure 5.1 illustrates the average effect of campaign Web site use on sending e-mails without reference to a particular candidate. The percentage that users are engaged is higher than that of nonusers in most strata.

The recursive bivariate probit model (RBPM) of sending e-mails telling people to vote without reference to a particular candidate fits the data well and has a significant correlation between disturbances (first column in table 5.6). Campaign Web site use and sending e-mails to vote appear to be jointly determined. Use of campaign Web sites has a positive and significant effect on sending e-mails without reference. The left plot of Figure 5.2 depicts conditional predicted probabilities that campaign Web site users and nonuser will send e-mails urging people to vote without reference to a particular candidate. The discrete change, that is, the gap between two curves, is the impact of campaign Web site use on this engagement. Users who are moderately mobilized at .5 are 10.1 percent more likely than nonusers to send e-mails urging others to vote, holding all other variables at their reference points. As citizens are more mobilized, the effect of campaign Web site use on this engagement increases (figure 5.2).

Political knowledge and mobilization are important predictors of sending e-mails to vote, while partisanship does not make a substantial difference. Political knowledge has an overall effect of 15.7 percent; for a .1 increase from the intermediate level of political knowledge, the conditional

TABLE 5.5

Average Effect: Sending Emails Urging to Vote and Attendance at a Rally

Civic engagement	Pairs	Treated	Control	Effect	S.E.	T	P-value
E-mails to vote	282	.2943	.1206	.1738	.0334	5.2006	<.0000
Campaign rally	296	.2061	.1014	.1047	.0294	3.5643	<.0004

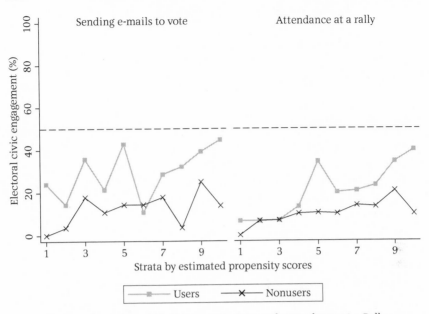

FIGURE 5.1 Average Effect: E-mails to Vote and Attendance at a Rally

predicted probability of users' engagement will increase by 1.6 percent, holding other variables at their reference points. The indirect effect of 11.8 indicates that political knowledge influences sending e-mails largely by facilitating use of campaign Web sites. Political mobilization has significant direct and indirect effects.

Gender and race have marginally significant direct effects. Age has positive direct and negative indirect effects that cancel each other out to make its overall effect negligible. Internet experience and online use intensity facilitate use of campaign Web sites and thus indirectly influences sending e-mails urging to vote without reference to a particular candidate. Family income, education, and broadband use do not affect this engagement significantly.

Attendance at a Campaign Rally

PSM suggests that campaign Web site users are 10.5 percent more likely than nonusers to attend a campaign rally (table 5.5). The right plot of Figure 5.1 illustrates that campaign Web site users attend a rally more than nonusers in most strata.

The RBPM of attending a campaign rally fits the data well and has a large correlation coefficient of disturbances (second column in table 5.6). Use of campaign Web site has a positive and significant effect on attendance at a rally. The right plot of figure 5.2 illustrates that conditional predicted

TABLE 5.6

Sending E-mails to Vote and Attendance at a Rally (RBPM)

	Sending E-mails to vote		Attendance at a rally	
	Engagement	Web site use	Engagement	Web site use
Political knowledge	.1381	1.0104***	.2975	1.0384***
	(.1909)	.1461)	(.1844)	(.1401)
Mobilization	.5161**	.8813***	.3282	.7050***
	(.2636)	(.1903)	(.2034)	(.1795)
Partisanship	−.0353	.0132	.0738	.0929
	(.1241)	(.1162)	(.1343)	(.1119)
Family income	−.0013	−.0001	−.0012	.0003
	(.0018)	(.0018)	(.0018)	(.0017)
Education (college)	−.0407	−.0956	.0757	−.0782
	(.1259)	(.1128)	(.1208)	(.1088)
Gender (male)	−.2262*	−.1514	.1566	−.1928*
	(.1186)	(.1031)	(.1184)	(.1005)
Race (white)	−.2619*	−.1271	−.1324	−.0321
	(.1497)	(.1451)	(.1508)	(.1387)
Age	.0044	−.0173***	.0127***	−.0178***
	(.0040)	(.0037)	(.0040)	(.0036)
Campaign Web site	1.4731		1.6364***	
	(.2893)***		(.2499)	
Internet experience		.0691***		.0449**
		(.0231)		(.0197)
Online use intensity		.0216***		.0227***
		(.0060)		(.0057)
Broadband use		.0529		.0438
		(.1123)		(.1147)
Intercept	−1.5157***	−1.2097***	−2.4550***	−1.1276***
	(.2310)	(.2438)	(.2717)	(.2381)
Rho (correlation)		−.5049		−.6993
		(.1569)		(.1232)
Wald test (rho)		6.9689***		12.8987***
Log Likelihood	−1571.9885		−1520.9568	
Wald test (model)	318.60***		416.97***	
N	933		980	

Note: Standard errors in parentheses. *p < .10 **p < .05 ***p < .01.

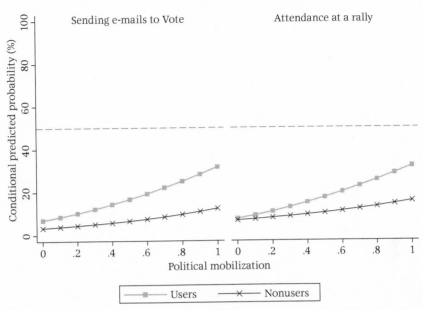

FIGURE 5.2 Conditional Predicted Probability: E-mails to Vote and Attendance at a Rally

probability of campaign Web site users is about 7.2 percent higher than non-user, holding all other variables at their reference points.

Political knowledge and mobilization have significant indirect effects on attendance at a rally without significant direct effects. Age has positive direct and negative indirect effects on attendance at a rally; young generations are more likely to use campaign Web sites but less likely to attend a rally than older counterparts in each equation. However, the overall effect is negligible because direct and indirect effects cancel each other out.[5] Internet experience and online use intensity indirectly influence attendance at a rally, while gender has a marginally significant indirect effect. Other variables do not affect this engagement significantly.

Solicitations for Votes

Use of campaign Web sites has a positive average effect on solicitations for votes. Users send e-mails urging people to vote for a particular candidate 14.8 percent more than nonusers (table 5.7). The average effect on solicitation for votes by making telephone calls or visiting at home is 8.9 percent. Figure 5.3 illustrates these average effects.

Both RBPMs of solicitations for votes fit data but do not have significant correlations between disturbances (table 5.8). As a result, the binary probit model is estimated to consider direct effects. Both binary probit models fit

TABLE 5.7

Average Effect: Solicitations for Votes

Civic engagement	Pairs	Treated	Control	Effect	S.E.	T	P-value
E-mails with reference	283	.2792	.1307	.1484	.0334	4.4431	<.0000
Phone call/visit	296	.1824	.0946	.0878	.0282	3.1135	<.0020

the data well and report statistically significant effects of campaign Web site use on solicitations for votes.

Campaign Web site users are 17.4 percent more likely than nonusers to send e-mails urging people to vote for a particular candidate, holding other variables at their reference points (first column in table 5.8). The left plot in figure 5.4 depicts discrete changes of campaign Web site use at different levels of political mobilization. Political knowledge and mobilizations significantly influence sending e-mails for a particular candidate, while partisanship and education have marginally significant effects. Other variables do not make a substantial difference.

For urging people to vote for a particular candidate by making telephone calls or visiting at homes, campaign Web site use has a discrete

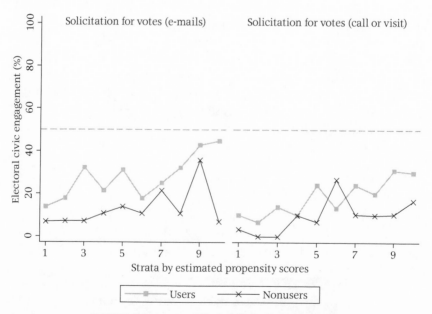

FIGURE 5.3 Average Effect, Solicitations for Votes

TABLE 5.8

Solicitations for Votes, Contributions, and Voting (binary probit model)

	Solicitation (e-mails)	Solicitation (calls or visit)	Financial contribution	Voting
Political knowledge	.9427*** (.1564)	1.0491*** (.1511)	.8535*** (.1452)	.4543*** (.1662)
Mobilization	1.0189*** (.2229)	.5193** (.2258)	.6912*** (.1923)	.7878*** (.2168)
Partisanship	.2565* (.1355)	.2592* (.1377)	.4263*** (.1276)	.4472*** (.1110)
Family income	−.0010 (.0019)	−.0059*** (.0020)	.0046** (.0019)	.0026 (.0019)
Education (college)	−.2232* (.1261)	.1694 (.1258)	.3186*** (.1188)	.2464** (.1202)
Gender (male)	−.0033 (.1177)	.0432 (.1212)	.2726** (.1079)	−.0713 (.1108)
Race (white)	−.2485 (.1730)	−.2770* (.1520)	.3049* (.1723)	.2972** (.1378)
Age	.0048 (.0040)	.0014 (.0045)	.0276*** (.0041)	.0189*** (.0042)
Campaign Web site	.6415*** (.1282)	.3070** (.1354)	.3589*** (.1196)	.0734 (.1365)
Intercept	−2.1519*** (.2647)	−1.8997*** (.2910)	−4.1322*** (.3275)	−.8661*** (.2242)
Log likelihood	−327.3350	−295.6216	−344.9291	−440.1983
Wald test	135.25***	90.06***	153.41***	97.50***
Pseudo R^2	.1842	.1370	.2314	.1366
N	1027	1090	1088	1093

Note: Standard errors in parentheses. *$p < .10$ **$p < .05$ ***$p < .01$

change of 7.9 percent at the reference points (second column in table 5.8). Two curves in the right plot of figure 5.4 have a similar slope, as if they were parallel lines. Political knowledge and mobilization have positive effects, while partisanship and race marginally affect solicitations by phone calls and visit. The more family income users have, the less likely they are to urge people to vote for a particular candidate. Education, gender, and age do not have a significant effect.

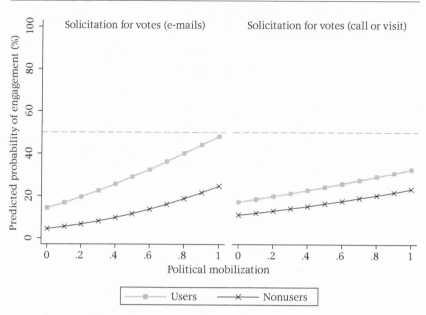

FIGURE 5.4 Predicted Probability of Solicitations for Votes

Financial Contributions

PSM suggests that campaign Web site users are 11.2 percent more likely to give money to a political candidate than nonusers (table 5.9). This average effect is depicted in the left plot of figure 5.5. Users show a higher level of contributions than nonusers in most strata.

The RBPM of financial contributions fits the data well but has a small correlation coefficient of disturbances. Accordingly, the binary probit model is used. Campaign Web site users are 13.6 percent more likely than nonusers to donate money, holding all other variables at their reference points. Discrete changes of campaign Web sites use are illustrated in the left plot of figure 5.6. The engagement curves appear to be parallel lines. All independent variables turn out statistically significant. In particular, family income, college education, and age positively influence financial contributions.

TABLE 5.9
Average Effect: Financial Contributions and Voting

Civic engagement	Pairs	Treated	Control	Effect	S.E.	T	P-value
Contributions	294	.2925	.1803	.1122	.0348	3.2259	<.0014
Voting	296	.8851	.8682	.0169	.0271	.6236	<.5334

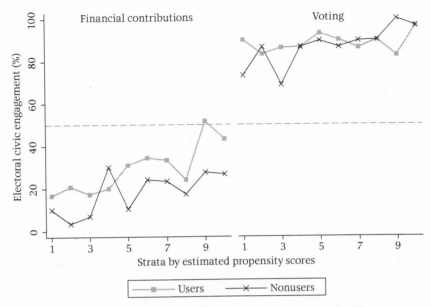

FIGURE 5.5 Average Effect: Financial Contributions and Voting

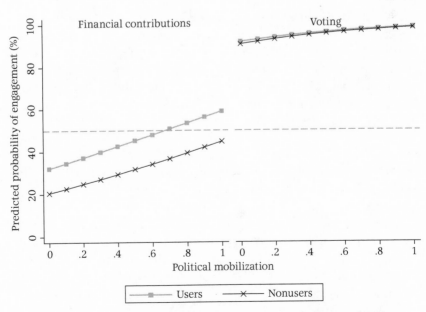

FIGURE 5.6 Predicted Probability of Financial Contributions and Voting

TABLE 5.10

Summary of Empirical Analysis

Civic Engagement	LR test	Rho	Coefficient	Discrete change	Average effect
E-mails urging to vote	319***	−.5049***	1.4731***	.1013	.1738**
Attendance at a rally	417***	−.6993***	1.6364***	.0717	.1047***
Solicitations (e-mail)	135***[a]	−.3455	.6415***[a]	.1736[a]	.1484***
Solicitations (call/visit)	90***[a]	.2807	.3070**[a]	.0785[a]	.0878***
Financial contributions	153***[a]	−.2383	.3589***[a]	.1363[a]	.1122***
Voting	98***[a]	.3940	.0734[a]	.0063[a]	.0169

[a]Result of the binary probit model. $^*p < .10$ $^{**}p < .05$ $^{***}p < .01$

Voting

Voting has unique properties that cannot be simply modeled. PSM returns a negligible average effect of 1.7 percent, indicating that use of campaign Web sites does not matter much in voting. The right plot of figure 5.5 does not show a consistent difference in voting between campaign Web site users and nonusers.

The RBPM of voting has a small and insignificant correlation coefficient that calls for the binary probit model. The model fits the data well but does not report a significant coefficient of campaign Web site use. The discrete change remains less than 1 percent, holding other variables at the reference points. This negligible effect is illustrated in the right plot of figure 5.6.[6] Political knowledge, mobilization, partisanship, age, education, and race significantly influence voting.

Summary

The RBPMs of sending e-mails urging others to vote and attending a campaign rally have significant correlations between disturbances of two equations. Even after use of campaign Web sites is accounted for in the first equation, there still remains a part of variation in engagement that the endogenous variable can indirectly explain in the second equation. In order to evaluate overall impact of an independent variable, both direct and indirect effects are considered. The RBPMs of other engagements do not show a significant correlation coefficient between disturbances. Hence, the binary probit model is estimated.

Use of campaign Web sites is influential for giving money to political candidate and sending e-mails urging people to vote with and without reference to a particular candidate. Campaign Web site use has moderate effects on attendance at rallies and solicitations for votes through phone calls or visits at homes. However, its impact on voting is negligible.

Discussion

Individual civic engagements require different resources, convey different messages, and exert pressures to different degrees on politicians (Verba, Schlozman, and Brady 1995). Thus, civic engagements need to be distinguished from one another. The empirical analysis suggests that use of campaign Web sites influences individual electoral engagements differently depending on the type of civic engagement.

Use of campaign Web sites is endogenous in the models of sending e-mails urging to vote and attending a rally. These engagements and campaign Web site use appear to be jointly determined with significant correlation. The relationship may be reciprocal and form a virtuous circle (Norris 2000, 2001; DiMaggio et al. 2001). Campaign Web site use accounts for some variation of these engagements, but there must be another portion that is still left over and can be indirectly accounted by the endogenous variable. A single equation model such as the binary probit model could not take this indirect effect into account and thus would report an incorrect, if not misleading, result. For example, age has significant direct and indirect effects on attendance at a rally, but its overall impact is negligible. Use of campaign Web sites is exogenous in models of other electoral engagements such as financial contributions and solicitations for votes.

Why is use of campaign Web sites endogenous in some electoral engagements and exogenous in other engagements? Sending e-mails urging people to vote without reference to a particular candidate appears less partisan-oriented than sending e-mails urging people to vote for a candidate. The former is more likely to involve public deliberation than the latter. A campaign Web site may be used to organize campaign rally and other events. As a "technology of cooperation," a campaign Web site may be able to minimize the collective action problem by facilitating information exchange among attendants (Rheingold 2002). This speculation is consistent with Uslaner's (2000, 2004) notion that the Internet may positively influence public deliberation and information exchange within personal networks. In contrast, other engagements, such as financial contributions and voting, are based on individual choices (as opposed to collective actions) without public deliberation and information exchange involved.

It is surprising that use of campaign Web sites has a large effect on sending e-mails urging people to vote with and without reference to a particular candidate. In particular, the discrete change and average effect of campaign Web site use are respectively 17.4 and 14.8 percent in solicitations for votes by means of e-mails. These online electoral engagements appear to be correlated to whether citizens use the Internet and e-mail. Hence, the impact may be overestimated by the self-selection or incidental truncation problem. It is not, however, surprising that campaign Web sites are influential for financial contributions, since they provide easy ways to donate money through credit card, cellular phone, and other techniques.[7] Bimber (2003) and this study consistently suggest that Internet and campaign Web site use, as an exogenous variable, have a significant positive effect on financial contributions.

Target clients of campaign Web sites tend to be those who are politically acknowledged and mobilized, in particular party members and supporters rather than the general public (Bimber and Davis 2003). Political knowledge and mobilization are important indicators of civic engagement as well as use of campaign Web sites. Political parties often use campaign Web sites largely for disseminating information, fund-raising, and mobilizing volunteers. Candidates are likely to provide only information (such as profiles and election pledges) that they want constituents to see, in the format that they prefer. Politicians have no strong incentives to get involved in online two-way communications with supporters (Stromer-Galley 2000). Politicians often want to avoid furious debates on online forums and the overflow of e-mails and messages from constituents. Politicians tend to "narrowcast" favored information for the target audience who resort to the sources of favored information (Bimber and Davis 2003). Internet fund-raising through campaign Web sites is an example that satisfies the need of both politicians and supporters. Targeting clients and narrowcasting of campaign Web sites generally supports the reinforcement theory, that is, that information technology reinforces rather than transforms the existing patterns of political participation.[8]

Campaign Web sites cannot replace but instead supplement traditional electoral activities (Bimber and Davis 2003). Therefore, there may be limitations to the extent that use of campaign Web sites will influence electoral engagement, although information technology continues to progress over time. The limitations do not come from information technology itself but rather from the ways that people (both politicians and constituents) use information technology.

Conclusion

This chapter explores the 2004 Post-election Internet Tracking Survey data of the Pew Internet and American Life Project. Use of campaign Web sites has a positive effect on electoral civic engagement, but the effect differs by the type of civic engagement. Campaign Web site use is endogenous in the model of electoral engagements that involve public deliberation and collective actions through information exchange among citizens. Otherwise, use of campaign Web sites is exogenous and its impact is direct. However, campaign Web sites tend to focus more on mobilizing party members and supporters who are already engaged rather than on accosting the general public. This finding appears to buttress either the reinforcement theory of pessimism or the normalization theory of skepticism.

The propensity score matching and the recursive bivariate probit model were employed to handle the missing data problem and endogeneity of campaign Web site use. These methods improve methodological rigor in this field of study but do not deal with the incidental truncation problem that may occur when modeling online civic engagements such as posting messages to online forums. In future research, it will also be necessary to consider interaction among use of campaign Web sites, government portals, Internet broadcasting, and other information technology applications that are associated with exchange of political information.

APPENDIX 5.1. VARIABLES AND QUESTIONS REGARDING VOTER ENGAGEMENT

- [ ] *E-mails without reference.* Have you sent e-mails urging people to get out and vote without reference to a particular candidate? (q27c)
- [ ] *Attendance at a rally.* During this year's election campaigns, have you attended a campaign rally? (q27a)
- [ ] *Solicitation (e-mails).* Have you sent e-mails urging people to vote for a particular candidate? (q27d)
- [ ] *Solicitation (call/visit).* Have you made telephone calls urging people to vote for a particular candidate? (q27e)
- [ ] Have you visited people at their homes to urge them to vote for a particular candidate? (q27f)
- [ ] *Contributions.* Have you given money to a political candidate? (q27b)
- [ ] *Voting.* Did you happen to vote? (voto2)
- [ ] *Use of campaign Web sites.* Do you go onto campaign Web sites to get news or information about the 2004 elections? (q34a, q34b, q34c)
- [ ] *Political knowledge.* In the past year, have you read a book about current politics or national affairs? (q52a)
- [ ] In the past year, have you seen any documentary films related to the campaign or the candidates? (q52b)
- [ ] *Political mobilization.* In the past two months, have you received mail urging you to vote for a particular presidential candidate? (q23a)
- [ ] Have you received e-mail urging you to vote for a particular presidential candidate? (q23b)
- [ ] Have you received telephone calls urging you to vote for a particular presidential candidate? (q23c)

☐ Have you been visited at home by someone urging you to vote for a particular presidential candidate? (q23d)

☐ *Partisanship.* Do you consider yourself a Republican, Democrat, or Independent (polid). 1 for Republican and Democrat, and 0 otherwise.

☐ *Family income.* Last year, what was your total family income from all sources, before taxes? (inc)

☐ *Education.* What is the last grade or class you completed in school? (educ) 1 for college graduates and 0 otherwise.

☐ *Gender.* Gender (sex). 1 for male and 0 for female

☐ *Race.* What is your race? Are you white, black, Asian, or some other? (race) 1 for white and 0 otherwise

☐ *Age.* What is your age? (age)

☐ *Internet experience.* About how many years have you had access to the Internet? (q12)

☐ *Online use intensity.* How often do you go online from home? (q14)

☐ How often do you go online from work? (q16)

☐ *Broadband use.* Does the computer you use at home connect to the Internet through a dial-up telephone line, or do you have some other type of connection? 1 for a DSL-enabled phone line, a cable TV modem, a wireless connection, or a T-1 or fiber optic connection and 0 for dial-up telephone line and others (modem, q15). Internet users at work are assumed to have a broadband connection.

Note: Original variable name in parenthesis

NOTES

An earlier version of this chapter was published in *Social Science Computer Review* (2008) 26: 190–212. Reprinted by permission.

1. These descriptive content analyses are biased toward supply of Internet services without considering how citizens use the Internet.

2. This formulation is likely especially when Internet use itself is a part of civic engagement. For example, citizens may e-mail civil servants to make policy suggestions, post messages to online forums, and run political blogs.

3. Because individual questions included vary across surveys, it was not possible to get longitudinal data by combining the November 2000, 2002, and 2004 data sets.

4. The one-to-one matching without replacement matched 282 pairs of campaign Web site users and nonusers that have similar propensity scores.

5. A binary probit model would mistakenly report a positive effect of age on attendance at a rally.

6. "But the reality is not only that campaign sites fail to change the minds of citizens, but they also fail even to assist many undecided citizens in making up their minds" (Bimber and Davis 2003, 144).

7. Online fund-raising becomes one of the successful information technology applications adopted for political campaigns. According to Rainie, Cornfield, and Horrigan (2005), Howard Dean collected more than $20 million through the Internet, accounting for 40 percent of his total receipts. John Kerry earned $82 million (33 percent) from Internet fundraising, while George Bush received $14 million (3 percent) during the 2004 election.

8. "The more people like a candidate, the more likely they are to learn about him, and as they learn, their feelings toward the candidate are likely to strengthen" (Bimber and Davis 2003, 137).

REFERENCES

Angrist, J. 1998. "Estimating the Labor Market Impact of Voluntary Military Service Using Social Security Data on Military Applicants." *Econometrica* 66 (2): 249–288.

Arterton, F. 1987. *Teledemocracy: Can Technology Protect Democracy?* Beverly Hills, CA: Sage Publications.

Barber, B. 1999. "Three Scenarios for the Future of Technology and Strong Democracy." *Political Science Quarterly* 113 (4): 573–589.

Becker, S., and A. Ichino. 2002. "Estimation of Average Treatment Effects Based on Propensity Scores." *STATA Journal* 2 (4): 358–377.

Bimber, B. 2001. "Information and Political Engagement in America: The Search for Effects of Information Technology at the Individual Level." *Political Research Quarterly* 54 (1): 53–67.

———. 2003. *Information and American Democracy: Technology in the Evolution of Political Power.* New York: Cambridge University Press.

Bimber, B., and R. Davis. 2003. *Campaigning Online: The Internet in U.S. Elections.* New York: Oxford University Press.

Corrado, A. 1996. "Elections in Cyberspace: Prospects and Problems." In *Elections in Cyberspace: Toward a New Era in American Politics*, ed. Anthony Corrado and Charles M. Firestone, 1–31. Washington, DC: Aspen Institute.

D'Agostino, R. Jr., and D. Rubin. 2000. "Estimating and Using Propensity Scores with Partially Missing Data." *Journal of the American Statistical Association* 95 (451): 749–759.

Davis, R. 1999. *The Web of Politics: The Internet's Impact on the American Political System.* New York: Oxford University Press.

Davis, S., L. Elin, and G. Reeher. 2002. *Click on Democracy: The Internet's Power to Change Political Apathy into Civic Action.* Boulder, CO: Westview Press.

Dehejia, R., and S. Wahba. 1999. "Causal Effects in Nonexperimental Studies: Reevaluating the Evaluation of Training Programs." *Journal of the American Statistical Association* 94 (448): 1053–1062.

Delli Carpini, M., and S. Keeter. 2003. "The Internet and an Informed Citizenry." In *The Civic Web: Online Politics and Democratic Values*, ed. Michael Cornfield, and David M. Anderson, 129–153. Lanham, MD: Rowman and Littlefield.

DiMaggio, P., E. Hargittai, W. Neuman, and J. Robinson. 2001. "Social Implications of the Internet." *Annual Review of Sociology* 27 (1): 307–336.

Greene, W. 1998. "Gender Economics Courses in Liberal Arts Colleges: Further Results." *Journal of Economic Education* 29 (4): 291–300.

———. 2003. *Econometric Analysis.* 5th ed. Upper Saddle River, NJ: Prentice Hall.

Grossman, L. 1995. *The Electronic Republic: Reshaping Democracy in the Information Age.* New York: Viking Penguin.

Hahn, J. 1998. "On the Role of the Propensity Score in Efficient Semiparametric Estimation of Average Treatment Effects." *Econometrica* 66 (2): 315–331.

Heckman, J., H. Ichimura, and P. Todd. 1997. "Matching as an Econometric Evaluation Estimator: Evidence from Evaluating a Job Training Programme." *Review of Economic Studies* 64 (4): 605–654.

Jennings, M., and V. Zeitner. 2003. "Internet Use and Civic Engagement." *Public Opinion Quarterly* 67 (3): 311–334.

Kamarck, E. 2002. "Political Campaigning on the Internet: Business as Usual?" In *Governance.com: Democracy in the Information Age*, ed. E. Kamarck and J. Nye Jr., 81–103. Washington, DC: Brookings Institution Press.

Katz, J., and R. Rice. 2002. *Social Consequences of Internet Use: Access, Involvement, and Interaction*. Cambridge, MA: MIT Press.

Kavanaugh, A. 2002. "Community Networks and Civic Engagement: A Social Network Approach." *The Good Society* 11 (3): 17–24.

LaLonde, R. 1986. "Evaluating the Econometric Evaluations of Training Programs with Experimental Data." *American Economic Review* 76 (4): 604–620.

Long, J. 1997. *Regression Models for Categorical and Limited Dependent Variables: Advanced Quantitative Techniques in the Social Sciences*. Thousand Oaks, CA: Sage Publications.

Long, J., and J. Freese. 2003. *Regression Models for Categorical Dependent Variables Using STATA*. 2nd ed. College Station, TX: STATA Press.

Maddala, G. 1983. *Limited Dependent and Qualitative Variables in Econometrics*. New York: Cambridge University Press.

Maddala, G., and L. Lee. 1976. "Recursive Models with Qualitative Endogenous Variables." *Annals of Economic and Social Measurement* 5 (4): 525–545.

Margolis, M., and D. Resnick. 2000. *Politics as Usual: The Cyberspace*. Thousand Oaks, CA: Sage Publications.

Norris, P. 2000. *A Virtuous Circle: Political Communication in Post-Industrial Democracies*. New York: Cambridge University Press.

———. 2001. *The Digital Divide: Civic Engagement, Information Poverty and the Internet Worldwide*. New York: Cambridge University Press.

Pew Internet and American Life Project. 2004. November 2004 Tracking Survey.

Putnam, R. 2000. *Bowling Alone: The Collapse and Revival of American Community*. New York: Simon and Schuster.

Rainie, L., M. Cornfield, and J. Horrigan. 2005. The Internet and Campaign 2004. Pew Internet and American Life Project. http://www.pewinternet.org/ppf/r/150/report_display.asp.

Ramakrishnan, S., and M. Baldassare. 2004. *The Ties That Bind: Changing Demographics and Civic Engagement in California*. San Francisco: Public Policy Institute of California.

Rheingold, H. 1993. *The Virtual Community*. Reading, MA: Addison-Wesley.

———. 2002 *Smart Mobs: The Next Social Revolution*. Cambridge, MA: Basic Books.

Robbin, A., C. Courtright, and L. Davis. 2004. "ICTs and Political Life." *Annual Review of Information Science and Technology* 38:411–481.

Rosenbaum, P., and D. Rubin. 1983. "The Central Role of the Propensity Score in Observational Studies for Causal Effects." *Biometrika* 70 (1): 41–55.

———. 1984. "Reducing Bias in Observational Studies Using Subclassification on the Propensity Score." *Journal of the American Statistical Association* 79 (387): 516–524.

Scott, J. 2006. " 'E' the People: Do U.S. Municipal Government Web Sites Support Public Involvement?" *Public Administration Review* 66 (3): 341–353.

Selnow, G. 1998. *Electronic Whistle-Stops: The Impact of the Internet on American Politics*. Westport, CT: Praeger.

Shadish, W., T. Cook, and D. Campbell. 2002. *Experimental and Quasi-experimental Designs for Generalized Causal Inference*. Boston: Houghton Mifflin.

Stromer-Galley, J. 2000. "On-Line Interaction and Why Candidates Avoid It." *Journal of Communication* 50 (4): 111–132.

Uslaner, E. 2000. "Social Capital and Net." *Communications of the ACM* 43 (12): 60–64.

———. 2004. "Trust, Civic Engagement, and the Internet." *Political Communication* 21 (2): 223–242.

Verba, S., K. Schlozman, and H. Brade. 1995. *Voice and Equality: Civic Voluntarism in American Politics.* Cambridge, MA: Harvard University Press.

Ward, S., R. Gibson, and P. Nixon. 2003. "Parties and the Internet: An Overview." In *Political Parties and the Internet: Net Gain?* ed. R. Gibson, P.Nixon, and S. Ward, 11–38. New York: Routledge

Weissberg, R. 2005. *The Limits of Civic Activism: Cautionary Tales on the Use of Politics.* New Brunswick, NJ: Transaction Publishers.

PART TWO

Technology and
Voter Mobilization

Campaign organizations exist primarily to call voters to political action. The main aim is to persuade voters to support specific candidates over others and to mobilize them to vote, volunteer, and contribute. Technology-enabled tools, including e-mail, text messaging, and political advertising, are now available to help campaigns to facilitate these goals. Campaigns at all levels have started to rely increasingly on these tools to supplement traditional voter mobilization and persuasion tactics, but there is scant reliable evidence about the effectiveness of these techniques. Using a variety of methodological approaches, the authors investigate the impact of these tactics and discuss the nuances associated with deploying them in electoral campaigns. Overall, the authors offer mixed results about the effectiveness of various tactics in influencing political behavior. In some respects, the analyses debunk conventional wisdom, while other observations suggest it may be premature to render judgment, as the transition to incorporating these tools into contemporary campaign strategy is ongoing but in its infancy. In any case, the selections offer readers the most up-to-date insights based on rigorous empirical analyses.

6

Clicking for Cash

Campaigns, Donors, and the Emergence of Online Fund-Raising

COSTAS PANAGOPOULOS

DANIEL BERGAN

In the 2000 presidential election cycle, Senator John McCain, an unsuccessful contender for the Republican nomination, demonstrated that the power of the Internet could be marshaled effectively to raise campaign funds. McCain raised $2.2 million online in just four days after winning the New Hampshire Republican primary (Malbin 2006). Overall, the McCain campaign raised a total of $6.4 million on the Internet during the 2000 cycle (Cornfield 2004), representing nearly one-quarter of the $28.1 million total the campaign raised from individual contributors over the course of the campaign.

By 2004, the number of Americans who went online had surged past 200 million Americans for the first time, and three out of four Americans had access to the Internet (Nielsen 2004). Eighteen percent of registered voters reported that the Internet was their primary source of information about the presidential election in 2004, up from 3 percent in 1996 and 11 percent in 2000 (Rainie, Cornfield, and Horrigan 2005). Widespread access and innovative applications rendered the medium especially useful for organizational, communication, and fund-raising purposes in the 2004 elections, and the presidential campaigns capitalized on these developments. Both parties relied extensively on the Internet, sending out millions of communiqués via e-mail to enormous mailing lists. The Republican National Committee boasted an e-mail database of 6 million voters while the Democrats' list totaled 2.5 million (Malbin 2006). In the last six months of the campaign alone, the Institute for Politics, Democracy and the Internet collected more than 900 different e-mails sent from the two major campaigns or national parties (Graf et al. 2006). Many of these online communications included solicitations for financial support.

Fund-Raising in the 2004 Presidential Campaign

Technological developments partly explain the increased use of the Internet for political fund-raising in 2004. Americans had grown accustomed to performing financial transactions online, and fears about security and confidentiality had largely subsided (Fallows 2004). The stronger impetus that fueled elite strategies with respect to raising funds online probably resulted from the new regulatory context within which the 2004 elections were operating, however. The passage of the Bipartisan Campaign Reform Act (BCRA) in 2002—especially the elimination of soft money, which was a key provision of the law—had changed the landscape of political fund-raising considerably. Unable to attract large sums of unregulated soft money, political campaigns and parties were compelled to broaden their fund-raising bases and to solicit contributions from more donors. Overall, total contributions and number of donors surged in 2004 (Panagopoulos and Bergan 2006), as did the number of small donors (individuals who contributed $100 or less) and first-time donors (Graf et al. 2006). The Internet helped to facilitate these developments.

In many ways, Democratic presidential hopeful Howard Dean pioneered the modern use of the Internet for political fund-raising and organizing in 2004. His campaign placed the Internet center stage in its strategy and succeeded in attracting substantial sums from online contributors. Even after the collapse of the Dean campaign following the Iowa caucuses, the Internet was featured prominently in the fund-raising strategies of both the Kerry and the Bush campaigns. The Kerry campaign reportedly raised $82 million using the Internet during the 2004 cycle, while Bush's online fund-raising brought in $13 million total (Malbin 2006).

Data

Heavy reliance on new technology, primarily the Internet, for political fund-raising purposes is likely to be an enduring feature of contemporary political campaigns. At least in the short term, online political fund-raising is here to stay. In the sections that follow, we use available survey data to investigate online fund-raising strategies and to compare the attributes, attitudes, and motivations of online donors with offline donors.

Data for the analyses that follow were obtained from the Small Donors Survey conducted by the Institute for Politics, Democracy and the Internet and the Campaign Finance Institute from July 1 to November 30, 2005.[1] The sample of donors was composed of a random sample of 3,000 large donors (more than $200) and 3,480 small donors who contributed to the 2004 presidential campaigns. Survey instruments were mailed to respondents, who were given the option to respond via mail or online; 428 valid surveys were completed online, and 1,153 were received by mail. The overall response rate for the survey was 27 percent.[2]

For the purposes of this study, the key variable in the survey is whether the contributor gave online. Survey respondents were asked: "How many of your contributions were made online using a credit card, debit card, or online check?" The respondent could answer "All," "Some," or "None." We split the respondents into two groups based on responses to this question: those who made at least some of their contributions online ("Online contributors") and those who made none of their contributions online ("Offline contributors.") The online/offline distinction breaks the sample into two roughly even groups: 50.8 percent of the sample (776 respondents) were offline contributors, while 49.2 percent were online contributors (751 respondents). The analysis in the next section of this chapter compares these two types of donors with respect to the average size of their contributions, the recipients of their contributions, the contributor's demographics, ideology, activism in politics, and motivations for giving.

Analysis of Online and Offline Donors

In this section, we will compare various demographic and political characteristics of online and offline donors. One simple question is answerable at the outset, however: how large is the total amount of contributions from each type of contributor? One claim about the Internet is that it facilitates smaller contributions because it makes it easier for small contributors to give to a campaign and taps into younger contributors who may not be as wealthy as older, offline donors. We compared total contributions from offline and online contributors for the 2003–2004 presidential election cycle. The median total amount contributed by online donors was $150 versus $85 for offline donors. This is a surprising result given the emphasis in the media on raising small contributions online in the 2003–2004 campaign.

Who gives online? Table 6.1 compares demographic characteristics of online and offline donors. Both types of donors are similar in terms of gender, race and marital status: most donors are male, are white, and are married. The mean age for online givers is twelve years younger than offline givers, not surprising given the relatively recent advent of the Internet. Perhaps more surprisingly, online givers are wealthier: 58 percent of online donors have incomes of $100,000 or greater, while only 46 percent of offline givers have incomes this high. Online givers are also more likely to have at least some graduate education.

One would think that the ability to make online contributions would expand to pool of potentially donors to other demographic groups, but

TABLE 6.1

Demographic Characteristics of Off-line and Online Donors

	Off-line donors	Online donors
% Male	58.6	60.0
% White	92.5	93.2
% Married	69.1	68.1
Mean age	63.6	52.0***
% Income $100,000 or higher	45.9	58.1***
% At least some graduate education	54.3	63.7***

***Indicates statistically significant difference at .001, two sided t-test.

table 6.1 suggests that this expansion has not been extremely wide. On many demographic characteristics, online donors do not differ from offline contributors. They are, in fact, wealthier and more highly educated than offline contributors. One notable exception is age; the ability to contribute online has appeared to increase political contribution behavior in a younger demographic.

What is the ideological makeup of online donors compared to offline donors? Table 6.2 presents the partisan and ideological characteristics of online and offline donors. The table shows that online donors are predominantly Democratic.[3] There are also separate questions that track ideology. Respondents were asked to place themselves on a scale from conservative to strong liberal. While the typical offline donor is a moderate, the typical offline donor is a liberal. Similar results hold when comparing an additive scale of respondent ideology (see the appendix to this chapter for questions included in this scale). The scale ranges from 6 for extreme conservatives to 30 for extreme liberals. Offline donors have a mean score of 20 while online donors have a mean score of 25.

What about the extremism of contributors? In the past, innovations in campaigns caused some alarm because it was feared that some technologies went hand in hand with polarizing rhetoric. For example, Godwin (1988) found that the most successful fund-raising direct mail from citizen groups and from some candidates featured emotive, polarizing rhetoric. One could imagine that the Internet could introduce the possibility of polarizing donors along ideological lines. For example, those visiting candidate Web sites and other sites with a partisan slant could be exposed to more polarizing rhetoric than those who get their political news from newspapers and network television.

To gauge this, we compared the percentage of self-described "strong liberals" and "strong conservatives" among online and offline donors. We find that there is not a large gap between the two types of donors with respect to extremism: 34 percent of offline donors have strong ideological stances while 39 percent of online donors have strong ideological stances. This is not a statistically significant difference, suggesting that the growth of online contributions should not give rise to concerns about a parallel rise in donor extremism.

The overall liberal ideology of online donors seems to reflect the efforts on the part of Democratic candidates, such as John Kerry and Howard Dean, to solicit online contributions. We can explore this further by looking at the recipients of online contributions. Table 6.3 shows proportion of online donors among contributors to selected candidates. Because individuals in the sample could give to more than one presidential candidate, the table reports data on the first contribution the respondent gave in the 2003–2004 presidential campaign. The table reports the percentage of online donors among those who gave their first contribution in the election cycle to each candidate listed. Only 20.7 percent of contributors to George W. Bush were

TABLE 6.2

Party Identification and Ideology of Online and Off-line Donors

	Off-line donors	Online donors
Party identification		
% Republican	41.4	12.4***
% Democrat	46.4	70.1***
Ideology		
Mean self-reported ideology (7-point scale, 7 = strong liberal)	4.0 (2.1)	5.4*** (1.7)
Mean additive index score (range: 6–30; higher scores = liberal)	19.8 (7.0)	34.7*** (5.4)
Extremism		
% Strong liberal or conservative	34.2	38.5

Note: Standard deviations displayed in parentheses with means.

***Indicates statistically significant difference at .001, two sided t-test.

online donors. Some Democratic candidates, such as Joseph Lieberman and Dick Gephardt, also received a small percentage of contributions from online donors. Other Democratic candidates, such as John Kerry, Wesley Clark, John Edwards, and Howard Dean received large percentages of the first contributions made by online donors, reflecting their efforts to pursue online contributions. In addition, Ralph Nader received a large percentage of these online contributions. These numbers probably reflect efforts on the part of these campaigns to raise online funds more than any characteristics of the donors.

The mobilization of potential donors is reflected in the high percentages of donors who were asked to give to a campaign. A large percentage of both types of donors were asked to give to a candidate or party; 67.7 percent of offline donors and 74.5 percent of online donors were asked personally to contribute to a candidate or party. One difference between online and offline donors may be the way that they are encouraged to contribute. Table 6.4 shows how donors were motivated to make their first contribution of the election cycle (respondents could check more than one item on the list). Most means of mobilizing do not differ substantially across donors; for example, there is no major difference in being motivated by attending a meetup.com event or house party, seeing a television ad, or seeing something in the television news. The major differences are in the first three rows of the table. Online donors are more likely to be mobilized to give by

TABLE 6.3

Recipients of Online Contributions

	Percentage of contributions from online donors
George W. Bush	20.7
John Kerry	66.2
Wesley Clark	79.9
John Edwards	65.1
Richard Gephardt	33.3
Howard Dean	67.0
Joe Lieberman	26.0
Ralph Nader	64.2

Note: Includes only first contribution of election cycle.

TABLE 6.4

Influences on Online and Off-line Contributors

	Off-line donors	Online donors
Received letter from candidate or party	58.6	25.2***
Received telephone call from candidate or party	18.0	8.7***
Received e-mail from candidate or party	8.0	29.2***
Saw candidate in person	11.9	13.2
Saw political advertisement on TV	9.8	6.1**
Saw political video online	2.2	5.9***
Family member/friend/colleague encouraged me to	11.9	9.2
Someone I know told me he/she made contribution	2.6	3.7
Attended meetup.com event or house party	4.5	6.8

***Indicates statistically significant difference at .001, two sided t-test.

**Statistically significant at .01, two-sided t-test.

an e-mail, while offline donors are more likely to be motivated to give by a letter or phone call.

The result in the first column is worth considering. Most offline donors were motivated to give at least in part by a letter they received from a candidate or party. A relatively small number—only about a quarter—of online givers were mobilized by a letter. This suggests that individuals who contribute online would not have been reached by fund-raising letters, a more traditional means of fund-raising.

How active are online donors in politics, aside from making campaign contributions? One possibility is that online contributors are not active in traditional domains (such as writing an elected official or belonging to a political group), and may not have the same social networks as activists but are able to be active in politics through the impersonal, low-cost medium of the Internet. One could also imagine that such individuals would be more active politically on the Internet—that is, more likely to read news online, participate in chat rooms, read blogs, and so on. One reason to suspect that online donors may be less active in traditional political activities is that a larger proportion of online donors are giving for the first time. Respondents

TABLE 6.5

Activism Among Online and Off-line Donors

	Off-line donors	Online donors
Mean activism scale	2.90	4.04***
	(2.24)	(2.12)
Mean online activism scale	1.78	4.13***
	(1.78)	(1.68)
Did you ask anyone to give money to a candidate or party? (% yes)	17.2	33.4***
Did you ask more than three people to give money to a candidate or party (% yes)	62.4	73.4*

Note: Standard deviations displayed in parentheses with means.

***Statistically significant difference at .001, two sided t-test.

**Statistically significant at .01, two-sided t-test.

*Statistically significant at .05, two-sided t-test.

were asked if the 2003–2004 election cycle was the first time they made a campaign contribution. Among online donors, 27.3 percent responded yes, compared with 15.1 percent for offline donors.

Table 6.5 explores the offline and online political participation of online and other contributors. The table presents mean scores for an activism scale that is an additive scale of traditional political behaviors such as writing a political candidate or attending a rally (see the appendix to this chapter for questions included in the scale). The scale ranges from 0 to 8, with an additional point added for each activity. The scale reliability index is .77. The table also displays online activity, including using the Internet to gain political information and visiting the Web site of a candidate (see the appendix to this chapter for activities included). The scale ranges from 0 to 7 with a reliability coefficient of .8. In addition to displaying online and offline behavior, the table presents responses to questions about asking other individuals to give. Respondents were asked if they asked anyone to give money to a candidate or political party, and if so, how many people they asked.

Online donors, unsurprisingly, engage in more online activity; they take on average more than two online actions than offline donors. What is surprising is that online donors are more likely to participate in other ways as well. Online donors take on average one additional action on the activism scale. They are more likely to ask someone to contribute to a political candidate or party, and on average ask more people to contribute.

TABLE 6.6
Logit Regressions of Online Contributing Behavior

	Model 1	Model 2
Demographics		
Male	.413**	.308
	(.140)	(.157)
White	.412	.100
	(.256)	(.284)
Married	.045	−.069
	(.156)	(.173)
Age	−.072***	−.048***
	(.006)	(.006)
Income (9-category)	.019	.047
	(.034)	(.038)
Education (6-category)	.017	−.022
	(.057)	(.065)
Party/ideology		
Democrat	.149	.307
	(.203)	(.224)
Liberalism self-reports	.406***	.326***
	(.053)	(.058)
Extreme	−.047	−.155
	(.148)	(.165)
Activism		
Activism		−.019
		(.037)
Online activism		.590***
		(.046)
Constant	1.31**	−0.984
	(.491)	(.566)
N	1274	1274
LR chi2(10)	400.5	622.2
Prob>chi2	.000	.000
Pseudo (r) squared	.23	.35

Note: Standard errors in parentheses. Dependent
variable = 1 if contributed online, 0 if off-line.

***Statistically significant difference at .001, two sided t-test.

**Statistically significant at .01, two-sided t-test.

*Statistically significant at .05, two-sided t-test.

What do these results mean? While it is possible that the Internet could draw inactive citizens into politics, in the 2003–2004 presidential campaign it appears that those who contributed were active in other ways already. Online activists are in fact more active in traditional forms of participation, such as signing petitions and writing elected officials, than offline contributors.

Table 6.6 presents logit regressions, allowing us to determine the predictors of online giving versus offline giving. The dependent variable equals 1 if the respondent was an online donor, and equals 0 for offline donors. The models control for demographic variables, party, self-reported ideology, and individuals with extreme ideologies (strong liberals and strong conservatives). The second model adds the two indices of activism discussed in the text, traditional and online activism.

Age, unsurprisingly, has a robust effect on online giving. Gender is a statistically significant predictor of online giving, although the effect is not robust, The differences discussed earlier relating to education and income are not statistically significant.

In the second model, activism is not statistically significant, although a difference between the two types of contributors was noted. Online activism, however, is a robust predictor of online contributing.

The key finding of both of the models is that liberalism is a statistically significant predictor of giving. This result holds even when controlling for party and extreme ideology. Ideology is statistically significant, although party identification not; although an indicator for identifying with the Democratic Party is statistically significant in a model without control for ideology; this result is not shown in the table. This suggests that candidates on the left were successful at mobilizing liberal donors to give online.

Conclusion: Online Fund-Raising in 2008 and Beyond

This chapter has analyzed the characteristics of online contributors and compared them to traditional, offline givers. We have found that online contributors do not differ substantially from offline givers in that they are predominantly male, white, highly educated, and wealthy. The data suggest, however, that a younger demographic has been tapped by the candidates and parties in attempting to raise more funds online. Online contributors are more liberal than offline givers, suggesting that the Democratic (and perhaps Green Party) presidential candidates have been better at soliciting funds from online donors than the Republicans.

Has the Internet drawn a new class of otherwise inactive contributor into politics? The data here suggest that the answer is no. Online contributors are more active politically than offline contributors, but it appears that the advent of the Internet is responsible for bringing in younger donors who are asked for funds through e-mail rather than traditional (such as direct mail) means. These contributors are more active online than are offline contributors.

One point that we have made in this chapter is that contributing behavior is driven by the efforts of parties and candidates to raise funds. Candidates who have put more efforts into raising funds online have been successful at attracting more online donors. One question that remains to be answered is: Are there certain types of candidates who will be more successful at raising funds online? Howard Dean raised a large proportion of funds online, a strategy that perhaps went hand in hand with his attractiveness to younger, progressive activists. Can all candidates take advantage of the Internet, or is this a strategy that only works for candidates who appeal to a certain ideology or age group? Future strategies will reveal the possibilities and limitations of the Internet for raising funds.

Fund-raising during the 2008 presidential primaries offers some insights. The initial evidence suggests online donations are increasing in number and importance. Moreover, online contributors are frequently first-time givers and small donors; there are also indications, however, that not all candidates perform equally well in raising online contributions.

In this chapter, we have discussed Howard Dean's success at raising online funds in the 2004 campaign. Several candidates in 2008 have followed suit. At the time of this writing, Barack Obama has tripled the number of Dean's online donors (Malone 2008). As Howard Dean's campaign manager, Joe Trippi, remarked, "We may have invented [online fund-raising]. But it was the Wright brothers with a flimsy plane that proved you could fly." According to reports early in 2008, the Obama campaign had brought in $28 million online, with 90 percent of those donations from individuals who gave $100 or less. Senator Hillary Clinton, the other main contender for the Democratic nomination, also raised unprecedented sums online. On the Republican side, Texas Congressman Ron Paul, who lagged way behind in opinion poll and election support, captured national attention when his campaign raised $4.2 million in one day from 37,000 donors contributing online in November 2007. His campaign described the achievement as "the largest, single-day online primary fund-raising effort by a presidential candidate in United States election history" (Memmott and Lawrence 2007).

The experiences of these candidates suggest that online donors can be a major source of funds. Not all candidates have been successful at raising funds online, however. In the 2008 primaries, the three leading contenders for the Democratic nomination raised more than doubled the amount raised online by the three Republican frontrunners in the first six months of 2007 (Luo 2007). Rudy Giuiliani, the frontrunner in national polls in early 2007, raised the least online of all major candidates—only $1.3 million.

Why are some candidates more effective than others at raising online contributions? The results of our analysis suggest that demographics play a major role. As online donors are on average younger, candidates who appeal to younger voters appear able to raise more funds online. Campaigns seem to anticipate this by experimenting with online fund-raising. For example, a number of campaigns have used social networking sites to solicit volunteers and campaign contributions: the Obama campaign's MySpace.com and Facebook.com pages had more than 100,000 friends each by the summer of 2007. In addition, at rallies the campaign made an effort to solicit e-mail addresses, which have been used to raise funds. Liberal sites like ActBlue.com allow individuals to contribute to Democratic candidates. Other candidates, perhaps anticipating the online behavior of key supporting demographics, have not taken advantage of these features. For example, the Giuliani campaign's MySpace page was accessible only to individuals who receive approval, and the campaign did not maintain a Facebook page (Luo 2007).

Technology is also facilitating other innovations and fund-raising opportunities. A new program, Text2Help, first used after Hurricane Katrina to solicit contributions, enables donors to make political contributions using their cell phones (Strom 2007). Mobile fund-raising for political campaigns is currently in its nascent stages, but the technology may eventually emerge as an effective option.

APPENDIX 6.1. QUESTIONS USED IN ADDITIVE SCALES

Activism Scale:
Here is a list of things some people do about government or politics. Please indicate if you have done any of these in the past year. Check all that apply.

- [ ] Written or called any politician at the state, local or national level
- [ ] Attended a political rally, speech, or organized protest of any kind
- [ ] Attended a public meeting on town or school affairs
- [ ] Served on a committee for some local organization
- [ ] Served as an officer for some club or organization
- [ ] Signed a petition
- [ ] Worked for a political party
- [ ] Written a letter to the editor to a newspaper or magazine or called a live radio or TV show to express an opinion
- [ ] Been an active member of any group that tries to influence public policy or government

Online Activism Scale:
Do you ever go online to access the Internet or to get e-mail? (If yes: In the past year, did you do any of the following? Check all that apply.

- [ ] Go anywhere to get political information?
- [ ] Visit the Web site of your political party or candidate?

☐ Visit the Web site of another party or candidate?
☐ Visit a political discussion group or chat room online?
☐ Visit a news Web site, such as CNN.com, MSNBC.com, or NYTimes.com?
☐ Visit a Web log (or blog) that discusses politics or current events?

In the 2004 campaign did you do any of the following? Check all that apply.

☐ Attend a Meetup.com political event?

Ideology Scale:
What are your views on the following statements? (1 = strongly agree, 2 = agree, 3 = neutral, 4 = disagree, 5 = strongly disagree). Reversed items are coded so that 1 = strongly disagree and 5 = strongly agree:

___ Taxes should be cut even if it means reducing public services.
___ People should be able to invest some social security funds.
___ Government should enact laws to restrict gay marriage.
___ Government should provide health insurance for the uninsured (reversed).
___ Mandatory death penalty for murder should be the law.
___ Government should spend more to reduce poverty in the U.S (reversed).

NOTES

An earlier version of this chapter was published in *Social Science Computer Review* (2007) 25: 484–493. Reprinted by permission.

1. One of the authors (Panagopoulos) was part of the research team that conducted and analyzed the 2005 survey. See Graf et al. (2006) for details.

2. For details about sampling and methodology, see Graf et al. (2006).

3. Respondents were assigned to a party based on a seven-point scale. Individuals could claim to be independent, to be strong party identifiers, party identifiers who were not strong, and independents who lean toward a particular party. Strong and not strong identifiers and leaners were coded as party identifiers.

REFERENCES

Cornfield, M. 2004. *Politics Moves Online: Campaigning and the Internet.* New York: The Century Foundation Press.

Fallows, D. 2004. *The Internet and Daily Life.* Report issued by the Pew Internet and American Life Project (accessed April 24, 2007, at http://www.pewinternet.org/pdfs/PIP_Internet_and_Daily_Life.pdf).

Godwin, R. 1988. *One Billion Dollars of Influence: the Direct Marketing of Politics.* Chatham, NJ: Chatham House Publishers.

Graf, J., G. Reeher, M. Malbin, and C. Panagopoulos. 2006. "Small Donors and Online Giving." Report issued by the Institute for Politics, Democracy and the Internet.

Luo, M. 2007. "Democrats Take the Lead in Raising Money Online." *New York Times.* July 13.

_____. 2008. "Small Online Contributions Add Up to a Huge Fund-raising Edge for Obama." *New York Times.* February 20.

Malbin, M. 2006. "A Public Funding System in Jeopardy." In *The Election After Reform: Money, Politics and the Bipartisan Campaign Reform Act,* ed. M. Malbin. Lanham, MD: Rowman and Littlefield.

Malone, J. 2008. "Obama Donor List Makes History." *Philadelphia Daily News*. February 28.

Memmott, M., and J. Lawrence. 2007. "Ron Paul Says He's Broken One-Day Online Fundraising Record." *USA Today*. November 6 (accessed March 10, 2008, at http://blogs. usatoday.com/onpolitics/2007/11/ron-paul-says-h.html).

Nielsen. 2004. Three Out of Four Americans Have Access to the Internet. Press release (accessed April 24, 2007, at http://www.nielsen-netratings.com/pr/pr_040318.pdf).

Panagopoulos, C., and D. Bergan. 2006. "Contributions and Contributors in the 2004 Presidential Election Cycle." *Presidential Studies Quarterly* 36 (2): 155–171.

Rainie, L., M. Cornfield, and J. Horrigan. 2005. "The Internet and Campaign 2004." Report issued by the Pew Research Center. March 6 (accessed April 20, 2007, at http://www.pewinternet.org/pdfs/PIP_2004_Campaign.pdf).

Strom, S. 2007. "Group Questions Cellphone Fund-Raising." *New York Times*. April 11 (accessed March 10, 2008, at (http://www.nytimes.com/2007/04/11/us/11cell. html?emc=eta1).

7

The Impact of E-Mail Campaigns on Voter Mobilization

Evidence from a Field Experiment

DAVID W. NICKERSON

Howard Dean's innovative use of the Internet for political campaigning caught the nation's attention during the beginning of the 2004 Democratic primary. According to the *Washington Post*, Dean raised much of his $41 million online, and 185,000 supporters signed up on Meetup.com (Faler 2004a). In the past, a candidate's Web site only served as a place to download press releases and donate money. Dean built a Web site that offered a virtual community for his supporters, and many campaigns have since adopted many of its features. It took years for politicians to utilize television as a campaign tool, and candidates are just now beginning to figure out how to use the Internet.

An intuitive place to begin is by using the Internet to accomplish work previously done with older technology such as mail, phones, or face-to-face. The low transaction costs and massive economies of scale of the Internet could radically alter the strategies campaigns employ in every facet of campaigning. In principle, once the initial list of e-mail addresses is compiled and database infrastructure is in place, there is no cost to contacting voters via e-mail. The same economics that push businesses to move online are also present in the political realm.

The specific campaign goal this chapter considers is voter mobilization. Leading up to Election Day, political parties and nonprofit groups engage in get out the vote (GOTV) activities. The low rates of voter turnout in the United States make GOTV work critical to successful campaigning. Occasionally, the challenge is not to persuade voters, but rather to ensure that one's supporters turnout at higher rates than the opponent's supporters.

E-mail is the GOTV technology studied in this chapter. Direct mail has been shown to be an effective, albeit expensive, means of increasing voter turnout (Gerber, Green, and Green 2003). Examining all known randomized experiments evaluating direct mail, Green and Gerber (2004, 60) estimate it takes 133 pieces of mail to create one vote and at fifty cents per mailing the cost for each vote is sixty-seven dollars. By saving on printing, supplies, and postage, one would think that e-mail is likely to be more cost-effective than direct mail at mobilizing voters.

This logic guided the spending of millions of dollars during the 2004 presidential election. Entirely Web-based groups such as MoveOn.org grabbed headlines for their pioneering use of the Internet for political mobilization, but traditional campaigns also engaged in significant online mobilization. During the final week of the election campaign roughly one-third of e-mail contact from both parties focused on encouraging turnout (Reich 2005).[1] After the election, one of the pressing questions in the Democratic Party was the future of the 2.7 million supporters on Kerry's e-mail lists (Faler 2004b). The utility of the Web for collecting donations is evident, but whether e-mail lists engage voters and increase participation is more difficult to measure.

To test this hypothesis seven experiments were conducted by a nonpartisan organization during the 2004 presidential election to determine the usefulness of e-mail for voter registration and increasing voter turnout.[2] Members of the organization signed up online to receive reminders for both registration and mobilization. The members who signed up were randomly divided into a treatment group, which received a series of e-mails encouraging registration and turnout, and a control group, which received no attention from the organization. Given that the seven combined experiments involve 161,633 subjects, any differences in registration and turnout between the treatment and control groups will be directly attributable to receipt of the e-mail.

Ultimately, this chapter concludes that mass opt-in e-mails are unlikely to be a cost-effective means of increasing voter turnout. In reaching this conclusion, I first describe and explain the experimental methodology. Next I describe the experimental setting, design, and implementation. The results are discussed in the third section and the chapter concludes by proposing future avenues for research.

Method

How much does receiving a series of e-mails encouraging voter turnout increase a person's likelihood of voting? Political scientists attempting to answer this question might be tempted to rely upon observational data and draw incorrect inferences as a result. The typical observational study might begin with a survey of registered voters in a city, asking questions about the respondent's contact with political campaigns, attitudes across a range of political questions, and a range of political behaviors. In order to avoid self-reporting errors, a good study would rely upon official county clerk records to determine which of the respondents abstained from voting. In a perfect world, the researcher would also contact political campaigns and nonprofit groups to verify whether the respondent was contacted by e-mail (and the content of the contact), thereby avoiding measurement error on the independent variable of interest. Despite all of these efforts, the results of such an observational study are potentially biased and uninformative.

The reason the hypothetical study is biased is that multiple causes of voting behavior can account for an observed result. Suppose that the hypothetical survey demonstrated that the set of people who received e-mail from campaigns voted at a higher rate, say 2 percent, than those persons who did not receive e-mail. One possible explanation for the 2 percent difference is that receiving e-mail boosts turnout much in the same manner as door knocks (Green, Gerber, and Nickerson 2003), mail (Gerber, Green, and Green 2003), and phone calls (Nickerson 2006 and 2007). However, a second explanation is that the campaigns targeted likely voters in the first place, so the difference in turnout is evidence of good targeting by the campaign more than the effectiveness of the e-mail. A third explanation could be that voters with e-mail have higher income and therefore were more likely to vote in the first place. Similarly, it is also possible that the campaign sent e-mail only to those individuals who opted into a list. These self-selected individuals are likely to be more interested in politics and the election than the general populace, so the difference in turnout may be measuring the correlation between interest in the election and voter turnout. In short, there are numerous possible explanations of the findings, and observational studies have no good way of adjudicating between them. The effect of e-mail could be the full 2 percent, but it could also be zero or even negative.

Randomized experiments bypass concerns about unobserved causes of voter turnout. In an experiment, the variable of interest is manipulated by the researcher and applied to particular subjects. When the application of the treatment is randomized, the researcher can be confident that the treatment and control groups are roughly similar to one another in relation to all other factors, both seen and unseen. That is, experimental subjects in the group who were sent an e-mail encouraging voter turnout have the same age, interest in the election, exposure to outside campaign materials, and Internet savvy as the people in the control group, who do not receive the e-mail. Thus, by simply comparing the rates of voter turnout in the treatment and control groups, the causal effect of the e-mail on voter turnout can be estimated. As a practical matter, the estimate is derived by simply subtracting the control group's turnout from the treatment group's turnout.

The key is the random assignment, which protects against selection bias and unobserved heterogeneity.

Setting and Design

Working Assets is a progressive citizen action group that directs member activism and donates a percentage of revenues from long distance and credit card services to nonprofit groups. In order to increase participation rates among its members, Working Assets asked its members to sign up for registration reminders and forms with mobilization e-mails to follow. Working Assets sent e-mail only to those individuals who came to the Working Assets Web site and specifically requested to be on a mailing list reminding individuals to register and vote. People signed up from all over the nation, but 161,633 people signed up from the seven experimental areas. After individuals entered name and address information into the Web site, the subject possessed a 68.5 percent chance of being assigned to the treatment group and receiving a series of e-mails from Working Assets encouraging registration and turnout (see figure 7.1 for an example).[3] Open rates were not recorded, but given the trusted nature of the e-mail source and the vibrant nature of Working Assets' online community, it is likely that the e-mails were read by a large percentage of the subjects assigned to the treatment group. The self-selection of subjects into the experiment limits the external validity (that is, it can say nothing about people who would receive unsolicited e-mail), but the vast majority of e-mails sent by the Bush and Kerry campaigns in 2004 went to voters who provided their e-mail addresses to the campaigns.

The seven experimental areas included the states of California (N=108,600), Colorado (N=11,926), Michigan (N=11,918), Minnesota (N=8,750), Missouri (N=4,331), and North Carolina (N=13,558). A small sample of subjects from Clark County, Nevada, was also included in the experiment (N=2,550). These areas are not a random sample of the American electorate but do represent a cross-section. Neither California nor North Carolina was a battleground state during the 2004 presidential election, but Minnesota, Missouri, Colorado, and Clark County were tightly contested. The experiments will shed light on the efficacy of e-mail GOTV outreach in these states but will remain silent on its performance in other states. That said, there is no good reason to believe the performance in other states would be different.

Voter registration and turnout were measured by matching the randomized Working Assets volunteer file to official voter registry databases. The chief complication of the Working Assets experiments is the self-entered data. Data entry fields (for example, street number, street direction) helped to standardize the data, but irregularities still occurred in naming conventions. For instance, a voter might be listed as "Robert" on the voter file but

Your vote matters. That's why we're emailing to remind you that your state allows same day registration. That means, in most cases, you can vote even if you haven't yet registered. If you plan to register to vote at your polling place on election day, make sure you bring the required identification. For detailed information about your state's same day voter registration policy, click here to find your Secretary of State's contact information and web site.

One vote can make a difference! Just ask the folks in Florida, where the margin of victory in the 2000 presidential election was 537 votes.

Please note!

This email is intended to provide information and as a reminder only. If you have questions or concerns about voter registration or voting, please consult your Secretary of State or the Federal Elections Commission.

YourVoteMatters.org is a non-partisan voter registration web site brought to you by Working Assets.

FIGURE 7.1 E-mail from Working Assets encouraging registration and turnout

typed "Bob" for Working Assets. Efforts were made to cross-check standard name and address variants, but there was no way of avoiding a lower match rate. Ultimately, 44,681 experimental subjects, or 28 percent of the subjects in the Working Assets experiments, were positively identified on the official list of registered voters. Since these individuals were randomly assigned to treatment and control groups, there is no threat to internal validity in the truncated sample for the mobilization experiment. External validity is another matter, and the experiment is silent on the ability of e-mail to mobilize individuals who did not accurately input name or address information. It should be pointed out, however, that the self-entered data was used to create printable voter registration cards for each subject in the treatment group. Thus, if the e-mailed voter registration form was effective, the names and addresses should match up with the official county records well.

The one advantage of the self-entered data is that Working Assets possessed the most accurate information about the subject's residence. Voter registration rolls often contain deadwood, and consumer databases possess a lag in updating addresses for individuals.[4] If a person were to use Working Assets' registration tool to register at a new address, consumer databases may not know where to find the individual, and voter files would only be updated if the person moved within the same state or county. In contrast, Working Assets would know the address to match against turnout lists because the person provided Working Assets with the most up to date information at the beginning of the campaign.

Results

Because the receipt of the e-mails was randomly assigned, one can measure the effect of the e-mail campaign by simply comparing registration and turnout rates for the treatment and control groups for each experiment. Figure 7.2 and the top half of table 7.1 report the results for voter registration. In every one of the seven experiments, the treatment group was registered to

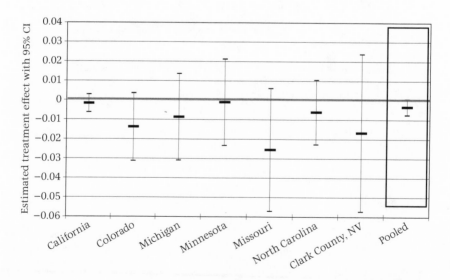

FIGURE 7.2

TABLE 7.1

Voter Registration and Turnout Results from the Randomized Controlled E-mail Experiment

Site	California	Colorado	Michigan	Minnesota	Missouri	North Carolina	Clark County, NV	Pooled
Control registered	15.2% [34,062]	72.4% [3,802]	53.4% [3,722]	58.8% [2,750]	60.7% [1,352]	31.0% [4,351]	63.9% [793]	
Treatment registered	15.1% [74,538]	71.0% [8,124]	52.5% [8,196]	58.7% [6,000]	58.1% [2,979]	30.4% [9,207]	62.3% [1,757]	
Registration treatment effect	-0.2% (0.002)	-1.4% (0.009)	-0.9% (0.011)	-0.1% (0.011)	-2.5% (0.016)	-0.6% (0.008)	-1.7% (0.021)	-0.3% (0.002)
Control voted	87.1% [5,192]	90.1% [2,753]	89.5% [1,986]	94.2% [1,617]	56.8% [820]	86.6% [1,349]	87.8% [507]	
Treatment voted	86.5% [1,1237]	89.9% [5,771]	90.2% [4,303]	94.4% [3,522]	56.1% [1,731]	85.4% [2,799]	88.1% [1,094]	
GOTV treatment effect	-0.6% (0.006)	-0.2% (0.007)	0.7% (0.008)	0.1% (0.007)	-0.7% (0.021)	-1.2% (0.012)	0.3% (0.017)	-0.2% (0.003)

Note: Numbers in brackets report cell counts. Numbers in parentheses report standard errors. Pooled results estimated by precision weighted averaging.

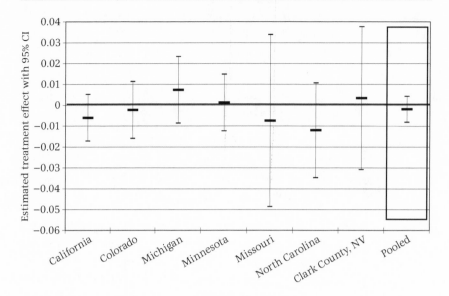

FIGURE 7.3

vote at a lower rate than the control group. None of these results is statistically significant, but each experiment provides evidence for the view that
sending e-mail to supporters does not boost rates of voter registration.
Pooling the results of the seven experiments together, the estimate is that
sending e-mail lowers rates of voter registration by −0.3 percentage points
(s.e.= 0.2). Given the implausibility of the argument and the high degree of
uncertainty, it would be premature to conclude that e-mail lowered rates of
voter registration, but there is no evidence whatsoever that e-mail can cause
voter registration.

Restricting our analysis to only those subjects who could be found on
the official voter registry, the effect of e-mail on voter turnout can also be
measured. The null finding is not quite as emphatic for voter turnout, but
e-mail shows a similar lack of potency for this goal as well (see figure 7.3 and
the lower-half of table 7.1). In only three of the seven experiments did the
treatment group turn out to vote at a higher rate. If the true effect of e-mail
on voter turnout was zero and the experiment was replicated hundreds of
times, one would expect precisely half of the experiments to estimate a
small but positive treatment effect and half of the experiments to provide
a small but negative estimated treatment effect. Thus, the roughly even
split between positive and negative results is consistent with e-mail's impo-
tence upon turnout. When the results of the seven experiments are pooled
together, the estimated effect of e-mail on voter turnout is −0.2 percentage

points (s.e. = 0.3). Thus, the experiments provide no evidence that e-mail can be effective at raising rates of voter turnout.

Discussion

Given the similarity between direct mail and e-mail, the null finding is surprising. Both forms of contact are highly centralized and highly impersonal. The fact that Working Assets is a trusted source for the subjects in the experiment makes the lack of a demonstrable effect even more confounding. Using e-mail to register and mobilize voters was a sensible strategy to employ, but no evidence of its efficacy could be detected.

This chapter should not be taken to imply that e-mail is ineffective as a campaign tool. E-mail is an extremely efficient way of communicating information and instructions to supporters. The Internet as a whole has proved invaluable as a fund-raising tool and is beginning to be used as a platform for advancing a campaign's message through advertising and as an organizational tool. This chapter casts doubt upon the value of centralized mass e-mails as a means of registering individuals and moving voters to the polls.

Despite the enormous size of the experiments, this chapter does not prove that centralized mass e-mails are valueless as a GOTV technique (though it comes very close for registration).

Figure 3 depicts the estimated mobilization and 95 percent confidence interval for each experiment. For all seven elections examined, the confidence intervals overlap with zero (that is, no effect). It is possible, but unlikely, that e-mail has a mobilization effect that is too small for these experiments to detect. In fact, the upper tip of the 95 percent confidence interval for the pooled estimate is 0.4 percent. If this extremely optimistic guess were true, a campaign would need to send 250 e-mails to supporters in order to generate one vote. If collecting the e-mail addresses, managing the databases, crafting the e-mails, and sending the e-mails cost a campaign an average of twenty cents per subject, it would cost fifty dollars per vote. So, while it is extremely unlikely for e-mail to be as cost effective as direct mail at increasing turnout, it is not impossible. In contrast, there is no chance that e-mail has the same bang for the buck as knocking on doors and volunteer phone, banks which cost between twenty and thirty dollars per vote (Nickerson 2007).

The experiments presented here are only a preliminary step. More questions are opened than are answered and several follow up projects present themselves naturally. First, the sample studied is limited to members of an organization who opted into the campaign. People who volunteer to be mobilized may be sufficiently engaged that it is impossible to mobilize them

further. The extremely high rates of voter turnout exhibited in Table 7.1 suggest this is the case. It is possible that e-mail could be effective among non-
volunteers. To test this hypothesis, a study where unsolicited e-mail (i.e.,
SPAM) is sent could be conducted.

Secondly, a much bigger experiment is needed. The whole logic behind
the e-mail voter mobilization is that it is possible to contact millions of registered voters instantly. An experiment with 1 million subjects split evenly
between treatment and control groups would yield estimates with a standard
error of 0.1 percent, thus allowing very precise estimates. Such a large experiment would also provide a platform for testing different types of messages.
It is likely that some messages work better than others.

Thirdly, the use of e-mail to accomplish other campaign goals should
be considered. Voter mobilization is only a small part of political activity.
Email could provide information to supporters, organize rallies, raise donations, and solicit volunteer labor. Rigorous experiments could be designed
to study any and every one of these activities. The value of e-mail may not
lie in GOTV work, but it likely can serve a useful purpose for a campaign.

Finally, other Internet technologies could be used to move voters to the
polls. Email is only technology associated with the Internet and one of the
most rudimentary. Perhaps peer-to-peer networks can effectively move people to vote in elections. The most personal old-fashioned grass roots mobilization techniques (e.g., face-to-face canvassing) work better than the least
personal techniques (e.g., direct mail). It stands to reason that the most personal Internet strategies will be more successful than the least personal. The
challenge is to harness and rigorously evaluate these personalized methods.

NOTES

An earlier version of this chapter was published in *Social Science Computer Review*
(2007) 25: 494–503. Reprinted by permission.

I would like to thank the Tides Center, Pew Charitable Trusts, and the Institute for
Social and Policy Studies at Yale University for their financial support. I would also
like to thank Working Assets for cooperation in the execution of the experiments.

1. Kim and Margolis (2005) collected ninety-nine e-mails sent in total from the Kerry
   campaign from July 1 through Election Day. The Bush campaign utilized e-mail
   slightly less, sending only seventy-three messages during this period.
2. All of the experiments were nonpartisan in nature, but prior research indicates that
   there is little difference between partisan and nonpartisan messages concerning
   voter mobilization (Nickerson, Friedrichs, and King 2006; Panagopoulos n.d.).
3. Randomization checks comparing treatment and control groups for age, missing data, and past voter history when available found no systematic differences
   between the two groups.
4. When an individual fills out a National Change of Address (NCOA) form, the lag in
   updating consumer databases is typically one to two months. Most people do not

fill out the form making the consumer data firms rely upon magazines and credit cards to update the address. They purchase these lists far less frequently, so the file takes longer to update—often a year or more.

REFERENCES

Faler, B. 2004a. "Dean Leave Legacy of On-Line Campaigning." *Washington Post.* February 20, p. A12.

_____. 2004b. "Kerry's Email List Continues to be Valuable Resource." *Washington Post.* December 25, p. A02.

Gerber, A., D. Green, and M. Green. 2003. "The Effects of Partisan Direct Mail on Voter Turnout." *Electoral Studies* 22:563–79.

Green, D., A. Gerber, and D. Nickerson. 2003. "Getting Out the Vote in Local Elections: Results from Six Door-to-Door Canvassing Experiments." *Journal of Politics* 65:1083–96.

Green, D., and A. Gerber. 2004. *Get Out the Vote: How to Increase Voter Turnout.* Washington, DC: Brookings Institution Press.

Kim, J. and M. Margolis. 2005. "Deploying E-mail Lists in the 2004 Presidential Campaign: Simple Enhancements or New Necessities?" Paper presented at the State of the Parties: 2004 and Beyond Conference, Akron, OH.

Nickerson, D. 2006. "Volunteer Phone Calls Can Increase Turnout: Evidence From Eight Field Experiments." *American Politics Research* 34:271–292.

Nickerson, D. 2007. "Quality Is Job One: Professional and Volunteer Mobilization Calls." *American Journal of Political Science* 51:269–282.

Nickerson, D., R. Friedrichs, and D. King. 2006. "Partisan Mobilization Campaigns in the Field: Results from a Statewide Turnout Experiment in Michigan." *Political Research Quarterly* 59:85–97.

Panagopoulos, C. N.d. "Are Partisan Voters More Responsive to Partisan or Nonpartisan GOTV Messages?" Institute for Social and Policy Studies, Yale University. Manuscript.

Reich, B. 2005. "E-Strategies that Worked." *Campaigns and Elections* 26 (February): 34–35.

8

Mobilizing the Mobiles

Text Messaging and Turnout

ALLISON DALE
AARON STRAUSS

Political campaigns use television advertising to reach large segments of voters with their persuasion and mobilization messages. To deliver targeted messages to individual voters, however, campaigns have traditionally used U.S. mail, landline phone calls, or in-person canvassing. These forms of direct voter contact are particularly important in "get out the vote" (GOTV) efforts leading up to an election. A successful GOTV program can add up to 8 percent to a campaign's vote total on election day (Nickerson 2007). Having accurate information about how to contact key voters is critical to these efforts. We argue in this chapter that the rise of mobile technology in the electorate presents a challenge to conventional campaign GOTV efforts. We also show how campaigns can respond to an increasingly mobile electorate by incorporating mobilization text messages into a broader GOTV strategy.

Political campaigns build databases of voters by purchasing public records of registered voters. Although they vary by state, these "voter files" uniformly contain the name, street address, and age of the registered voter. This basic, though useful, information is augmented by matching the public records to landline phone number directories and other commercial data such as magazine subscriptions. Campaigns use this information to contact voters through mail, phone banks, and canvassing, with the goal of identifying supporters and persuading uncommitted voters to become supporters. As Election Day approaches, voters who are flagged as supporters receive direct mobilization messages to encourage them to visit the polls and vote for the desired candidate.

There are several known shortcomings of public voter files; in this chapter, we focus on two. First, voter registration records are not automatically updated when a voter changes address or moves to a new election jurisdiction. For voters who are highly mobile, voter file records are likely to be out-of-date and inaccurate. This problem is particularly prevalent in urban areas, college towns, and among younger voters. Secondly, mobile phone records are generally not available for campaigns to match with the voter files. As a result, campaigns are unable to call the growing percentage of Americans without landlines who rely exclusively on cell phones.

Young people are particularly likely to use only their mobile phone: a quarter of Americans under the age of twenty-five were mobile-only in the second half of 2006 (Blumberg and Luke 2007). The growth in the mobile-only population, however, is not strictly limited to young people. A 2007 study announced the passing of a communications milestone in United States. Individuals who rely solely on cell phones for voice communication now outnumber those who only have a landline. Analogously, a greater percentage of households have at least one cell phone than have at least one landline. Over 20 percent of individuals ages thirty-five through sixty-four in single-person households are exclusive cell phone users. Finally, the study shows that Hispanics and African Americans are more likely than the population at large to have a cell phone and not a landline (Arthur 2007).

Campaigns envisioning a universe of potential voters as those who can be contacted through voter files are, then, going to miss the opportunity to court mobile voters, young voters, and those who rely primarily on cell phones for communication. Ironically, these are voters who, under some theories of voter mobilization, would benefit most from a reminder to vote (Wolfinger and Rosenstone 1980; Highton and Wolfinger 2001). But because they are not reliable voters, campaigns have little incentive to invest in turning them out. With the trends toward mobile-only communication increasing across all segments of the population, there is a growing imperative for campaigns to resolve this technology disconnect. Text messaging offers a promising avenue for communicating with an increasingly mobile electorate.

The Possibility of Mobile GOTV

Given that mobile phones are so prevalent in American society, it is not difficult to imagine how these devices could be used to benefit political campaigns. Cell phones have a captive audience; users pay attention to incoming messages on their mobile phones, whereas they may screen out junk mail spam e-mail, or landline calls. Jed Alpert, a political text messaging consultant, noted that text campaigns "get response rates that are 10, 20 even 30 times what response rates are to e-mail because open rates are so high with text messaging" (quoted in Goldfarb 2006).

Additionally, mobile phone users can be contacted anywhere they take their phone. While conventional GOTV tactics require voters to be in their home to receive a message, mobile phone communication can reach voters wherever they are. Mobile phone GOTV campaigns can also deliver political information in a format that is relevant to voters with a mobile lifestyle. Information that is catchy, direct, and accessible empowers young and mobile voters to participate in the electoral process.

A final advantage of text messaging over face-to-face communication is the low cost of delivering the message. The cost of sending text messages is, at most, ten cents per recipient, which translates into a per-vote cost of only three dollars. In contrast, the cheapest per-vote cost of conventional campaign activities—a professional, personalized phone bank—is nineteen dollars. Door-to-door canvassing and leafleting programs both run about $30 per additional vote generated (Nickerson 2007).[1]

Evidence in Support of Text Messaging GOTV

We conducted a three-part study in the 2006 general election to determine how a text campaign could be executed and to discern the effectiveness of this strategy. First, we conducted a large-scale field experiment that tested the general effects of text messaging on voter turnout. This main experiment had over 8,000 participants. Second, we conducted a smaller pilot experiment with about 1,300 participants to test the feasibility of including personalized voting information in each mobilization text message. Finally, we used a postexperiment survey to detect the magnitude of possible backlash against the text messaging treatment. Taken together, these findings can instruct voter mobilization organizations on how to implement effective text messaging campaigns for future elections.

To identify a sample for this field project, we partnered with three voter registration organizations that registered 150,000 individuals for the 2006 election. The three partner organizations were Student PIRGS, Working Assets, and Mobile Voter. The Student PIRGS registered individuals to vote through tabling and canvassing on college campuses. Working Assets registered people to vote through a Web site. Traffic to the Web site was generated by Google keyword searches and e-mails sent by nonprofit organizations to their members. Mobile Voter collaborated with Working Assets on the registration Web site and also registered individuals through text messaging. The majority of the registration information we collected from these three groups was included in the main experiment.

The first part of the study, the main experiment, examines the difference in turnout rates between participants in the treatment group and those in the control group. Treatment group participants received one text message reminding them to vote in the 2006 general election; control group participants did not receive a message. Overall results indicate that text messaging is an effective mobilization tool. The text messaging treatment increased the likelihood of voting by a statistically significant 3.0 percentage points. The control group turnout was 55.9 percent, while the treatment group turned out at a rate of 58.9 percent.

The results indicate that there was no significant difference between the types of messages that voters received (a "close election" message or a "civic duty" appeal). Finally, adding a polling place hotline number in the text message did not significantly increase the likelihood of voting when compared to a more generic message. Somewhat surprisingly, those who received the hotline information voted at a lower rate than even the control group. While we have little confidence in this finding because it is not statistically significant, the result suggests that simple and direct messages are preferred to messages directing recipients to another source for information.

Participants not included in the main experiment were part of the second part of the study: a pilot experiment that tested the possibility of integrating a personalized polling location into the reminder text message. The pilot study provides an alternate test to the inclusion of a voter information hotline in the main experiment. While the hotline in the main experiment directed voters to a phone number to get polling location information, the pilot study treatment delivered that information directly to voters' cell phones. The treatment group received a text message reminder that included the voter's specific polling location (for example, First Presbyterian Church) and that location's address (for example, 57 State St.). The control group in the pilot study (half of the total universe) received a generic text message reminder. The turnout rate for those who received the name and address of their polling location was 54.7 percent, similar to that of the control group, whose participants received a generic text message (52.8 percent).

While the sample is too small to make any inferences with reasonable certainty, it appears that added polling information does not increase the likelihood of voting any more than a generic message does. This result, taken with the main experiment's negative result for including the polling hotline, suggests that short messages are best for increasing turnout. Additional information about polling locations may distract from the primary message, which is: go vote.

The pilot study proved useful in testing technology that matches a voter's information to a polling location. We found that automated matching using nine-digit zip codes connected less than 70 percent of the sample records to the correct polling location with 100 percent certainty. Manual matching (such as visiting secretary of state Web sites and entering addresses) increased this match rate to 73 percent. Statewide redistricting, local determination of precinct lines, last-minute polling location changes, and (perhaps most importantly) the lack of a nationwide data standard all hinder the successful creation of a nationwide "Where Do I Vote" Web application that would make matching more accurate and complete. Since mobilization organizations are wisely hesitant to disseminate incorrect information, large-scale text message campaigns that seek to include accurate polling place locations may need to wait for technology and standards to improve.

Because voters may not appreciate receiving a political text message on their personal mobile phone, we conducted a follow-up survey as the final phase of our study to test for a backlash to the text messaging treatment. The mobile medium used in this survey is relatively new. The Pew Research Center has been a pioneer in cell phone opinion research (2006b). To increase the response rate, Pew provides a monetary incentive to potential mobile phone respondents, as these individuals may be disinclined to converse with a caller from an unknown number. Pew also leaves messages with a response number in mobile phone voice mail. We followed Pew's lead, adopting several of these procedures.

Our survey was conducted on the two weekends immediately following the 2006 general election. Of those willing to complete the survey, we only interviewed individuals who recalled that receiving the treatment text message. One problem with this approach is that a voter's propensity to respond to a cell phone survey is likely correlated with a positive reaction to receiving a political text message. Likewise, participants unwilling to take the survey are more likely to have had a negative reaction to receiving the text message. To account for this pernicious nonresponse bias among participants unwilling to take a survey on their cell phone, the initial "disposition" (for example, annoyed or pleasant) of every person who answered their cell phone was recorded. This information was used when weighting the survey.

To induce annoyed participants to take the survey, a five-dollar amazon.com gift certificate was offered to those individuals who initially declined to complete the survey. This offer was also extended to those whose cell phone service did not include unlimited weekend calling. In general, the amazon.com offer was not an effective incentive. Of the 72 participants whose dispositions were recorded as being "somewhat annoyed," nineteen were willing to take the survey without the gift certificate; only one person decided to stay on the line after agreeing to take the gift certificate. Overall, exactly three hundred respondents were interviewed.

The results of the survey are promising for practitioners, as the backlash to the text messages was dwarfed by percentage of the population with a positive reaction to the text messages. When asked to report their reaction to receiving the text messages (an open-ended question), a plurality (about 40 percent) reported a positive reaction, a quarter said they were surprised

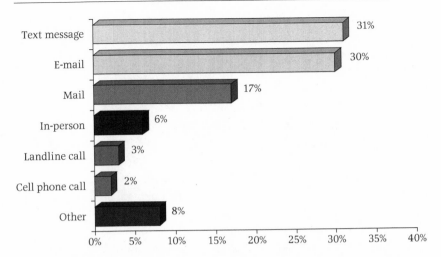

FIGURE 8.1 Respondents' Ranking for Preferred Form of GOTV Contact

Question was: Imagine that a political organization wanted to remind you to vote just before Election Day. How would you prefer that they contact you?

by the message, and only a tenth had a negative reaction. In fact, a quarter of respondents specifically said that the text message helped remind them to vote.

The reminder aspect of a mobilization text message should not be overlooked. Of respondents who did not vote, a near-majority reported that a "lack of time" prevented them from casting a ballot. A similar percentage of nonvoters in a much larger U.S. Census study reported that they didn't vote because they were "too busy" or had a "conflicting schedule" (Holder 2006). The text messages in the randomized field experiment were likely successful because the recipients were reminded to vote in a convenient way that they could not avoid noticing. Sending the messages on a Monday reminded recipients to include voting as one of their activities for Tuesday, Election Day.

Finally, the survey demonstrates that voters actually prefer text messaging to other forms of voter contact (Figure 8.1). When asked to choose their preferred method of get-out-the-vote contact, respondents ranked text messaging (31 percent) and e-mail (30 percent) at the top of the list. Perhaps surprisingly, only 6 percent of individuals listed a personal visit as their favorite contact, despite the proven effectiveness of such personal methods of mobilization.

In sum, the results of this study show text messaging to be a promising and cost-effective form of voter mobilization. The two experiments suggest that short and direct text messages can increase voter turnout by

3 percentage points. The postexperiment survey shows that there is little backlash to receiving text messages. In fact, voters prefer text message mobilization messages to more conventional forms of voter contact.

Barriers to Using Mobile Technology

Although these results show that text messaging can be effective in mobilizing voter turnout, a number of challenges prevent this technology from being easily implemented under current conditions. First, and perhaps most importantly, mobile phone numbers must be collected through voluntary submission by the voter. Unlike landline phone numbers, there is not a public directory available for mobile phone numbers. Campaigns can encourage strong supporters to provide their mobile number, with reasonable success. It is a greater challenge, however, for campaigns to get mobile information from undecided voters. Text message communication, then, may be most effective for turning out voters who were already motivated to vote for a candidate in the first place. It is likely to be less useful for the targeted persuasion of undecided voters.

Further complicating the challenge of not having a mobile phone directory is the strategic imperative for campaigns to know something about the voter connected to a mobile phone number. While mobile phones can cross city and state lines, voter registration records do not. Campaigns will need to know that the individual connected to a mobile phone number is registered in a jurisdiction important to that campaign. This means that, in addition to capturing mobile numbers from voters voluntarily (by, for instance, having voters send a text message to a five-digit short code to get into a rally), political campaigns must also be able to connect those mobile numbers to a voter's basic information (name, address, and age). In the study reported here, mobile phone numbers were collected when individuals registered to vote with our partner organizations.

A second challenge facing campaigns seeking to reach voters through mobile technology is that cell phone numbers cannot legally be used in automated dialers. Automated dialing is used by survey and commercial phone bank operations to speed up the process of calling potential voters. The Federal Communications Commission has issued a permanent ban prohibiting vendors from using mobile phone numbers in combination with these tools (Silva 2007). This makes it difficult for campaigns to use paid phone banks to identify whether mobile-only voters support or oppose their candidate. Campaigns can, however, use volunteer phone banks to contact mobile-only voters. Additionally, campaigns may be willing to assume that a voter who was willing to give the campaign his or her mobile number supports their candidate.

Potential cost to the voter for receiving a text message is a fourth obstacle with which campaigns must contend. In spite of the fact that text messaging is a widespread form of communication, some mobile phone users do not have a prepaid text feature included in their phone service. This means that some users pay money for each text they receive (usually about ten cents), or for each text received over a certain threshold (such as one hundred messages). As texting becomes a more popular form of communication, unlimited text message plans are becoming more available and more widely adopted. But currently, campaigns must be wary of annoying voters with non-free communication, though our survey indicates that this hurdle to a successful mobile campaign is small.

What Campaigns are Doing

In spite of the challenges facing implementation of mobile technology campaigns, several candidates in the 2008 presidential primary have worked to harness the power of text messaging in creative ways. John Edwards used text messaging to make fund-raising appeals and to encourage supporters to sign a petition to end the war in Iraq. The Obama campaign asked supporters to text their mailing address to the campaign to get a free bumper sticker. This helped the campaign determine where the supporter may be registered to vote (Vargas 2007). Hillary Clinton's campaign asked supporters to vote for their favorite campaign songs with text messages. Additionally, the Clinton campaign encouraged volunteers to bring their cell phones to "phone banking" parties where the volunteer phones were remotely connected to an automated dialer. That allowed supporters to use their mobile phones to help in campaign efforts to contact voters with landline numbers.

Although text messaging has been used primarily by Democrats in the 2008 presidential campaign, several Republican candidates have used this technology in their campaigns, including Governor Arnold Schwarzenegger of California and former Senator Rick Santorum of Pennsylvania (Vargas 2007).

Political organizations may have something to learn from the television industry, which has used text messaging quite effectively. A study from the Mobile Marketing Association indicated that 30 percent of American television audiences participated in text message "voting" on TV programs in 2006 (Vargas 2007).

Conclusion

Our research demonstrates that text messaging can be an effective mobilization tool, boosting turnout by 3 percentage points. Not only was the backlash to receiving a text message small, but text messaging was cited as the most preferred form of GOTV communication by respondents. Although e-mail came in a close second as a preferred from of contact, prior research (Pew 2006a) found that a majority of voters consider campaign e-mail to be spam and readily ignore the message. The power of text messaging comes from its direct yet unobtrusive nature.

From a practical standpoint, there are still several hurdles for voter mobilization organizations to address in implementing campaigns using mobile technology. Joe Rospars, director for new media outreach with Barack Obama's 2008 presidential campaign, noted there is not "a campaign or a political organization right now that has figured out how to smartly use this technology. There's going to be a lot of experimentation" (quoted in Vargas 2007).

One of the complications in implementing this new form of voter communication is that it challenges the control that campaigns have exercised over conventional forms of voter contact. Voter file databases have been a centralized source of information that campaigns have used to dictate who gets contacted, and with what message. The power of mobile technology, by contrast, is that it builds political community by acting as a "gateway to users' core networks" (Chambers and Sebastian 2006). Individuals are at the center of these networks, not campaigns.

Decentralized social networks can be politically powerful, as evidenced through several cases outside the United States. In the 2004 general election in Spain, for example, a viral text messaging campaign is thought to have mobilized young and urban voters in a way that may have contributed to an unexpected victory by the Spanish Socialist Labour Party (Suárez 2005; see also chapter 11 of this book). In Korea and China, peer-to-peer text messaging is used to organize flash mobs and large protest rallies on short notice (Hong 2005). The challenge for campaigns wishing to strategically implement this powerful mobilization strategy lies in the inherently decentralized nature of viral campaigns.

Campaigns accustomed to more conventional forms of voter contact may be inclined to use mobile campaigns to direct traffic to other, more centralized, media such as the candidate's Web site. Justin Oberman, a consultant for mobile technology in politics, has noted that successful text campaigns will avoid this tactic and instead provide information pertinent to the recipient and encourage direct action that can be taken from the mobile phone (Vargas 2007). This does not mean that campaigns must abandon their basic goals of voter persuasion and mobilization. Rather, it means that campaigns need to acknowledge that changes in communication require a reenvisioning of how to meet those goals within an increasingly mobile electorate.

Given the increasing popularity of mobile forms of communication, campaigns can ill afford to ignore new strategies for contacting mobile voters. We have shown that text messaging mobilization is an effective method for increasing turnout but that there are several hurdles to implementing a successful text campaign. In addition to the practical challenges of conducting a text messaging campaign, mobile technology challenges campaigns to think creatively about how they can tap into the culture of social networking facilitated by new forms of media. A failure to harness this new technology will result in political campaigns being unable to communicate effectively with the next generation of participants in the political process.

NOTES

We are extremely grateful for the help of our many partners. We received generous support from the following organizations and individuals: Working Assets; Mobile Voter; Student PIRGs; the UMass Donahue Institute Civic Initiative; Young Voter Strategies; the Mellman Group; Survey Sampling International; Catalist; Kieloch Consulting; Professor David Nickerson; Professor Donald Green; Professor Ray LaRaja; Professor Craig Thomas; Professor Marty Gilens; and Professor Chris Achen.

1. It is important to note that the low cost of text messaging reported here assumes that there is not an additional cost of collecting the mobile numbers (thus increasing the cost of the program). The specifics of creating a text messaging program are discussed below. The cost of our 2006 text messaging experiment was about $1.50 per vote.

REFERENCES

Arthur, A. 2007. "The Birth of a Cellular Nation" Mediamark Research Inc. (accessed March 1, 2008, at http://www.mediamark.com/PDF/WP%20The%20Birth%20of%20 a%20Cellular%20Nation%20Revised.pdf).

Blumberg, S., and J. Luke. 2007. "Wireless Substitution: Preliminary Data from the January-June 2006 National Health Interview Survey." National Center for Health Statistics: Centers for Disease Control and Prevention. January 18.

Chambers, T., and R. Sebastian. 2006. "Mobile Media in 21st Century Politics." New Politics Institute (accessed March 1, 2008, at http://www.newpolitics.net/sites/ ndn-newpol.civicactions.net/files/NPI-Mobile-Media-Report.pdf).

Goldfarb, Z. 2006. "Between Polar Opposites is this Equator: Text Me." *Washington Post.* July 2.

Highton, B., and R. Wolfinger. 2001. "The First Seven Years of the Political Life Cycle." *American Journal of Political Science* 45 (1): 202–209.

Holder, K. 2006. "Voting and Registration in the Election of November 2004." Current Population Reports, US Census Bureau.

Hong, C. 2005. "New Political Tool: Text Messaging." *Christian Science Monitor.* June 30, 2005 (accessed March 1, 2008, at http://www.csmonitor.com/2005/0630/p13s01-stct.html?s=u2).

Nickerson, D. 2007. "Quality Is Job One: Professional and Volunteer Voter Mobilization Calls." *American Journal of Political Science* 51 (2): 269–282.

Pew Research Center. 2006a. "Pew Internet Project Data Memo." May 15 (accessed March 1, 2008, at http://people-press.org/reports/display.php3?ReportID=276).

_____. 2006b. "The Cell Phone Challenge to Survey Research." April 3 (accessed March 1, 2008, at http://people-press.org/reports/display.php3?ReportID=276).

Silva, J. 2007. "FTC Works to Quash Call List Urban Legend." *RCR Wireless News*. October 22.

Suárez, S. 2005. "Mobile Democracy: Text Messages, Voter Turnout, and the 2004 Spanish General Election." Paper presented at the 2005 annual meeting of the American Political Science Association, Washington, DC.

Vargas, J. 2007. "Text-Friendly Hopefuls Vie For Hearts And Thumbs." *Washington Post*. June 30.

Wolfinger, R., and S. Rosenstone. 1980. *Who Votes*. New Haven, CT: Yale University Press.

9

Online Political Advertising

MICHAEL CORNFIELD
KATE KAYE

Several types of online communication have enjoyed breakout moments in U.S. political campaigning and public affairs, including e-mail (Jesse Ventura 1998), fund-raising (McCain 2000), blogging (the Trent Lott resignation 2001), the organization of in-person meetings (MeetUp/Howard Dean 2003), and Web videos (the "macaca" incident, 2006). After these successes received notice, adoption of the practices behind them spread among campaigners and activists. They became standard equipment in the online politics toolkit.

Online advertising would seem a likely candidate for this social treatment. As Henry Copeland and Megan Mitzel of Blogads.com point out, the interactivity, accountability, iterability, and targeting capacities of online ads—not to mention their relative low cost—make them an attractive complement to campaign advertising in print, broadcast, and cable media (Copeland and Mitzel n.d.). Yet despite steady growth in overall online advertising, at a rate of roughly 1 percent additional share of total advertising spending per year since the dawn of the millennium, and steady if not comparable growth in online political advertising expenditures at the presidential level, there has been no breakout moment of social discovery and adoption.

In this chapter we examine the state of the craft of online political advertising in the 2004 presidential campaign and the 2007 phase of the 2008 presidential campaign. We contend that online political advertising remains in a prehistoric era. It exists. It is maturing in sophistication of strategy and message. But it lacks a killer application and good public metrics. To borrow an image and sound from one of the most famous scenes in film history, the ape has not tossed the bone into the air to the fanfare from "Also Sprach Zarathustra."[1]

2004: Banner Ads and Ambient Persuasion

Our 2004 analysis begins by drawing from a report written for the Pew Internet and American Life Project; it relies on data from Evaliant Media Resources, an affiliate company of TNSMI/Campaign Media Analysis Group (Cornfield 2004). Evaliant used "spidering" technology to search thousands of Web sites for brand-related banner advertising. Banner ads fall into the category of online advertising known as display. Along with such other display templates as skyscrapers and rectangles, the banner ad is a purchased space on a Web site intended to be viewed by Internet users who have come to the Web site to see other content and do other things. Display advertising online, like street billboards, yard signs, broadcast commercials, and print ads, interrupts the gaze of people to make an impression on them. Evaliant collected banner ads, coded them according to their site locations (per page) and daily frequency, then estimated the price paid for each perceived exposure based on available rate information.

In the first eight months of 2004, the time period for which data are available, the presidential candidate campaigns, national parties, and major 527 advocacy organizations spent an estimated $2.66 million on banner ads. This amounted to less than 1 percent of the buy for television ads in the top hundred markets during the same time period. The Kerry campaign alone raised twice as much money as this total online in one day: $5.7 million on July 29, when he gave his speech accepting the Democratic nomination for president.

In placing their banner ads, the two presidential campaigns appeared to prefer local to national and global news outlets, and Web sites of traditional media properties to those of online companies. It's unknown whether the buys at national and global outlets were targeted to particular segments. The Bush campaign aimed its online advertising at middle-class women, Hispanics, and voters in battleground states in one big blast in May, which cost approximately four hundred thousand dollars. Its top five ad buys were at KPTV Oregon'si2.tv.com (the Fox network affiliate in Portland, Oregon), Parents.com (*Parents* magazine), KNVA-TV.com (WB network in Austin, Texas), ElNuevoHerald.com (Miami, Florida), and KPHO CBS 5 News.com (Phoenix, Arizona). The Kerry campaign concentrated on raising money from progressive outlets in metropolitan areas. Its top five ad buys were at SFGate.com (Chronicle newspaper, San Francisco), Newsweek.com, Village Voice.com, Reuters.com, and L.A. WeeklyMedia.com.

An examination of 137 display ads in the archive attributable to the Bush and Kerry campaigns and the Democratic and Republican national committees (DNC and RNC) between January and July 2004 reveals mostly slogans and graphics of the kind found on bumper stickers and billboards, although the texts were longer.[2] Forays into flash animation were rare. No ad announced a political endorsement, issued an invitation to rallies and meetings, or referred to upcoming events such as primaries, television appearances, and financial disclosure deadlines. While the display ads were targeted, the contents were, on the whole, generic. Only one ad asked viewers to click through to a specific message: a two-and-a-half minute video featuring Laura Bush talking about education. There was no discernable pattern in the use of negative, contrast, and positive ads.

We know something about the strategies and results behind some of these ad buys thanks to an article by Michael Bassik (2004). The DNC, the Kerry campaign, and the consulting firm Malchow Schlackman Hoppey & Cooper (where Bassik works) collaborated on several banner ad purchases. More interestingly, they ventured into an exercise in what might be termed ambient persuasion.

The goal was to shape public opinion about the outcome of the first presidential debate between Bush and Kerry. The method: in the hours just after the debate concluded, strew display ads on more than fifty Web sites where Internet users were likely to soak up news accounts of the debate, including the home pages of the sites operated by Reuters, the *New York Times*, the *Washington Post*, *USA Today*, MSNBC, and even the Weather Channel. The banners read like headlines: "Debate Shows Kerry's Strength—Bush Fails To deliver Plan for Iraq"; "Kerry Presents Strong Plan for America—Bush Won't Admit Failures." The mind's eye would presumably gloss over the distinction between ad and news content and thereby be inclined to take the former with the credibility of the latter. A study commissioned by the collaborative found that 55 percent of those who saw the ads thought Kerry won, compared with 49 percent of a similar survey group who did not see the ads. As a bonus, more than one million dollars in contributions flowed into the DNC via the "Debate Center" landing page reached by viewers who clicked on the banners. The DNC sustained the online advertising campaign until the election.

2008: Early Patterns and Prospects

The online world had changed in several respects by the time the next presidential campaigns began to advertise. Video portals and social networking sites were providing new forms and forums for content. More companies were offering data on advertising results, including ads on search engines. As in 2004, a majority of Web users (52 percent) told interviewers that they encountered campaign news and information while online doing something else. But the percentage of Americans saying they learned something about the campaigns through the Internet almost doubled between 2004 and 2008 (13 to 24 percent). ("Internet's Broader Role" 2008) More voters had broadband connections, and they had more experience as consumers and producers of online political information. Clearly, the opportunities for online political advertising had improved.

Among the large number of entrants in the presidential nomination races, three stood out in 2007 for spending on Internet display advertising: Republicans Mitt Romney and John McCain, and Democrat Barack Obama. Combined, the campaigns for Romney (37 percent) and McCain (34 percent) ran over 70 percent of the online display ads purchased by the candidates between January 1 and December 16, 2007, according to data from Nielsen Online AdRelevance. Obama's campaign ran more than a quarter (27 percent) of all presidential campaign ads in that time, beginning in the summer. Display ads for Hillary Clinton, Mike Huckabee, and the others accounted for just 1 percent. All told, the candidates ran more than 277 million display ad impressions (Kaye 2007i); an ad impression marks one view by a Web user.

While we have a relatively solid estimate of which political campaigns, particularly presidential candidate campaigns, ran online display advertising in 2007, some ads running on small sites such as blogs and ads that were not correctly categorized may have fallen through the cracks. Also, when it comes to tracking other types of online advertising formats, no public data track ads in any systematic manner. So we only have anecdotal information and interview material to ground our analysis of nondisplay political advertising formats, including in-stream video advertising (whereby spots play before a requested clip on a local news site, YouTube, or elsewhere), and text ads placed on the return pages supplied by Google, Yahoo, MSN, and other search engines according to user requests.

Display Ad Content Broadens

In contrast to 2004, display ads in 2007 featured a wider array of messages and purposes. Fund-raising in small donations remained a popular approach, as it was in 2004; Mitt Romney asked Web viewers to "Donate $44 for the future 44th President." But other ads run early in the year by the Romney for President campaign pushed local campaign events, urging people to "Join the Rally Today" (Kaye 2007h). Many of Barack Obama's display ads later in the year were also intended to get people to attend campaign events, perhaps banking on curiosity about the candidate's famed oratorical skills and glamorous presence: "Get to Know Barack Obama. Attend Invitations to Campaign Events" and "Show your Support. Attend Local Campaign Events." Most of the Illinois senator's ads culminated with a plea to "Join Us."

Before his candidacy became official, the John McCain 2008 Exploratory Committee ran video ads on AOL in conjunction with the interactive technology firm PointRoll (Kaye 2007d). "Be There From the Start" read a small display ad running on the conservative community, news, and opinion site Townhall.com, as well as on a collection of sites selected via Google's AdSense service. The McCain ads featured invitations to view three thirty-second videos presenting the potential candidate. Users submitted contact information as they clicked through the ad to the videos, including physical and e-mail addresses. After the viewings, they could link to a donation page on the precampaign site. The advertisements thus simultaneously tested messages, acquired data on prospective supporters, raised funds, and promoted the idea of the candidacy.

McCain also gathered grassroots information by promoting online petitions and surveys. "Surrender is not an option," declared one ad, asking people to "Sign the Petition Today" in a show of support for the U.S. military mission in Iraq (Kaye 2007c). McCain was not alone in using this technique at this time over this issue. A display ad run by the Hillary Clinton campaign called upon its viewers to "Sign the Petition" expressing opposition to President Bush's veto threat against Iraq War–related legislation. "Sign the petition to stop the Bush veto of the will of the people. Start bringing our troops home," read another such ad, which was placed on CNN's News and Politics sections. A third version told Web users, "Your signature can be as powerful as President Bush's. Tell Bush: listen to the people on Iraq. Sign the Petition. End the Veto threat."

When it came to the issue of congressional (over)spending, McCain's online ads adopted a lighter tone. One that ran for several months showed googly-eyed cartoon nuts and citrus fruit leaving the Capitol. "$74 million tax dollars for peanut storage costs? That's Nuts! $100 million tax dollars for citrus assistance? Orange You Outraged?" On it went, flipping to salmon and, of course, pork.

In June 2007, Republican presidential hopeful Congressman Tom Tancredo briefly ran display ads on the Drudge Report news portal focusing on his signature issue, immigration (Kaye 2007b). The ads were timed to coincide with a Senate vote on an immigration reform bill that, in Tancredo's view, offered amnesty to illegal immigrants. A petition was attached so that electronic signatories would declare "Here is my message for any politician who supports an amnesty bill: I will commit myself to working for your defeat!" The year before, grassroots activists employed the Internet to stop a similar bill in the face of bipartisan congressional and White House backing.

Branding, the marketing term that represents the experiences associated with a good or service, was an evident purpose behind the display ads of lesser-known candidates. In political terms, the purpose of the ads might be best categorized as name recognition or persuasion. In one ad placed days before the Iowa caucuses, Democratic Governor Bill Richardson directed viewers of the Web site of the *Ackley (Iowa) World Journal* to "Read Bill Richardson's plan for behavioral health care" on his Web site. The ad summarized the plan so as to depict Richardson as a detail-oriented pro–government services candidate: "A Heroes Health Card for veterans, ensuring them the quality care they deserve. Quality health care for PTSD [Post-Traumatic Stress Disorder] and other mental trauma. Access to afford-able behavioral health care for all Americans." To a degree, this was more a re-branding than an introductory stamp, given Richardson's series of mock job interview television and Web spots in which he humorously advanced an image as the candidate with the best qualifications for the presidency.

Attack ads seemed sharper than in the previous campaign cycle. In ads served in October 2007 on FoxNews.com and such conservative blogs as Power Line, Biblical Womanhood, and Hugh Hewitt's blog on Townhall.com, Republican Fred Thompson's campaign urged readers to "Support the Real Conservative." The ads promoted the brand by taking aim at both Romney, questioning his fidelity to a pro-life stance, and Rudy Giuliani's pro-choice position. The ads suggested that these Thompson rivals were feigning con-servative values to garner support from important far-right Republican primary voters. "This is not a time for philosophical flexibility, it is a time to stand up for what we believe in," noted the animated display ads, which linked to the Fred08.com campaign contribution page. The effort came just in time for a Fox News debate among GOP presidential hopefuls and a Values Voter Summit hosted in Washington, DC, by the pro-marriage and family group Family Research Council.

In what appeared to be the first use of video overlay advertising by a pres-idential campaign, Romney ads reprised—or, in online lingo, "repurposed"—television spots running concurrently on the air in Iowa (Kaye2007a). Web users watching videos related to family life would suddenly see an image overlaid on top of the video inviting them to watch a Romney ad about the same subject. (The "Our Home" ad combined reality-TV-style footage of the former Massachusetts governor bouncing grandchildren on his knee with family film archives of his wife, Ann, with their children.) Clicking on the overlaid image would start the ad video, pausing the originally selected video clip. The Romney campaign bought time for these overlay ads through the technology firm ScanScout, targeting them based on socially conserva-tive and family-related keywords identified in the audio tracks of the Web videos. This type of ad placement is known as contextual targeting, because it keys off the subject matter of editorial content.

The Romney campaign and others also ran display ads on blogs. Blog ads can serve the purposes already discussed in this section while advancing two additional strategic goals: the goodwill of influential bloggers (some of whom depend heavily on ads to sustain their chosen vocation of contemporary pamphleteering) and rapid responses to charges that bloggers discuss in real time. Blog ads are inexpensive even by Internet standards: a top slot on DailyKos, attracting more than six million impressions a week, costs fifteen thousand dollars.

Ad Networks: Smart Placements . . . and Placements That Smarted

Ad networks offer placements in a multitude of Web sites, according to targeting criteria. They are a rational development, a huge time-saver given the gigantic number of possible locations to reach Web users. These ad networks offer choices not just of specific sites, but also of Web pages, times of the day and week, and designated groupings of users by demographic, geographic, and behavioral categories. (Behavioral targeting entails delivery of ads or other Web content to computers whose users have previously viewed certain editorial content, clicked on an ad, or taken another such detectable action.) Hundreds of online ad networks exist, from Google's fortune-making AdSense to ValueClick and Advertising.com.

In 2007, the presidential campaigns ran the bulk of their ads on the big-name portals and news media sites, including FoxNews.com, the *New York Times*, MSNBC, Newsmax, and HuffingtonPost.com. According to AdRelevance, the top site for presidential campaign ads was Yahoo!, which ran 32 percent of the ads the monitoring operation identified. The ads ran on news and politics pages, but also in Yahoo!'s movies, sports, and e-mail sections. MSN served about 11 percent, Excite 6 percent, and AOL 4 percent.

Some ads may have appeared as well on the "long tail" of the distribution curve, where traffic can number in the hundreds or even dozens of impressions. Although we lack the data to substantiate that phenomenon, AdRelevance data showed some online ad network buys helped push political ad dollars out to niche content sites. The three top display ad spenders, Romney, McCain, and Obama, had ads show up in unlikely Web nooks and crannies. McCain ads appeared on RealityTVWorld.com, Southern Living Online, and HowStuffWorks, while ads for Obama ran on GoComics, Hoover's Online, and CNET TV.com. Romney for President ads were also seen on the gaming community site Allakhazam's Magical Realm.

Since the ad network placement process is abstracted through the selection of key words or audience demographic categories and often relies on automation, ads can show up alongside inappropriate content. Buying through an ad network embarrassed conservative Mitt Romney when his campaign ads surfaced on Gay.com, Advocate.com, and PlanetOut.

Social Networking Sites: Hot Spots of the 2008 Cycle

Candidates have flocked to establish presences on social networking sites, especially MySpace and Facebook, which have experienced astronomical growth in participation during the past few years. Most presidential campaign Web home pages sport iconic links to social networking sites, a sharp break from the tradition of not putting up any exit gates to tempt visitors. Some candidates and their family members (especially those in the eighteen to thirty age group) have put up profile pages, videos, and blog entries on social networking sites, and their campaigns have worked with members to promote the activity which gives this type of site its name. But with some exceptions, most campaigns did not buy ads on these sites. Democrat John Edwards did purchase approximately 170,000 impressions on MySpace in October 2007, according to AdRelevance. It was a simple, single-image ad with the caption "Join the campaign to change America. Join Senator John Edwards at www.JohnEdwards.com." McCain ads also showed up on MySpace during the primary season.

How to explain this combination of reluctance and enthusiasm? The fact is, commercial and political advertisers alike are concerned about having their ads appear alongside offensive user-generated content. We know that, in its deal with social network site publisher Community Connect, Obama's campaign sought to minimize the risks of ads served by ad networks by obtaining the assurance that only house banners promoting Community Connect itself would be posted on Obama profile pages. The goal was to prevent inappropriate ads from showing up on those profile pages. For example, other profiles on AsianAve.com might show text ads served by Google promoting "Asian Girl Photos."

The publisher also agreed to run homepage display ads to drive traffic to those pages on its family of networking sites, which span several identity cultures. (In addition to AsianAve.com, Community Connect owns BlackPlanet. com, the gay community network site Glee.com, Latino-oriented MiGente. com, and the Christian networking site FaithBase.com.) Community Connect also sent out e-mail alerts to site members notifying them about the official Obama presence. Yet a full-fledged paid ad campaign on the network's sites was not part of the deal; a Community Connect representative expressed the hope that advertising would come in time. The Clinton and Edwards campaigns subsequently contacted the publisher in efforts to obtain similar deals.

Meanwhile, as one might expect, the Obama campaign tailored the content added to each site. Obama's Glee.com profile included a post about National Coming Out Day, while his MiGente page touted the endorsement of his energy plan by former U.S. Secretary of Energy Federico Peña.

The candidate's profiles on AsianAve.com, MiGente and BlackPlanet.com spotlighted education and family issues, while statements on Glee.com highlighted environmental issues. FaithBase.com and AsianAve.com noted Obama's thoughts on faith and politics. The candidate's main "personal message" on all the sites was the same, noting, "I was fortunate to be able to grow up seeing America from varied viewpoints."

Search Engine Ads

Sponsored links or search ads are purchased directly from the companies that design and operate the engines powering this near-universal online activity. The ads appear according to how relevant they are to a user's search request, or how much the advertiser is willing to pay for a particular slot, or a negotiated combination of the two criteria. They are usually text-based, although Google's AdSense and a few others offer programs whereby image-based ads can be targeted according to keywords users search for. Most search advertising is sold on a cost-per-click or cost-per-action basis, meaning that the advertiser pays only to the extent a viewer clicks on the ad or performs a "conversion" activity such as signing up for a newsletter.

Click-throughs and conversions have become widely accepted metrics of success in the online world. But there are no measurement services that comprehensively disclose who is paying how much for what kind of search ads with whom, on what sites, with what results. A report by the search engine marketing firm iCrossing, published in July 2007, stated that presidential campaign involvement in this major activity remained sparse ("How America Searches" 2007). To make its assessments, iCrossing analyzed 126 election-related issue keywords along with candidate site URLs. The company also factored in rank and coverage data from search marketing research firm AdGooroo and Google AdWords data on keyword costs. In addition to estimating search ad spending and visibility, it commissioned Opinion Research Corporation to survey more than one thousand Web users concerning their search habits when it comes to election-related information.

In May 2007, McCain's presidential campaign spent less than half what the Edwards campaign did on issue-based search ads, but McCain got far more bang for his buck. McCain came out ahead in visibility, appearing prominently in searches for "stem cell research," "pro-life," "campaign finance," "electoral reform," "ethics reform," "government accountability," "government reform," "lobbyist," "special interests," "tort reform," "DNC," and "RNC." Edwards's ads were highly visible only in results for searches on "Iraq" and "war in Iraq." Romney also expended funds on search ads: 5

percent of the detected and calculated total, according to the report, compared with Edwards's 64 percent share and McCain's 29 percent. Ads for the former Massachusetts governor surfaced in search results for "ethics," "family values," "war in Iraq," and "social conservative." Obama's campaign accounted for 4 percent of spending, with sponsored links appearing in searches for "Iraq" and "war in Iraq." Giuliani showed up in searches on "flat tax;" and Paul for "war in Iraq" queries.

The report's survey found that 89 percent of voters using search engines to track down election information have conducted searches on a relevant issue. Most searches followed party lines. Obama was the most-searched candidate of all, prompting searches by more than 50 percent of all people using search engines for election information, and 60 percent of the Democrats in that group. Forty percent of all election searchers sought information on Clinton, and about 57 percent of Democrats in that segment did. Thirty-seven percent searched for Giuliani, while 51 percent of Republicans in that segment searched for the Republican candidate. About 23 percent of all searched for McCain, and 28 percent of Republicans did.

Independents searched for lesser-known and potential candidates more than the self-identified partisans. Republican Newt Gingrich was sought by 18 percent of Independents, and just 10 percent of Republicans. Huckabee (a second-tier candidate at the time of the survey) drew searches from less than 5 percent of Republicans compared to 12 percent of Independents. Dennis Kucinich was searched on by just 5 percent of Democrats, but drew searches by 14 percent of Independents.

The online consulting firm Connell Donatelli, which placed the search ads for McCain, claimed the campaign has reaped $4 in fund-raising cash for every $1 spent on search advertising (Kaye 2007g). As of July 2007, search ads had accounted for around 40 percent of the campaign's online donations. The campaign also ran display and video ads through Google's AdSense network, which places keyword-targeted text and display ads on non-Google Web sites.

Conclusion

Social adoption of a new technology or technique often soars upon demonstration of its superiority, repeatability, and verifiability (Rogers 2003). The new mousetrap, in other words, must not only be seen as better, it must be better when prospective adopters try it themselves. When these and related criteria are met, a community embraces a killer application: a utility so compelling that in order to take advantage of it people will purchase new equipment and incorporate it into their lives. (When it sits on the shelf, it doesn't count as adopted.) As we have seen, the Internet provides a host of advertising formats, methods, and measurements. What might be a winning combination capable of providing online political advertising with its breakout moment?

Finding the right combination will be tougher than it looks. While measurements abound in the world of the Internet (which is, after all, a network of computers), statistics alone are insufficient persuaders of value. Head to the online politics news site TechPresident.com, and you will see a "Charts" bar. Each tab on the bar leads to interactive graphs with brightly colored data points detailing the number of the presidential candidates' "MySpace Friends," "YouTube Views," "Facebook Supporters," "Technorati Tracks," "Eventful Demands," "Hitwise Traffic," and "Meetup Members." The bar reinforces our argument at the elemental level: there is no tab with statistics about ads. It also helps us make a subtler point: these statistics are fun to ponder, but hard to use, because a formula to derive value from the data has not been devised, demonstrated, and accepted. They are not yet success metrics.

To professional politicians the worth of online metrics, as with poll data, depends on their reliability as indicia of expected dollars and votes, the supreme measures of value to campaigners. To political scientists and other students of democratic politics, the most valuable correlations are with voter knowledge and participation. So, for example, most professional pollsters regard the "is this country going in the right direction or headed down the wrong track" question as valuable because they have a good idea, if not a solid calculating formula, of how well responses to that question correlate with the electoral prospects of incumbents and challengers.

The most obvious candidate for a valuable metric of measuring the state of online political advertising is spending. When spending rises considerably, that may be a sign that more professionals appreciate what online ads can do for their campaigns. Reports released in late 2007 and January 2008 indicate the lack of a clear gauge of online political ad spending. Late in 2007, the market research firm PQ Media forecast a 150 percent increase in spending by political campaigners on Internet advertising, marketing and promotional efforts (Kaye 2007f) However, the estimated $73 million expected to go toward the Web in 2008 represents a 1.6 percent sliver of the projected campaign media spending pie. And, according to PQ, the majority of dollars spent by political advertisers on the Web will go toward e-mail marketing efforts, a primary method for online fund-raising pitches, rather than for display, search, or video advertising. Other reports released in January 2008, sometimes including public policy advertising in addition to candidate and advocacy group campaigns, suggest online ad spending by political advertisers will total anywhere from $20 million to $110 million in 2008, a huge discrepancy caused by varying methodologies.

Yet given the relative efficiency of Internet communication compared with other media (including transportation costs for face-to-face meetings), raw spending is not the best indicator of value. A better approach to measurement is already employed by commercial advertisers, who consider a variety of metrics to determine return on investment (ROI). In fact, all advertisers can measure ROI for online ads much more directly than they can for broadcast and print ads, and even more than for the impact of such online assets as having a MySpace page.

ROI is a familiar concept among commercial advertisers, but foreign in the political sphere, where returns connote election returns, which come once or twice every two years, at most. And, as we have shown in our review of current practices, ROI on online ad spending encompasses multiple types of returns: informational sign-ups, name recognition, opinion change, rally attendance, and, of course, donations and donors. How should these returns be combined into a valuable formula? And who can be trusted with the often proprietary data to plug in the numbers?

Commercial ad veterans like Eric Frenchman of McCain's consulting firm Connell Donatelli already rely on ROI-based metrics. For example, in the case of search ads, John McCain 2008 compared the number of fundraising dollars collected after someone clicked on a search ad with the amount spent on the ad to determine ROI. Mitt Romney's online campaign staff measured ad success by the number of "Team Mitt" volunteer sign-ups gathered as a result of ad click-throughs, in addition to contributions collected after supporters clicked on the ads, according to Director of eStrategy Mindy Finn.[3] Another way the campaign measured online advertising was by devising a formula based on the number of potential voters in a particular region or state reached per dollar spent on Web ads.

We hope that effective and standardized metrics for measuring the impact of online political advertising are not long in coming. Because online ads can readily elicit responses from viewers, they have the potential to merge the professional values of campaign money and votes (and the secondary value of journalistic attention) with the idealistic values of voter knowledge and participation. The killer application, in other words, could be a rise in grassroots activity generated per dollar invested. Like any political practice and business enterprise, online political advertising will have its greedy and venal side. But the civic benefits are not just theoretical wishes; they are already evident in the scattershot and sporadic results we have seen.

Someone should pick up that bone and figure out what to do with it.

NOTES

1. The scene referenced, from Stanley Kubrick's 1968 film *2001: A Space Odyssey*, may be viewed at www.youtube.com/watch?v=sdoA3AJ6zGE&feature=related. This quintessential representation of technological discovery occurs in the last two minutes of the clip.

2. Examples of display ad contents: "Victory is Ours," combined with fireworks and confetti; "Education is my passion. And the President's too. Let me explain why." This was the text of the one ad with a link, to the Laura Bush video. "Give $50 Now: If You Want Kerry to win in November we need your help today." "Every Vote Counts: 20,000 votes decided four states in 2000—Make a Difference."

3. Kate Kaye interview with Mindy Finn, December 2007.

REFERENCES

Bassik, M. 2004. "What John Kerry Taught Us About Online Advertising." *Campaigns & Elections* 25 (10) (accessed March 1, 2008, at http://findarticles.com/p/articles/mi_m2519/is_10_25/ai_n8583728).

Copeland, H., and M. Mitzel. n.d. "The Huge Opportunity For Online Political Ads." *New Politics Institute* (accessed March 1, 2008, at www.newpolitics.net).

Cornfield, M. 2004. "Presidential Campaign Advertising on the Internet." Pew Internet and American Life Project. October (accessed March 1, 2008, at www.pewinternet.org/pdfs/PIP_Pres_Online_Ads_Report.pdf)

"How America Searches Election '08." 2007. *iCrossing.com*. July. Opinion Research Corporation (accessed March 1, 2008, at http://www.icrossing.com/articles/how_america_searches_election_2008.pdf).

"Internet's Broader Role in Campaign 2008." 2008. Pew Research Center. January 11 (accessed March 1, 2008, at http://people-press.org/reports/display.php3?ReportID=384).

Kaye, K. 2007a. "Conservative Values Are Onstage in New Republican Video and Blog Ads." *ClickZ News*. October 23 (accessed March 1, 2008, at http://www.clickz.com/showPage.html?page=3627382).

_____. 2007b. "McCain and Romney Simplify Ads in June, Tancredo Goes on Attack." *ClickZ News*. July 19 (accessed March 1, 2008, at http://www.clickz.com/showPage.html?page=3626467).

_____. 2007c. "McCain Sticks with No Surrender Message in Web Ads." *ClickZ News*. September 27 (accessed March 1, 2008, at http://www.clickz.com/showPage.html?page=3627149).

_____. 2007d. "McCain Takes to Video and Search Ads, Dems to Blogs." *ClickZ News*. January 25 (accessed March 1, 2008, at http://www.clickz.com/showPage.html?page=3624702).

_____. 2007e. "Obama Works With Ethnic Social Sites to Remove Bad Ad Potential," *ClickZ News*. October 19 (accessed March 1, 2008, at http://www.clickz.com/show-Page.html?page=3627352).

_____. 2007f. "Online Political Spending to Hit $73 Million in '08 Cycle." *ClickZ News*. December 7 (accessed March 1, 2008, at http://www.clickz.com/showPage.html?page=3627811).

_____. 2007g. "Politicos Weigh In on McCain's Woes and Web Campaign." *ClickZ News*. July 20 (accessed March 1, 2008, at http://www.clickz.com/showPage.html?page=3626479).

_____. 2007h. "Presidential Hopefuls Go on Attack With Most Ads Ever in October."
  ClickZ News. November 15 (accessed March 1, 2008, at http://www.clickz.com/
  showPage.html?page=3627610).

_____. 2007i. "Romney, McCain, Obama Dominate Presidential Display Ads This Year."
  ClickZ News. December 27 (accessed March 1, 2008, at http://www.clickz.com/
  showPage.html?page=3627978).

Rogers, E. M. 2003. *Diffusion of Innovations.* 5th ed. New York: Free Press.

PART THREE

International Perspectives

The following two selections reflect on the use of modern technology in campaigns abroad. The objective is to demonstrate that new technology can be–and is–applied in electoral contexts beyond the United States, often, but not always, in similar ways and to the same effect. It is useful to keep in mind that innovative uses of technology in campaigns may originate abroad, and scholars and political operatives are wise to follow these developments closely. Electioneers may discover creative and effective uses of the technology on the campaign trail or derive lessons that would help to avoid mistakes.

The case studies that follow serve as examples of the ways in which technology is being deployed in campaigns in an international context are designed to provide readers with a glimpse of what is happening elsewhere in the world. Although it is beyond the scope of this volume to provide more comprehensive coverage of developments abroad, pioneering uses of new technology in campaigns overseas abound. As analysts and operatives alike study these developments, it is useful to take into consideration the variation in institutional, structural, cultural, legal, or political constraints within which campaigns operate in nations across the world. In some cases, these may be conducive to the use of certain technologies; in others they may act as barriers.

10

"Under Construction"

Weblog Campaigning in the German Bundestag Election 2005

STEFFEN ALBRECHT

MAREN LÜBCKE

RASCO HARTIG-PERSCHKE

Election campaigns are an extreme form of political communication. During these periods, the mass media and the electorate devote more attention to the statements of politicians and their parties than at any other time. The stakes are high, indeed; elections are at the core of the political process: the allocation of political power. Because of their importance, campaigns can act as catalysts for new forms of political communication.

This chapter examines how campaign communication is being changed by a new technological medium: Weblogs. By offering easy-to-use content management software and an attractive presentation, Weblogs have revolutionized the way information is distributed on the Internet. In contrast to traditional mass media, Weblogs support the interaction of authors—bloggers—with their readers by offering services to comment on articles (so-called blog posts). Furthermore, they support the interaction with other bloggers by facilitating hyperlinking to other blogs and blog posts. The totality of Weblogs, the "blogosphere," today forms a new communicative space on the Internet.

While research in political communication has shown that changes in communication technology strongly influence campaigns (Mancini and Swanson 1996; Schulz, Zeh, and Quiring 2005), little is yet known about the effects of Weblogs. On the one hand, authors view Weblogs as alternative channels for the distribution of information as well as mobilization tools, because of their ability to spread news very quickly (Ito 2004; Kahn and Kellner 2004). Bloggers are seen as a "fifth power" that increasingly occupies the control function of the mass media (Gillmor 2004; Himmelsbach 2005), contrasting established news values with a more personal, direct, and often location-specific style of reporting. Blogs can be a tool for opinion formation, as they are said to influence agenda setting and framing processes (Drezner and Farrell 2004).

On the other hand, hyperlinking on Weblogs might foster political fragmentation by connecting only like-minded bloggers, who, as a consequence, avoid dealing with diverging views (Howard 2005). Blogs are said to destroy the reflective quality of public political communication by letting everyone share their more or less concise thoughts. Blogs are also expected to worsen the inequality of voices in the public sphere by supporting a star culture with few prominent authors (so-called A-listers) and a large number of unknown bloggers (Shirky 2003).

This chapter tries to further the state of research by empirically analyzing political communication with Weblogs in the campaign for the German Bundestag election in 2005. Starting with mediatization theory, it explores how the logic of the mediatized political field collides with the logic of the Weblogging culture in the campaign blogosphere. Next we introduce our research methodology and provide information about the study case. Finally we discuss the empirical results and present the conclusions.

Background: Mediatized Politics

Research on political communication and, specifically, on campaigns has yielded evidence of a fundamental change of political practices as an effect of mass media's evolution. This process is described analytically by mediatization theory (see Mazzoleni and Schulz 1999). According to this theory, "big media" follow their own logic of presenting news to their audiences: For example, research on news values and gatekeeping (Bennett 2004) has shown that some forms of information have a better chance of being presented than others. Driven by the need to get attention from recepients, the mass media are said to focus on events like political scandals (in contrast to long-term political processes), on surprising and conflict-laden content (instead of discourse and argumentation), and on prominent individuals (in contrast to newcomers and bystanders).

The theory of gatekeeping explains how this logic actually shapes the media field, emphasizing the role of institutionalized practices and their reproduction (Bennett 2004). With the increase in media usage—especially television—the political field had to adapt its procedures and preferences to comply with this "media logic" (Altheide and Snow 1979). The political field turned into a "media democracy," a novel regime in which media logic increasingly determines the political process (Meyer 2002).

One important question in this theoretical framework is the role technology plays in the process of mediatization. As Bennett (2004) demonstrates in his analysis of gatekeeping, new technology leads to new kinds of usage and to new forms of presentation. These new formats affect the media logic and, according to mediatization theory, the whole field of political communication (Bennett 2004, 301). This model assigns technology an important part in the process of mediatization, but one that is played through interaction with institutionalization and reproduction.

Our study on the effects of Weblogs on campaign communication starts from mediatization theory's assumption that the political and media fields together have shaped the logic of today's media democracies. We then ask how Weblogs, as a new technologically enabled genre, change campaign communication. Building on the role of technology in the theory of mediatization, we first explore the logic of Weblogs. Our research question is how this logic will interact with the logic of mediatized politics. Will one of these logics dominate the forms of communication? Will Weblogs actually change campaigning or will they merely reinforce the structures of mass mediatized campaigns?

Blogging Practices

To regard Weblogs as merely a new technology would discount the Internet as a social phenomenon. Rather, the whole range of Weblog culture—from production to reception of information—has to be considered when analyzing the consequences of Weblogs. In order to describe the logic of blogging, we can determine the characteristics of blogging practices, that is, the "shared routines and expectations that emerge within . . . groups of people who use social software" (Schmidt 2007, 34). We identify four dimensions of Weblog use (based on Schmidt and Wilbers 2006): the activity of blogging (who posts, and to what extent?); the interactivity between authors and readers (feedback received on blog posts); the connectedness of Weblogs with the blogosphere by means of blogrolls—lists of hyperlinks to other Weblogs; and the authenticity of the bloggers' expression, that is, a personal, subjective style.[1]

According to a survey of German Weblog users (Schmidt and Wilbers 2006), Weblogs are expected to be updated daily or at least several times a week. Weblog readers expect to be able to comment, although in practice, few posts are commented on. About half of the bloggers consider blogrolls typical elements of a Weblog, and a slight majority has a blogroll. This combination of blogging routines and users' expectations shapes a certain practice that establishes a new format of public expression. This format, in turn, follows its own logic: it rewards active involvement in Web publishing, orientation toward dialogue, and efforts to establish lasting social relations. Our hypothesis is that this blogging logic overrides the dominant logic of media democracies in shaping campaign communication.

Weblogs in Election Campaigns—Literature Review

The 2004 U.S. presidential campaign is often cited as a reference point for the political impact of Weblogs and even as "a breakout year for the role of the Internet in politics" (Rainie, Cornfield, and Horrigan 2005). Howard Dean demonstrated how such a tool could be used to mobilize supporters and funding, although his candidacy was not successful in the end (Kerbel and Bloom 2005). During the campaign, Weblogs were used intensively as a source of information and for the purpose of political debate. Weblogs were often cited in the mass media and even influenced their agenda (Cornfield et al. 2005).

In the last few years, campaign blogging has become an international trend, at least in western democracies. Studies have examined campaign blogging in the 2004 U.S. presidential election (Ackland 2005; Adamic and Glance 2005; Cornfield et al. 2005; Hargittai, Gallo, and Kane 2007; Kerbel and Bloom 2005; Lawson-Borders and Kirk 2005; Rainie, Cornfield, and Horrigan 2005), the 2005 United Kingdom general election (Auty 2005; Coleman and Ward 2005; Jackson 2006; Stanyer 2006), the 2005 Danish parliamentary election (Klastrup and Pedersen 2007), the 2005 New Zealand general election (Hopkins and Matheson 2005), and the 2005 German Bundestag election (Abold and Heltsche 2006; Ott 2006). The recent French election has also demonstrated the sustained use of Weblogs as a campaign instrument (Arnold 2007).

These studies show that blogging is widespread among candidates, partisans, and campaign observers. Most of them document that blogs help new actors enter the public sphere, making their voices heard (Coleman and Ward 2005; Hopkins and Matheson, 2005; Klastrup and Pedersen 2007; Rainie, Cornfield, and Horrigan 2005; Stanyer 2006). These new actors do not take new political positions, but they add new information and viewpoints to the debate (Stanyer 2006), as the investigations on military service of presidential candidates in the U.S. showed (Rainie, Cornfield, and Horrigan 2005). On the other hand, many politicians use Weblogs as mere soapboxes for self-marketing, as the 2005 United Kingdom election showed (Coleman and Ward 2005). These results match the view of German Weblog readers, who perceived Weblogs as an alternative source of information, but were disappointed by most politicians' blogs (Abold and Heltsche 2006).

The public reception of Weblogs is generally assessed as marginal. According to a survey by the Pew Internet & American Life Project, only 5 percent of the American population says that they used Weblogs at least sometimes during the campaign (Rainie, Cornfield, and Horrigan 2005). Lawson-Borders and Kirk (2005) also note that the actual impact of blogs on the election has been small. This is even more evident in other countries, where the blogging culture is not as widespread as in the United States. In the United Kingdom no less than 312 blogs reported about the election (Stanyer 2006), but the wider public, by and large, did not take any notice (Coleman and Ward 2005; Jackson 2006). The same holds true in New Zealand (Hopkins and Matheson 2005).

Several authors have studied the connectedness of Weblogs. This research is driven by the thesis of Sunstein (2001) and others that discourse on the Internet tends to attract like-minded participants. As a result, separate arenas emerge, which are each ideologically homogeneous. In the blogosphere, such clusters are apparent from the link pattern among Weblogs.

In their study on the 2004 U.S. presidential election, Cornfield and his colleagues (2005) do not find a clustering of blogs along ideological divisions of liberals versus conservatives. This finding contrasts with those of Adamic and Glance (2005), who studied the linking behavior of more than fourteen hundred political U.S. Weblogs with a conservative or liberal orientation. They diagnose an "unmistakable division between the liberal and conservative political (blogo)spheres" (4) that is also evident in a more in-depth analysis of forty of the most popular political blogs. Their findings are corroborated by Ackland (2005), who studied the same sample of forty blogs, although with a different methodology. Both studies are based on data collected after the 2004 U.S. presidential election.

Hargittai and her colleagues (2007) also investigated the fragmentation of the political blogosphere and arrive at a more nuanced picture. Whereas blogroll linking indeed follows the "friend or foe" scheme, blog posts contain surprisingly many cross-ideological links. The authors conclude that there is a tendency in political Weblogs to link to others who are like-minded, but find "no support for the claim that IT will lead to increasingly fragmented discourse online" (Hargittai, Gallo, and Kane 2007, 24).

This moderate position is also found in studies on campaign Weblogs in Germany, the United Kingdom, and Denmark. In the 2005 Bundestag campaign, Ott (2006) notices that blogrolls primarily linked to their own party's blogs. Stanyer (2006) observed a certain degree of partisan skewing within blogrolls in the United Kingdom, particularly among the left-wing blogs and among MPs and candidates. The partisan skewing was not as strong as that reported by Adamic and Glance (2005) for the United States, however. In Denmark, only a few campaign blogs linked at all to others. Klastrup and Pedersen (2007) conclude that politicians adopted Weblogs as a decentralized campaign tool but did not contribute to the spread of political debate.

Finally, a number of studies directly compare blogging activity to the media's coverage of the campaigns. The general picture is that Weblogs have had only a small role to play in the campaign but filled a niche within the mediascape (see Rainie, Cornfield, and Horrigan 2005 for the United States in 2004; Stanyer 2006 for the United Kingdom in 2005; Hopkins and Matheson 2005 for New Zealand in 2005).

In summary, our literature review indicates that along the dimension of activity, Weblogs allow new actors with new views to participate in the campaign discourse, filling a niche within the mediascape. This finding suggests that the logic of blogging affects campaign communication. But along the dimensions of interactivity and of connectedness, Weblogs seem to follow the logic of the mediatized political field. They are subject to the same economic logic that directs attention to well-known actors. And, if not deepening the cleavages, they mirror the fragmentation of the political field. This similarity of blogging practices to the media–political logic makes sense given that, at least in the United States, many campaign bloggers were journalists (Lawson-Borders and Kirk 2005), and many journalists use blogs as a guide to the sources of information on the Internet (Cornfield et al. 2005).

Data and Methodology

Our study seeks to systematically and empirically assess the impact of Weblogs on the 2005 German Bundestag campaign. The campaign blogosphere is our object of study, defined as all Weblogs focusing on issues related to the election in the last two months of the campaign. We confine our empirical observation to the campaign blogosphere because it represents the intersection of the media–political field and blogging culture.

This case study is explorative in nature because of the novelty of campaign blogging in Germany. It is guided by the analytical dimensions of activity, interactivity, and connectedness. In contrast to other studies of the Bundestag campaign, we do not limit our observation to blogs of political actors in the narrower sense (that is, candidates and parties), but consider all campaign blogs. In our sampling strategy, we also follow explicit methodological guidelines and do not employ online surveys, as their results are often biased when used in campaign research, reaching primarily "campaign junkies" (Schoen and Faas 2005, 328).

We first analyze blogging activity during the campaign, focusing on the characteristics of blog authors, quantity of postings, and Weblog age. We then investigate the level of feedback candidate Weblogs receive from readers, that is, their degree of interactivity. The independent variables are the prominence of the author and the type of service hosting the Weblog. Finally, we analyze the connectedness of Weblogs by means of blogroll links to determine how similar the blogosphere's structure is to the political field.

At the time of the campaign, the blogging culture in Germany grew slowly. The political blogosphere was still "under construction" (Albrecht et al. 2005). Lacking an adequate index, we employed a combination of sampling strategies, including search engines and pertinent lists published on dedicated Web sites, as well as snowball sampling techniques in order to collect as many campaign blogs as possible (see Albrecht et al. 2005 for further details on the sampling process). Only campaign Web sites with entries in chronologically reverse order and at least two of the following features were chosen for the sample: they are explicitly characterized as a Weblog or online diary, they link to other Weblogs in their blogrolls or posts, and they allow readers to comment on their posts directly on the site.

This process yielded a sample of 317 Weblogs. For each Weblog, blogroll links were archived every two weeks during the last two months of the campaign. The content of the Weblogs was surveyed once in the week following the election, and all blog posts were saved for further analysis. Weblogs that were completely deleted by their owners immediately after the election are treated as "missing."

Context and Electoral System of the Bundestag Election

While German campaigns are said to mirror the presidential campaigns in the U.S. (Korte 2006), the electoral system differs considerably from the American model (see Drück 2004; Wüst et al. 2006). It is characterized by mixed-member proportional representation and a multiparty system with strong party organizations. The role of candidates in the campaign is to lend a face to the campaign and to fight for votes locally. Members of the Bundestag are elected either through their party's list or directly within their constituency.

The 2005 Bundestag election was historically peculiar for several reasons (cf. Wüst and Roth 2006). Chancellor Gerhard Schröder called an early election after his party had lost the election in North Rhine-Westphalia in May 2005. The legal problems of this decision occupied government institutions until less than one month before Election Day on September 18, 2005, and the campaign phase was short and intense. The voters basically had to choose between two options: the incumbent Social Democratic Party (SPD) and Green Party coalition and the challenging Christian Democrats (CDU/CSU) and Liberal Democrats (FDP) coalition. The governing coalition scored low in polls compared to their opponents, reversing the traditional positions of incumbent and challenger, and had to run a campaign to prove they were still able to lead the country. A third competitor, the Left Party—formed by the East German PDS and West German WASG—represented a new force on the left that threatened to take votes from the SPD (Roberts 2006).

The result of the election was also historically significant, as neither of the two opposing coalitions succeeded in forming the government. Instead, SPD and CDU/CSU were forced to build a grand coalition, with the latter taking the lead under the new chancellor, Angela Merkel. Analysts expect this election to have fundamental consequences for the German party system (Roberts 2006; Wüst and Roth 2006).

Empirical Results: Overview of the Campaign Blogosphere

Although online campaigning in Germany is sometimes regarded as a mere supplement to or mirror of the "real world" campaign (Bieber 2005), parties and politicians are extending their Web presence and experimenting with new forms of communication (Hebecker 2002; Schweitzer 2005, 345). The use of Weblogs in the 2005 campaign is a case in point. Against the background of the lively debate about Weblogs in the U.S. presidential campaign, several German politicians and strategists were eager to use this new medium (Lianos and Schröder 2005). With a total of about sixty thousand to one hundred thousand Weblogs in Germany as of the summer of 2005 (Sixtus 2005) and the potential to reach 64 percent of the German electorate via the Internet (Forschungsgruppe Wahlen Online 2005), the blogosphere promised to resonate well with modern campaigning.

Between the end of May and the beginning of September, the number of Weblogs covering the election grew steadily, as figure 10.1 shows. The fastest growth was observed after July 21, when president Horst Köhler decided that the election would actually be held. In the last days of the campaign, only a few journalists set up new blogs to cover the final phase. About a quarter of the Weblogs in our sample were established before the election was called. Some of the blogging ambitions were not realized: nineteen Weblogs (6 percent) were set up but no posts published.

Six Weblogs were run by specialists (for example, design agencies or political communication experts) who did not take an active part in the campaign; fifteen blogs were written by journalists; ninety-three were written by politically interested citizens, thirty of whom supported one or another party. Furthermore, we found that seventy-six bloggers belonged to party organizations, eighty-three were candidates for a seat in parliament, and thirty-eight were existing members of parliament. Finally, six blogs were written by a collective of laypeople and politicians—both incumbents and challengers.

The number of laypeople in comparison to journalists and political professionals is remarkably high (also compared to the 2004 U.S. election—see Lawson-Borders and Kirk 2005). This suggests that Weblogs in the Bundestag campaign indeed helped new actors to enter the public sphere on an equal footing with established politicians—especially politically interested citizens and less prominent politicians. The blogosphere appears more diversified than the set of actors that appears in traditional news media.

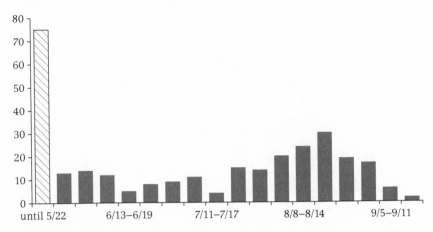

FIGURE 10.1 Growth of the Campaign Blogosphere in 2005. Bars represent the number of new blogs per week.

The formats of the campaign blogs in our sample are further evidence of such diversity. Journalists used their Weblogs to cover local campaigning. Citizens commented on the campaign and analyzed the strategies of the different parties from a personal perspective. Another Weblog format consists of several authors with opposing political standpoints, a kind of ongoing online panel discussion. These sites were initiated by politically independent actors who were generally interested in promoting Weblogging. However, the largest part of the sample consists of Weblogs written by politicians.

The campaign blogosphere covered the entire range of the political spectrum (see figure 10.2). The plurality of blogs supported the SPD (eighty-one Weblogs, 26 percent), while the CDU/CSU and Left Party only had a small number of partisan blogs (sixteen and eighteen blogs, representing 5 percent and 6 percent, respectively). Two small parties, the FDP and the Greens, were in between, with thirty-nine (12 percent) and forty-eight (15 percent) blogs, respectively, supporting them. The sample contains only one blog supporting the far right National Democratic Party (NDP). As we assume a certain amount of covert online activity in this part of the political spectrum, this might underestimate the number of blogs supporting the far right.

The parties' blogging strategies varied substantially. The Weblogs of the CDU/CSU were predominantly written by politicians themselves. Only the CSU had an official blog ("Blog for Berlin"), while the Weblog "CDUnion" was written by independent partisans. The SPD, in contrast, offered a broad range of Weblogs, from several central campaign blogs, to rapid-response and negative campaigning blogs, to individual blogs hosted on the party's

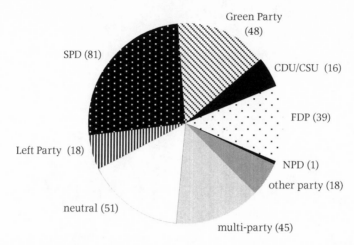

FIGURE 10.2 Campaign Weblogs According to Party Affiliation and Orientation (Absolute Frequencies in Parentheses)

own blogging platform. The SPD purportedly abstained from controlling whether these hosted blogs conformed with its campaign strategy (see Lianos and Schröder 2005).

The smaller parties fit in between these strategies, with a combination of several personal Weblogs and a few official Weblogs, such as Weblogs of the parties' youth organizations (Greens, FDP) and Weblogs to raise money for the campaign (FDP). The overrepresentation of the small parties in the blogosphere (except for the Left Party) marks another difference from the media–political field, where the big parties have a stronger presence.

A Tool for Campaigning, or for Sustained Dialogue?

We wanted to find out whether campaign blogs were mainly used for the short period of the campaign, characteristic of media democracy's focus on events, or rather as a tool for building up and managing long-term social relations, characteristic of the blogging culture (Schmidt 2007). To answer this question, we revisited each Weblog on May 22, 2006, one year after the election had been called. Ninety-three Weblogs were still active (at least one new posting in the last four weeks). Sixty-five bloggers had not posted anything since the election, and forty-three blogs were offline. Sixty-one Weblogs stopped their activity before the end of the 2005.

Looking at the Weblogs of candidates and MPs, only 15 out of 121 (9 candidates and 6 MPs) were kept up to date through May 2006. Therefore, while many blogs were created as a part of the 2005 campaign in Germany, most of them were used as a campaign tool, and this holds especially for Weblogs of parties and politicians.

Only a few political actors attempted to establish a long-term Web presence with their Weblogs. Similar to the 2005 British elections, Weblogs had once again only become the " 'latest and safest' media-friendly tool used by those who wanted to give the impression of being comfortable with getting up-close-and-personal with the public" (Ferguson 2005, 33). Nevertheless, the fifteen Weblogs still active show that at least some politicians are exploring the potential of political blogs, trying to establish sustained dialogue with their constituency.

Politician's Blogs: Just Active or Interactive?

Politicians are the largest subgroup in our sample.[2] How did Weblogging influence their style of political communication? More specifically, we are interested in how they complied with the blog readers' expectations, and in how their commitment and their position in the political field influenced the feedback they received.

The average activity on candidate Weblogs was 14.5 posts over the last four weeks of the campaign. There was a median of nine posts and the distribution of activity was right-skewed. Only seven Weblogs (7 percent of all politicians' blogs) had at least one post per day.

Activity and interactivity are not correlated in our sample: bloggers who wrote frequently did not earn a higher amount of responses. Further, readers made use of their ability to comment on blog posts to varying degrees, depending on the prominence of the author or the Weblog.

Among the ten most active bloggers, most were taking a back seat in their party or were independent candidates (see table 10.1). But with exception of Petra Pau, a well-known left politician—they received less feedback from their readers than average, with four of the most active bloggers receiving the fewest average responses per post.

In contrast, among the bloggers who received the largest amount of feedback, the most important determinants of response seem to be the visibility and prominence of the Weblog or its author. Eight of the ten Weblogs most frequently commented on were hosted by Focus Online and AOL, among the most visited Web portals in Germany (with a total of eleven Focus Online and AOL blogs in the sample). These portals were able to draw a lot of traffic to their Weblogs. All eight of these Weblogs were written by prominent politicians. Although this result is not surprising, the two exceptions are interesting because they show that some actors succeeded in bypassing the dominant logic. Their Weblogs were hosted on their own server or on "wahl.de," a special hosting service for politicians.

TABLE 10.1

Activity and Interactivity of MPs' and Candidates' Weblogs, Categorized by Party Affiliation, Actor Type, and (for the ten highest ranked Weblogs) Blog Hoster

Activity (number of posts)			*Interactivity (comments per post)*		
Left Party	mean	25.2	SPD	mean	8.9
Other party	mean	20.1	CDU/CSU	mean	7.9
Green Party	mean	13.2	FDP	mean	4.7
SPD	mean	12.4	Green Party	mean	4.7
FDP	mean	11.4	Left Party	mean	2.8
CDU/CSU	mean	8.4	Other party	mean	1.3
MPs	mean	14.6	MPs	mean	7.0
Candidates	mean	14.5	Candidates	mean	3.7
Dirk Schneider, Independent (M)		107	Andrea Nahles, SPD (F)		67.4
Stefan Liebich, Left (M)		96	Oswald Metzger, Green (F)		44.9
Helmut Gobsch, Independent (W)		76	Katherina Reiche, CDU (A)		24.3
Martin Hohmann, Independent (M)		59	Niels Annen, SPD (A)		22.5
Anna Lührmann, Green (M)		41	Hildegard Müller, CDU (F)		16.6
Gesine Lötzsch, Left (M)		34	Marco Buschmann, FDP (W)		15.1
Cornelia Pieper, FDP (W)		33	K. Göring-Eckardt, Green (A)		13.8
Petra Pau, Left (A)		31	Ulrich Kelber, SPD (M)		10.7
Gerhard Schick, Green (M)		29	Petra Pau, Left (A)		10.3
Sebastian Weigle, SPD (M)		29	Hermann-Otto Solms, FDP (A)		9.1
Overall mean		14.6	Overall mean		4.8
Overall median		9	Overall median		2.3

Blog hoster: A = AOL; F = Focus Online; W = wahl.
de; M = miscellaneous/self-designed.

These findings indicate that the news values and gatekeepers of the mass media are of considerable importance for Weblogs in this field. The prominence of politicians and the degree of popularity of gatekeepers such as news portals affect their Weblogs' visibility on the Internet, thus drawing the attention of potential readers. As to the two exceptions to this, the bloggers tried to meet the expectations of Weblog readers, keeping their Weblogs up-to-date and interacting with their audience. This indicates the potential of Weblogs to cross mass media's logic of attention, which dominates the political field both off- and online.

Network Structure of the Bundestag Campaign Blogosphere

Interestingly, bloggers' prominence was an attractor for comments as well as for blogroll hyperlinks. Blogs had an average of 8.7 hyperlinks, with a median of 2. A majority of the blogs (187, or 59 percent) had no blogroll links to other campaign blogs. Most of the remaining blogs referred to just a few others: 23.2 percent contained one to six links, 11.3 percent seven to fifteen links, and a mere 5.5 percent had more than fifteen links. The longest blogroll in our sample pointed to seventy-three other blogs. Links within the blogrolls were set to ideologically related Weblogs (for example, to Weblogs of the own party), according to the personal interests of the owner, or regardless of their political orientation. In some cases, blog providers set links automatically. For example, Focus Online Weblogs always contained links to other Focus Online blogs but did not refer to blogs hosted by other providers.

By following these links, one is able to trace the network structure of the Bundestag campaign blogosphere (see Marlow 2004, for a similar approach). A total of 195 Weblogs are part of the interconnected network of campaign blogs.[3] Of these, 113 were mutually connected to each other, 11 were only sending out links, and 71 were only receiving links. Another 116 Weblogs neither sent nor received links.

The density of this network (the relation of actual versus possible links) is 1.12 percent, which means that 1,081 links out of 96,410 possible were established between the 311 blogs. This number of realized connections indicates a complex and heterogeneously structured network. The distribution of blogroll links points to a widespread network with a large, sparsely connected periphery and a strongly connected core. Figure 10.3 shows the structure of the network.

Differences between central and peripheral blogs can be described in detail with the so-called indegree centrality, an index that counts the number of links pointing to a blog. The more incoming links a blog gets, the more likely it is that it will be found by a reader. The centrality of a Weblog can be interpreted as the amount of attention it gets within the blogosphere. Again,

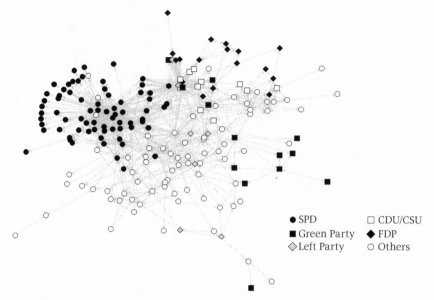

FIGURE 10.3 Blogroll Network of Campaign Weblogs, Categorized According to Party Affiliation (Spring-Embedded Layout)

the distribution of indegrees across Weblogs was highly skewed. Among all the blogs, 127 (40.8 percent) did not receive any links, 152 received between one and 10 links and the remaining 32 blogs received between 11 and 30 links. Focusing on the subgroup of blogs receiving links, there was an average of 5.9 links and a median of 3.5 links for each blog.

On the one hand, Weblogs from well-known politicians and Weblogs hosted by large Web portals were able to gain attention—matching the results we found for interactivity. On the other hand, three independent campaign blogs from bloggers with a long-established reputation also attracted much attention. They started at an early stage of the election campaign (two of them within hours of the call) and thus had time to build up a central standing.

Our analysis shows that the logic of the mass media dominate the blogosphere by mainly drawing attention to prominent actors. If we prescind from the individual blogger, the question arises whether the structure of the political field is reflected in the structure of the blogosphere as well. Hence, we analyze the blogroll network with regard to parties and their linkages. Table 10.2 shows the result of the network's segregation into blocks according to party affiliation. The relations between blocks were analyzed using a density matrix (see Wasserman and Faust 1994). Each cell represents the number of connections between two groups of Weblogs relative to the amount of possible connections. This method simultaneously takes into account the respective sizes of the Weblog groups sending and receiving links.

As we can see from table 10.2, no single party cut off from the others completely, although the SPD refrained the most from cross-party networking. Neither did the blogrolls mirror the traditional political camps: the would-be coalition of CDU/CSU and FDP entertained close links to each other, but there were also a number of links between the CDU/CSU and the rivaling coalition of SPD and Greens.

Thus we have to reject the assumption of a clear ideological division for the 2005 Bundestag campaign blogosphere. For the United States, Adamic and Glance (2005) recorded 91 percent of links directed to blogs within the same political camp. In contrast, only 77 percent of the links of SPD and Green blogs were directed to their own camp, and just 50 percent among CDU/CSU and FDP Weblogs. Nevertheless, the affiliation with a political group does have an important influence on the network's structure. Table 10.2 shows higher density values along the diagonal, which means that links between blogs belonging to the same group are more frequent than links to others. Additionally, we observe high-density values between the CDU/CSU and the FDP, whereas the SPD and Greens keep more of a distance. Both former governmental coalition partners were loosely connected by blogroll links, demonstrating self-reliance and an individual profile in the online campaign, which mirrors their offline strategy (Niedermayer 2007). The Left

TABLE 10.2

Density Matrix of Blogroll Links According to Party Affiliation (showing percentages)

Block name	N	CDU/CSU	FDP	SPD	Green	Left	Other
CDU/CSU	11	**16.4**	**9.1**	2.3	**4.9**	**3.9**	2.8
FDP	17	3.2	**11.8**	0.7	1.8	0.8	0.7
SPD	71	1.7	0.6	**7.9**	0.4	0.6	1.6
Green	13	3.5	3.2	1.0	**10.9**	1.1	0.5
Left	7	**7.8**	**5.9**	1.8	**5.5**	**7.1**	3.6
Other blogs	76	3.2	1.8	0.8	1.5	1.5	**3.9**

Note: Blocks with Weblogs sending links out are listed in the rows, those with Weblogs receiving links in columns. Density scores that are above average are printed in bold. The mean density across all blocks is 3.8 percent; the overall density of the network of Weblogs with blogrolls is 2.9 percent.

Party's position on the network is very similar to its political isolation (Roberts 2006). Its blogs are linked to various other groups but receive only a few incoming links. Thus, on closer examination, we find that the Bundestag campaign blogosphere indeed mirrors the structure of the political field.

To sum up, blogroll links draw an instructive picture of the structure of the blogosphere. Because a large proportion of blogs did not provide a blogroll, the overall network of blogs was only sparsely connected. The network is characterized by a center–periphery structure, and only Weblogs in the center exchanged links to a large degree. The network also showed that links are primarily to Weblogs of the same party. Furthermore, links were established primarily to prominent blogs within the blogosphere, depending on the prominence of the blog's platform, the recognition of the author, and the time the blog was online.

Conclusions

Our case study shows that Weblogs played an important role in the Bundestag campaign as far as we consider their active usage. All major parties and many candidates used this new mode of communication, although only a few attracted much attention. Campaign Weblogs were found to have a limited reach, at least in terms of the number of comments they provoke. Thus, our study confirms the results of previous studies on campaign Weblogging: Weblogs fill a niche in campaign communication.

Furthermore, we wanted to find out whether this niche position corresponds to a specific form of communication, a specific "Weblog logic" contrasting with the "media logic" documented in studies of political communication. Our results lead to different answers for the three dimensions we have distinguished. Along the dimension of activity, we found mixed evidence. On the one hand, Weblogs allow new actors to engage in campaign communication. This is in contrast to the media logic of gatekeepers limiting the scope of actors that appear on the public stage. On the other hand, Weblogs were mainly used as a campaign instrument with a short-term perspective, which is in line with the time horizon of mediatized politics.

Along the dimension of interactivity, the results clearly indicate that the campaign blogosphere has adopted the media logic. Weblogs of prominent actors or Weblogs hosted by well-known online portals receive the largest share of attention independent of their authors' activity. We confirmed this result with two different measures of attention, the number of comments per post and the indegree centrality score. Only few Weblogs with other characteristics were able to receive much attention from readers, indicating that sincerity and long duration of blogging can lead to higher levels of interaction with readers.

Finally, along the dimension of connectedness, the hyperlink structure of the campaign blogosphere very much resembled the ideological structure of the political field in general. This result supports the view of Weblogs as a mirror of the offline world. It rejects both the skeptical thesis implying that Weblogs worsen political fragmentation and the optimistic thesis implying that Weblogs foster dialogue across ideological divides.

In our interpretation, these results are an indicator that the logic of mediatized politics is strongly affecting Weblog communication in the campaign. But under certain circumstances, the distinctive logic of Weblogs interferes with this dominant logic, allowing actors from the periphery of the political field to gain a more prominent position. Based on our explorative study we suggest that the condition that would be decisive for this to happen is for the blogger to conform with the cultural norms of blogging. This includes posting regularly and with a long-term perspective to build social relationships, engaging in discussions with the readers who comment, and connecting to other bloggers by hyperlinking. Further studies are required to confirm this tentative conclusion.

We recommend that political actors with small reputation try to play against the rules of the mediatized political field. These actors will profit from using Weblogs if they adopt established blogging practices and persistently engage in communication with readers and fellow bloggers. At least, such a strategy was evident in the few cases in our study when Weblog logic prevailed over media logic and allowed actors to bypass gatekeepers in media and party organizations.

Assuming that campaigns act like a prism in making visible the special features of political communication (Holtz-Bacha 2004, 468), our findings are relevant not only for campaigns but also for the political process more generally. However, the novelty of blogging as a mode of communication limits the generalizability of the results. The field of campaign Weblogs was still under construction in Germany at the time of the Bundestag campaign 2005. Observations of the campaigns in the United Kingdom, New Zealand, and Denmark, where Weblog diffusion was at a comparable stage, support our findings; with more time and widespread adoption, the practices might come to resemble the pattern found in the United States, where the dominance of media logic was more evident.

To estimate the influence of Weblogs for political communication, one has to consider the whole public sphere, not just the political actors. Weblog use will increase the personalization of campaigns and speed up political communication. Politicians who report about their daily life and interact with their readers work against the impression of a disconnected political caste (Coenen 2005). Bloggers scrutinizing media reports and campaign information and engaging in political discussions across the blogosphere offer an alternative to highly professionalized campaigns. The impact of Weblogs on campaigns, and on political communication more generally, will depend on actual usage once campaign blogging reaches maturity. More comparative and follow-up studies are necessary to make assertions about these future developments.

NOTES

An earlier version of this chapter was published in *Social Science Computer Review* (2007) 25: 504–520. Reprinted with permission.

The authors would like to thank Björn Greve, Jan Hildebrandt, Judith Muster, Marco Schmitt, and Dr. Klaus Stein for their assistance in conducting the empirical research.

1. The fourth dimension, authenticity, is mentioned only for the sake of completeness. Because of our methodological focus on Weblogs rather than on their content, we were not able to investigate this dimension of usage empirically. Thus, we omit this dimension in our analysis.

2. The subsample for this analysis consists of all blog posts and comments on the 121 Weblogs of MPs and their challengers (that is, all candidates) that were published between August 18, 2005, and Election Day (September 18, 2005). Weblogs of 17 candidates, mostly relatively unknown politicians, were not active during the last month of the campaign. Four Weblogs were considered "missing cases" because the content had been deleted immediately after the election, before our observation took place. The remaining 100 active candidate blogs are the basis of our analysis.

3. The analysis refers to the blogroll lists found on the blogs close to Election Day. Six Weblogs are treated as missing data because they were observed only in retrospect. The constructed network was binary coded. Multiple links between blogs were excluded, as were links from blogs that were not part of our sample. We also excluded self-references.

REFERENCES

Abold, R., and M. Heltsche. 2006. "Weblogs in Political Campaigns—The Critical Success Factors." Paper presented at BlogTalk Reloaded, Vienna, Austria (accessed February 28, 2007, at http://blogtalk.net/Main/Papers?action=download&upname= Weblogspercent20inpercent20Politicalpercent20Campaigns.pdf).

Ackland, R. 2005. "Mapping the U.S. Political Blogosphere: Are Conservative Bloggers More Prominent?" Paper presented at BlogTalk Downunder, Sidney, Australia (accessed February 28, 2007, at http://acsr.anu.edu.au/staff/ackland/papers/pol blogs.pdf).

Adamic, L., and N. Glance. 2005. "The Political Blogosphere and the 2004 U.S. Election: Divided They Blog." Paper presented at 2nd Annual Workshop on the Weblogging Ecosystem—Aggregation, Analysis and Dynamics, Chiba, Japan (accessed February 28, 2007, at (http://www.blogpulse.com/papers/2005/AdamicGlanceBlogWWW. pdf).

Albrecht, S., M. Lübcke, R. Perschke, and M. Schmitt. 2005. "Hier Entsteht Eine Neue Internetpräsenz"—Weblogs im Bundestagswahlkampf 2005. kommunikation@

gesellschaft, 6 (accessed February 28, 2007, at (http://www.soz.uni-frankfurt. de/K.G/FI_2005_Albrecht_Luebcke_ Perschke_ Schmitt.pdf).

Altheide, D., and R. Snow. 1979. *Media Logic.* Beverly Hills, CA: Sage.

Arnold, M. 2007. "Contenders Go Online with Diverse Strategies." Financial Times. April 4.

Auty, C. 2005. "UK Elected Representatives and Their Weblogs: First Impressions." *Aslib Proceedings* 57:338–355.

Bennett, W. 2004. "Gatekeeping and Press–Government Relations: A Multigated Model of News Construction." In *Handbook of Political Communication Research*, ed. L. Kaid, 283–313. Mahwah, NJ: Erlbaum.

Bieber, C. 2005. "TV Kills the Internet Star" (accessed February 28, 2007, at http:// www.politik-digital.de/edemocracy/wahlkampf/bundestagswahl05/kommentar bieber050603.shtml).

Coenen, C. 2005. "Weblogs als Mittel der Kommunikation Zwischen Politik und Bürgern—Neue Chancen für die E-Demokratie? kommunikation@gesellschaft, 6" (accessed February 28, 2007, at http://www.soz.uni-frankfurt.de/K.G/B5_2005_ Coenen.pdf).

Coleman, S., and S. Ward, eds. 2005. *Spinning the Web. Online Campaigning in the 2005 General Election.* London: Hansard Society.

Cornfield, M., J. Carson, A. Kalis, and E. Simon. 2005. "Buzz, Blogs and Beyond. The Internet and the National Discourse in the Fall of 2004" (accessed February 28, 2007, at http://www.pewinternet.org/ppt/BUZZ_BLOGS__BEYOND_Final05-16-05. pdf).

Drezner, D., and H. Farrell. 2004. "The Power and Politics of Blogs" (accessed February 28, 2007, at from http://www.danieldrezner.com/research/blogpaperfinal.pdf).

Drück, H. 2004. "Germany." In *The Media and Elections. A Handbook and Comparative Study*, ed. B. Lange and D. Ward, 59–76. Mahwah, NJ: Erlbaum.

Ferguson, R. 2005. "Diving into the Shallow End." In *Spinning the Web. Online Campaigning in the 2005 General Election*, ed. S. Coleman, and S. Ward, 31–35. London: Hansard Society.

Forschungsgruppe Wahlen Online. 2005. Internet-Strukturdaten. Repräsentative Umfrage—III. Quartal 2005 (accessed February 28, 2007, at http://www.forschungs gruppe.de/Ergebnisse/Internet-Strukturdaten/Web_III_05.pdf).

Gillmor, D. 2004. *We the Media. Grassroots Journalism by the People, for the People.* Sebastopol, CA: O'Reilly.

Hargittai, E., J. Gallo, and M. Kane. Forthcoming. "Cross-Ideological Discussions Among a Group of Conservative and Liberal Bloggers." In *The Political Promise of Blogging*, ed. D. Drezner and H. Farrell. Ann Arbor, MI: University of Michigan Press (forthcoming).

Hebecker, E. 2002. Experimentieren für den Ernstfall. Der Online-Wahlkampf 2002. *Aus Politik und Zeitgeschichte* 49–50, 48–54.

Himmelsbach, S. 2005. "Blog. The New Public Forum." In *Making Things Public: Atmospheres of Democracy*, ed. B. Latour and P. Weibel, 916–921. Cambridge, MA: MIT Press.

Holtz-Bacha, C. 2004. "Political Communication Research Abroad: Europe." In *Handbook of Political Communication Research*, ed. L. Kaid, 463–477. Mahwah, NJ: Erlbaum.

Hopkins, K., and D. Matheson. 2005. "Blogging the New Zealand Election: The Impact of New Media Practices on the Old Game." *Political Science* 57:93–105.

Howard, P. 2005. "Deep Democracy, Thin Citizenship: The Impact of Digital Media in Political Campaign Strategy." *Annals of the American Academy of Political and Social Science* 597 (I): 153–170.

Ito, J. 2004. "Weblogs and Emergent Democracy, Version 3.2" (accessed February 28, 2007, at http://joi.ito.com/static/emergentdemocracy.html?).

Jackson, N. 2006. "Dipping Their Big Toe into the Blogosphere. The Use of Weblogs by the Political Parties in the 2005 General Election." *Aslib Proceedings* 58:292–303.

Kahn, R., and D. Kellner. 2004. "New Media and Internet Activism: From the "Battle of Seattle" to Blogging." *New Media & Society* 6 (I): 87–95.

Kerbel, M., and J. Bloom. 2005. "Blog for America and Civic Involvement." *The Harvard International Journal of Press/Politics* 10 (I): 3–27.

Klastrup, L., and P. Pedersen. 2007. "Blogging for Election. The Use and Function of Blogs as Communication Tool in a Danish Parliament Election Campaign." In *Internet research Annual 2005. Selected Papers from the Association of Internet Researchers Conference 2005*, ed. M. Consalvo and C. Haythornthwaite, 27–40. New York: Peter Lang.

Korte, K. 2006. "Model or Deterrence? The United States Presidential Election Campaigns and the Bundestag Election Campaigns." *German Politics* 15 (2): 153–165.

Lawson-Borders, G., and R. Kirk. 2005. "Blogs in Campaign Communication." *American Behavioral Scientist* 49 (4): 548–559.

Lianos, M., and T. Schröder. 2005. "Kampf im Netz. Roundtable-Gespräch zum Internet-Wahlkampf." *Politik & Kommunikation, Wahlkampf Special* 2:22–25.

Mancini, P., and D. Swanson. 1996. "Politics, Media and Modern Democracy: Introduction." In *Politics, Media and Modern Democracy: An International Study of Innovations in Electoral Campaigning and Their Consequences*, ed. D. Swanson and P. Mancini, 1–26. Westport, CT: Praeger.

Marlow, C. 2004. "Audience, Structure and Authority in the Weblog Community." Paper presented at 54th Annual Conference of the International Communication Association, New Orleans, Louisiana (accessed February 28, 2007, at http://www.overstated.net/media/ICA2004.pdf).

Mazzoleni, G., and W. Schulz. 1999. " 'Mediatization' of Politics: A Challenge for Democracy?" *Political Communication* 16 (3): 247–261.

Meyer, T. 2002. *Media Democracy. How the Media Colonize Politics.* Cambridge, England: Polity Press.

Niedermayer, O. Forthcoming. "Der Wahlkampf zur Bundestagswahl 2005." *Die Bundestagswahl 2005. Analysen aus Sicht der Wahlforschung, der Kommunikationswissenschaft und der Parteienforschung*, ed. F. Brettschneider, O. Niedermayer, B. Pfetsch, and B. Weßels. Wiesbaden, Germany: VS Verlag für Sozialwissenschaften (forthcoming).

Ott, R. 2006. "Weblogs als Medium Politischer Kommunikation im Bundestagswahlkampf 2005." In *Die Massenmedien im Wahlkampf. Die Bundestagswahl 2005*, ed. C. Holtz-Bacha, 213–233. Wiesbaden, Germany: VS Verlag für Sozialwissenschaften.

Rainie, L., M. Cornfield., and J. Horrigan. 2005. "The Internet and Campaign 2004" (accessed February 28, 2007, at http://www.wewinternet.org/pdfs/PIP_2004_Campaign.pdf).

Roberts, G. 2006. "The German Bundestag Election 2005." *Parliamentary Affairs* 59 (4): 668–681.

Schmidt, J. 2007. "Social Software: Facilitating Information-, Identity- and Relationship Management." *BlogTalk Reloaded. Social Software—Research and Cases*, ed. In T. Burg and J. Schmidt, 31–49. Vienna, Austria: Books on Demand.

Schmidt, J., and M. Wilbers. 2006. "Wie Ich Blogge?! Erste Ergebnisse der Weblogbefragung 2005" (accessed February 28, 2007, at http://141.13.22.238/fonkblog/pdf/fonkbericht0601.pdf).

Schoen, H., and T. Faas. 2005. "When Methodology Interferes with Substance: The Difference of Attitudes Toward e-campaigning and e-voting in Online and Offline Surveys." *Social Science Computer Review* 23 (3): 326–333.

Schulz, W., R. Zeh, and O. Quiring. 2005. "Voters in a Changing Media Environment: A Data-Based Retrospective on Consequences of Media Change in Germany." *European Journal of Communication* 20 (1): 55–88.

Schweitzer, E. 2005. "Election Campaigning Online. German Party Web sites in the 2002 National Elections." *European Journal of Communication* 20 (3): 327–351.

Shirky, C. 2003. "Power Laws, Weblogs and Inequality. Diversity Plus Freedom of Choice Creates Inequality." In *Exposure. From Friction to Freedom*, ed. J. Engeström, M. Ahtisaari, and A. Nieminen, 77–81. Helsinki, Finland: AULA.

Sixtus, M. 2005. Massenmedium. Blogosphäre: Kommunikationsgeflecht und Marketingfaktor. c't, 19, 148–152.

Stanyer, J. 2006. "Online Campaign Communication and the Phenomenon of Blogging. An Analysis of Web Logs During the 2005 British General Election Campaign." *Aslib Proceedings* 58:404–415.

Sunstein, C. 2001. *Republic.com*. Princeton, NJ: Princeton University Press.

Wasserman, S., and K. Faust. 1994. *Social Network Analysis: Methods and Applications*. Cambridge, England: Cambridge University Press.

Wüst, A., and D. Roth. 2006. "Schröder's Last Campaign: An Analysis of the 2005 Bundestag Election in Context." *German Politics* 15:439–459.

Wüst, A., H. Schmitt, T. Gschwend, and T. Zittel. 2006. "Candidates in the 2005 Bundestag Election: Mode of Candidacy, Campaigning and Issues." *German Politics* 15:420–438.

11

Mobile Democracy

Text Messages, Voter Turnout, and the 2004 Spanish General Election

SANDRA L. SUÁREZ

The purpose of this case study is to illustrate how the use of mobile phones to distribute political information, and its supposed impact on political mobilization and participation during the 2004 Spanish general election, has the potential of making this new technology a democratic force. The votes that gave the upset victory to the PSOE (Partido Socialista Obrero Español, or Spanish Socialist Labour Party) came from young voters and former absentee voters who were mobilized by the events of the preceding days. The opposition was galvanized by the belief that in an effort to hide the link to the Al Qaeda terrorist network the government of José María Aznar was blaming the Basque separatist and terrorist organization ETA for the March 11 bombs that killed 191 people and hurt 1,500. Some people perceived that government officials were trying to manipulate information because an Al Qaeda attack could be interpreted as evidence of the wrongness and futility of the policy of Spanish intervention in Iraq, and thus hurt the PP's (Partido Popular, or Popular Party) chances for reelection. On Election Day, voters were greeted by the astonishing news that thousands of protesters had gathered all over Spain the night before demanding the government to disclose the "truth" about the terrorist attacks. Protesters had been mobilized primarily by text messages transmitted via mobile phones, also known as Short Messaging System (SMS). On Election Day eve SMS messages—later magnified by TV and radio reports—set into motion a chain of events that ultimately contributed to the electoral defeat of the Popular Party.

Communication Technology and Democracy

With the spread of the Internet in the early 1990s, there was much discussion about the democratizing impact of the new information technologies

(Norris 2001, 60–61, 100–101; Papacharissi 2002). The argument was made that in democratic polities, where participation in the formal democratic process has been on the decline, the growth of the Internet would be a vehicle for a new kind of political participation. Globally the Internet has become a mobilizing tool providing political information instantly and economically. The extent of the transnational mobilization in protest of the World Trade Organization meetings in Seattle, Washington (1999), the IMF and World Bank meetings in Prague (2000), and the G8 summit in Genoa (2001) has been attributed to the Internet (Va Aelst and Walgrave 2002; Norris 2002). The Internet has also become an important tool of domestic political mobilization and participation. Many individuals routinely use the Internet to contact public officials, search government sites, register to vote, raise campaign funds, and coordinate grassroots activities (Best and Krueger 2005; Norris 2002). However, the democratizing impact of the Internet has fallen short of expectations, and the scholarly literature is split on the issue (Norris 2002; Putnam 2000; Dahlgren 2005). In democracies the patterns of participation that existed prior to the Internet revolution are simply replicated. Access to the Web does not help inform a previously apathetic electorate because individuals who search the Web for political news are "well informed to begin with, politically oriented and heavier users of other media" (DiMaggio et al. 2001, 320). The existence of a digital divide means that the political impact of the Internet is uneven. In the United States, affluent, urban, white, educated individuals are more likely to own a computer and have Internet access. A similar pattern is evident in Western Europe. For example, in the United Kingdom and France only 23 and 11 percent respectively of the lowest income brackets report using the Internet (DiMaggio et al. 2001; Carverth and Kretchmer 2002; U.S. Department of Commerce n.d.). Thus, the groups with the lowest levels of political participation are less likely to be mobilized politically by the Internet simply because they are less likely to use the Internet or have Internet skills (Best and Krueger 2005).

In contrast to the attention paid to the Internet, the political impact of mobile communication technology has received scant notice. A key similarity between the two media is that they enable the user to exercise discretion to access information and engage in exchanges with others. In addition, governments find it more difficult to censor free expression on the Internet or through the telephone than on television (Havick 2000). However, communication via mobile phones is more personal and direct than with traditional phones. As Ling explains, "with a traditional telephone, we call to a home or other location and then must often request a conversation with a particular individual. When we send a text message to a certain telephone number, we expect that it will reach a specific person regardless of where the person is at the moment" (Ling 2004, 151). Mobile phones are also easier to use than the Internet, which is typically accessed via a personal computer from a fixed location: "One does not need to deal with assembling various components and software. At the level of the user interface, the mobile telephone operates in much the same way as the traditional telephone: that is, you dial a number and the call is put through" (Ling 2004, 16; see also Best and Krueger 2005). Thus, unlike the Internet and traditional phones, mobile phone users are directly accessible at all times and locations (Fortunati 2002).

Another important difference between the Internet and mobile phones is that the latter have diffused to a larger proportion of the world population. Statistics compiled by the International Telecommunication Union as of the end of 2003, just before Spain's general election, indicate that for every Internet user worldwide there are two mobile phone users (see table 11.1). There are regional differences, however. The mobile phone is a relatively more important means of communication in Europe than in other regions of the world. For every European Internet user there are 2.4 mobile phone users. In Spain the discrepancy is even more extreme: for every Internet user there are 3.8 mobile phone users, surpassed only by Portugal with 4.6. By contrast, in the United States the ratio is exactly 1.0. More than 90 percent of the Spanish population use mobile phones, compared to just 24 percent who use the Internet.

The ability to send text messages to multiple recipients simultaneously is yet another distinction between mobile phones and traditional phones. But it is this ability that facilitates the access to a large number of people within a short period of time and without situational constraints, making this new technology exceptionally suited to contribute to flash protests and demonstrations. The growth of SMS worldwide has been an unintended consequence of the growth in mobile telecommunications. In 1995 there were about 91 million mobile phone subscribers worldwide and 689 million fixed telephone lines. By the late 1990s the number of mobile phone subscribers had surpassed the number of telephone lines in operation in Austria, Finland, Italy, and Portugal. Today, the number of mobile subscribers worldwide exceeds the number of fixed telephone lines (see table 11.1). SMS was initially conceived as a paging system that alerted the mobile phone owner to voicemail messages. Prepaid phone service (as opposed to contract service) took off in the mid-1990s and was a success with the teenage market because it kept costs under control. In time teens discovered that SMS messages were cheaper than the cost of a mobile phone call or voice messages. (Initially, they were free because the original billing systems were designed to charge for voice minutes, not text messages.) Teens began using text messages as the main way to communicate via a mobile phone and in the process created a new language (CMT 2002; ITU 2001; Deutsche Bank 2004;

TABLE 11.1

Telephone and Internet Use, Selected Countries, End of 2003

	Per 100 people			Ratio	
	Fixed lines	Mobile lines	Internet users	Mobile-to-fixed	Mobile-to-Internet
World	18.7	22.9	11.3	1.2	2.0
United States	62.4	54.6	55.6	0.9	1.0
China	20.9	21.5	6.3	1.0	3.4
India	4.6	2.5	1.8	0.5	1.4
Japan	47.2	67.9	48.3	1.4	1.4
South Korea	53.8	70.1	61.0	1.3	1.1
Philippines	4.1	27.0	4.4	6.6	6.1
Europe	41.2	59.2	24.2	1.4	2.4
Finland	49.2	91.0	53.4	1.8	1.7
France	56.6	69.6	36.6	1.2	1.9
Germany	65.7	78.5	47.3	1.2	1.7
Italy	48.4	48.4	33.7	1.0	1.4
Poland	31.9	45.1	23.2	1.4	1.9
Portugal	41.1	89.9	19.4	2.2	4.6
Spain	42.9	91.6	23.9	2.1	3.8
Sweden	73.6	98.1	57.3	1.3	1.7
United Kingdom	59.1	91.2	42.3	1.5	2.2

Source: International Telecommunication Union,
http://www.itu.int/ITU-D/ict/statistics.

Nokia Networks 2003). In Europe, Asia, and Australia SMS has become more popular than in the United States. More importantly, some reports suggest that men and women use it independent of their educational background. If levels of education do not affect SMS use, its democratizing impact can be potentially greater than that of the Internet, whose use is mainly driven by socioeconomic status and education (Smoreda and Thomas n.d.; Guillén and Suárez 2001).

These differences between the telephone and the Internet, and between mobile and fixed telephony, have implications for political behavior. Research on political mobilization shows that personal appeals have a strong impact on voter mobilization, although not on voter preference, and that the closer to the event or election that contact is made the greater the impact (Green and Gerber 2004; Piven 2002). Because mobile phones free users from situational constraints they enable individuals who may or may not know each other to act in concert in the spur of a moment and without previous planning (Rheingold 2002). There are already a number of studies reporting that mobile phones, together with the Internet, have become an instrument of political pressure and mobilization. In 2003, SMS messages disclosed the existence of the flu virus SARS and forced the Chinese government to stop the cover-up of the disease. According to news reports, the text message "There is a fatal flu in Guangzhou" was sent and re-sent numerous times via mobile phones and over the Internet, informing the population and foreign press long before the government acknowledged the spread of the virus (Pomfret 2003). Mobile phones were used to mobilize protestors against the Bush Administration during the Republican National Convention in 2004. These demonstrations organized via SMS messages have been referred to as "smart mobs," a term coined by Rheingold (2002), or "TXT-Mobs." During the Republican convention, TXTMob, an Internet mailing list of mobile phone numbers, distributed instant updates to the demonstrators about "route changes, street closures and police actions" (Di Justo 2004). What is exceptional about some of these demonstrations, however, is that they are not preceded by any advance planning and seem to have no identifiable leaders. For example, in May 2001, more than one million people prompted by SMS messages gathered on one of Manila's main highways and demanded the resignation of President Estrada amid corruption allegations. SMS messages not only encouraged the mobilization of Filipinos but, "bypassing the broadcasting media, cell phone users themselves became broadcasters, receiving and transmitting both news and gossip [about the culpability of Estrada], and often confounding the two" (Rafael 2003, 403). More recently, the Chinese used mobile phones, instant messaging, and Internet bulleting boards to encourage people to protest against Japanese history textbooks that minimize Japan's military aggression throughout East and South Asia prior and during World War II. Some reports indicate that the Chinese government, which was stunned by the scale of the demonstrations, was able to censor protest information on the Internet but seemed to have found it more difficult to screen text messages sent via mobile phones (Yardley 2005).

As was the case in the Philippines and China, the protests that preceded the Spanish general election of 2004 seemed to have no identifiable leaders, and new technologies—mobile phones and the Internet—bypassed traditional media as a source of information. In Spain and the Philippines the protests were not planned in advance. Rather, they were spur-of-the-moment, flash demonstrations of the kind that mobile phone technology appears to bring about more quickly and effectively than the Internet, given mobiles' more widespread use and reach.

Democratic Protests during the "Day of Reflection"

By the end of 2003, 92 percent of the Spanish population had a mobile phone, about 74 percent of households had at least one, and 20 percent used it as the only means of telecommunication.[1] Between 2000 and 2002, mobile phone traffic in Spain grew 70 percent (ITU n.d.; Noriega and Ariño Ortiz 2004).[2] The basic service allows the user to call almost anywhere in Spain, including the Canary and Balearic islands. As in the rest of Europe, young people are the heaviest users of SMS, although its growth is permeating all age groups. On March 11, while calls overwhelmed the three mobile phone operators, SMS messages went through. Messages like the ones sent on Election Day eve, also known as the "day of reflection," could be re-sent quite simply and efficiently to user-established lists of contacts.

At around 3:00 p.m. on March 13, a first SMS message was sent. The text was: "Aznar de rositas?[3] They call it Day of Reflection and Urdaci working? Today, March 13, at 18 hours, PP headquarters, Génova Street. No parties. Pass it on!" Urdaci was at the time the news anchor of the government-owned TV channel (TVE-1) whose coverage, in line with the government's view, advanced the theory that ETA was responsible for the bombings. The sender of the SMS message reportedly explained that he spent time trying to make sure that the message contained fewer than 160 characters so it could be sent all at once. He expected to meet only some of the people on his contact list, but by the time he arrived at the PP headquarters, located on Madrid's Génova Street, he was surprised to see hundreds of people. In a clear reference to the perception that the government may have been manipulating the information about the terrorist attacks, other messages read: "We want to know before we vote," and "The truth now, stop the manipulation, your war, our dead. Pass it on!" That evening there was a 20 percent abnormal increase in SMS traffic.[4] Messages were also picked up and sent via the Internet. As a result, there were flash protests in more than fifteen cities across Spain. Eventually, between three thousand and four thousand protestors gathered in front of the PP headquarters in Madrid, and three thousand in Barcelona. The party-picked successor to Aznar, Mariano Rajoy, complained that protests during the day of reflection were "illegal" and "anti-democratic." A judge later ruled that they were neither, but the fact that so many people driven by SMS messages came out to protest during the day of reflection appears to have helped mobilize the opposition on Election Day.

In 2004, the day of reflection was unlike others in the history of Spanish democracy because of the terrorist attacks. At 7:39 a.m. on March 11, a series of bombs began to explode in the Madrid commuter train system. The instinctive reaction of the Spanish public was that ETA had been the perpetrator of the attack. While ETA had been considerably weakened during the eight years of Popular Party rule, there was evidence that it was planning more attacks.

The government was adamant that ETA was responsible but its effort to prove it in spite of evidence to the contrary seemed dubious. By that evening, the interior minister, Angel Acebes, disclosed that a van containing detonators and a cassette with verses from the Koran had been found at around noon in the same town where some of the trains had originated. But while he stated that "no possibilities had been discarded," he maintained that the "government had no doubt that ETA was responsible." Additionally, foreign correspondents contacted by the government were told that ETA was responsible, and Spanish embassies around the world were instructed to say the same.

On Friday, March 12, the Basque TV station Euskal Telebista and the newspaper *Gara* reported that ETA was denying responsibility for the attack. Among the main media outlets, the newspaper *El País* and radio station SER, both partial to the PSOE, as well as some members of the opposition, started to suggest that the PP was manipulating the news about the investigation. Others, such as *El Mundo*, somewhat partial to the PP, were also cautiously considering the possibility of government manipulation. However, TVE-1, the national channel with the largest audience and the one most viewers watch when following important news events, persisted in its support of the government's ETA theory.[5] Thus, although in a few days all of the news media would confirm the responsibility of Al Qaeda, in the first forty-eight hours there was considerable confusion about the authorship of the attacks.

Whether the government truly believed it was ETA or was equivocal with the information it provided to the media, the political consequences of the discovery that the perpetrators were associated with Al Qaeda ought to have been as evident to members of the PP as they were to the protestors who gathered in front of the party's headquarters all over Spain on the day of reflection. To some, the terrorist attack was the direct result of the pro-American foreign policy promoted by Aznar since he was elected in 1996.[6] Opposition to Aznar's foreign policies, however, had not translated into electoral losses for the PP, and the party was confident that it would win the March 2004 general election.[7] Most of the opinion polls published prior to the terrorist attacks indicated that, although support for the PSOE was on the rise, the PP would be the winner (Michavila 2005). It is interesting that voter turnout was predicted to be low (CIS 2004; Díez Nicolás 2004a, 200b).

High Voter Turnout and Government Change in Spain

Postelection analyses of voting behavior suggest that the transfer of power from the PP to the PSOE occurred because there was high voter turnout. This seems to be the norm in Spain, where, in contrast to other Western European countries, voter turnout can oscillate between eight and ten percentage points in consecutive elections (Anduiza and Méndez 2001, 359–360; see table 11.2).[8] In 2004, the PSOE won the election because it received the support of almost 3 million more votes than in 2000. About half of the 3 million new PSOE votes came from former absentee voters, who tend to be young (ages eighteen to twenty-nine) as well as left leaning. The remainder came from voters who became eligible to vote for the first time in 2004 (there were 603,711 new eligible voters), former PP supporters who changed their vote, and the so-called tactical vote from IU (Izquierda Unida, or United Left) supporters, the former communists.[9]

Turnout, however, was not the only factor on Election Day. According to news reports, there were 40 percent more SMS messages than on the average day.[10] Information about the investigation and the protests was reportedly the topic of conversation among SMS users. There was also widespread press coverage of the demonstrations, but the role of traditional media (radio and TV) had been to report on the events of the previous day, rather than to contribute to them. Only CNN+, a cable channel partly owned by PRISA (which also owns El País and the SER radio network), had transmitted live images of the protests. When comparing the impact of traditional media versus mobile phones and the Internet, it is important to note that the information transmitted via new technologies was the catalyst for the protests. Prior to the day of reflection, PRISA-owned media outlets had suggested that the PP government was lying about the terrorists attack, and even the more sympathetic newspaper El Mundo had suggested as much; but these reports alone, while providing motivation for the protests, did not result in any. The political mobilization of voters during the day of reflection occurred when doubts about the credibility of the PP along with calls to demonstrate in protest were transmitted via mobile phones. Limited traditional media coverage of the protest, especially by the government-owned TVE-1, suggests as well that mobile communications had a snowball effect of reproducing the protests all over Spain.

Young voters use mobile phones for personal communication with family and friends. But research shows that personal appeals also have a strong impact on voter mobilization, although not on voter preference (Green and Gerber 2004). In Spain, the communication and distribution of information to and from protesters and friends was facilitated by mobile phones. Mobile phone users had an address book on the phone that allowed them to contact as many people as they wished. The recipients were, in turn, encouraged to

TABLE 11.2

Eligible Voters, Voter Turnout, and Electoral Outcomes in Spain's General Elections for the Congress of Deputies, 1982–2004

Election year	PSOE % of votes	PP[a] % of votes	Change of party in power?	Turnout (% of census)	Census of eligible voters	Increase in eligible voters from previous election (%)
2004	42.6	37.7	Yes	75.7	34,571,831	1.77
2000	34.2	44.5	No	68.7	33,969,640	4.42
1996	37.6	38.8	Yes	77.4	32,531,833	4.84
1993	38.8	34.8	No	76.8	31,030,511	4.82
1989	39.6	25.8	No	69.7	29,604,055	1.67
1986	44.1	26.0	No	70.5	29,117,613	8.46
1982	48.1	26.4	Yes	80.0	26,846,940	0.04

Source: Spanish Interior Ministry www.elecciones.mir.es.

[a]In 1982, Alianza Popular/Partido Demócrata Popular; in 1986, Coalición Popular.

contact their friends with the information.[11] Many people reported receiving their own message back two or three times as well as messages from all over Spain. By Election Day, voters knew that there had been unprecedented "illegal" demonstrations around the country stemming from the belief that the government was hiding information from the voters until after the Sunday elections. This seems to have further contributed to the mobilization of young voters. The terrorist attacks, mobile phone communication, flash demonstrations, and the reporting of traditional media outlets did not change the voting preferences of a large number of citizens. Estimates suggest that only 4 percent of the electorate who had planned to vote for the PP changed their minds after the terrorist attacks and the flash demonstrations, and 2 percent decided to support the PP instead of the PSOE (Díez Nicolás 2004c; Michavila 2005). Rather, a small but critical segment of the electorate chose voting over abstaining.

Conclusion

In this chapter I have argued that the diffusion of mobile phone use appears to have important consequences for participation and democracy. Mobile

phones and SMS messages enable users to maintain immediate, uninter-
rupted, and unmediated communication with people in their social network. Research shows that this type of personal communication has the
greatest impact on political mobilization. Computer-mediated Internet use
is more difficult, and hence less widespread, than mobile phone use. Still,
both media have been used successfully to stage demonstrations and protests in various countries around the world. Mobile phone technology, however, is more conducive to unplanned, flash demonstrations, because, as was
the case in Spain (and in China and the Philippines), text messages circulate
very quickly within and across overlapping social networks of contacts, and
the mobilization can be synchronized in real time.

The Spanish general election of 2004 was a unique event occurring in
the wake of an unprecedented terrorist attack. Thus, one must be careful
about generalizations. Still, it clearly represents a case study in the impact
of new information technologies on political participation and electoral
outcomes. The impression, although not necessarily the reality, that the PP
government was withholding information or presenting it in a self-serving
way outraged a relatively small number of voters who, empowered with
mobile telephones, organized flash demonstrations in front of the ruling
party's headquarters during "reflection day." In addition to mobile phones,
traditional media like TV, radio, and newspapers further contributed to the
creation of a growing chorus of citizens who felt misled. Those who tend to
abstain from voting, for example, young and newly registered voters, had
one more reason to come to the polls, and they disproportionately favored
the opposition party. The bombings and subsequent demonstrations did not
change the political preferences of Spanish voters as much as they encouraged them to go to the voting booths to express their views.

A democratic polity needs to allow and facilitate the formation and
expression of the popular will, which presumably translates into electoral
and policy outcomes. But in the case of new technologies, especially the
Internet, there is an inequality in the people's ability to access and distribute information. This is not the case with mobile phones because of their
greater diffusion compared to the Internet. Moreover, mobile phones are
a favorite means of communication among the young (the age group most
likely to abstain from voting), and their use is equally widespread across
socioeconomic and educational strata.

The question remains, however, whether new technologies are good
for democracy or not. It has been argued that "if we assume that one of the
essential characteristics of democracy is deliberation" as opposed to rushed
decisions, then new technologies are not likely to contribute to democracy
because what they provide us with is "speed" (Barber 2000/2001, 4). But it
is possible that our vision of deliberative democracy needs rethinking in an

era when more and more people are being offered the opportunity (or are being empowered) to participate in the political process via new information technologies (Dahlgren 2005). In the Spanish general election of 2004, mobile technology contributed to the quality of democratic practices in the sense that SMS messages helped provide citizens with more information about the rapidly unfolding events related to the terrorist attacks, including the reaction by the government and the opposition party as well as the investigation and the protests during the day of reflection. It is also possible that they contributed to higher voter turnout, a most welcome outcome in countries in which an increasing proportion of citizens feel alienated from political life and tend to withdraw from the political process. While mobile telecommunications had largely positive effects in Spain, it is possible that in other circumstances the same kind of political mobilization may not enhance the quality of the democratic experience. Peaceful flash demonstrations have the potential of turning violent, thus changing voter preferences in ways that have little to do with the actual pluses and minuses of the voting alternatives available, or even discouraging citizens from exercising their right to vote in the midst of political turmoil.

Like any technology, mobile telecommunication can have a wide variety of effects on political behavior and practices, and the fact that it has been around for only a relatively short period of time makes it impossible to reach general conclusions about its ultimate impact. The case of the Spanish general election of 2004 illustrates that, whether for good or for bad, mobile phones have the potential of changing certain aspects of political behavior, including people's desire to participate in the political process.

NOTES

An earlier version of this chapter was published in *Representation* (2006) 42(2): 117–128. Reprinted by permission.

1. Unless otherwise noted the sources used for this section are the following national newspapers *El País* and *El Mundo*, first and second in readership, respectively. While newspapers in Spain are known for their political leanings (*El País* readers are more likely to vote for the PSOE and *El Mundo* readers are more likely to vote for the PP) both agree on the basic chronology of what transpired during the days immediately following the terrorist attacks. They disagree on whether the PP government purposely lied to the Spanish people. There have also been accusations by the PP and other newspapers that the PRISA media conglomerate, part owner of the newspaper *EL País*, the cable channel CANAL+ and the SER radio network was promoting the idea that the Aznar government was hiding information from the public. For more on the structure and ownership of Spanish media see Trenzado and Núñez (2001).

2. Largely because of Western Europe's adoption of the Global System for Mobile Communications (GSM) standard, the United States and Japan no longer are world leaders in mobile phone penetration.

3. *Aznar de rositas* is slang for "departing unscathed."

4. "Paz: Un Clic Puede Hacer la Diferencia," Interpress Service News Agency (accessed March 1, 2008, at www.ipsnoticias.net).

5. "Telediarios en Retroceso," *El País*, April 12, 2004.

6. Aznar had faced considerable opposition to some of his legislative programs; however, it was his support for the Iraq war and for Spain's participation in it that resulted in unprecedented mass opposition. Approximately 90 percent of Spanish people were against Aznar's Iraqi policy. Other members of the coalition that supported the war also faced opposition at home, but none to the degree of Spain, where opposition never wavered (Pew 2003, 24). For more on Aznar's foreign policy see Aznar 2004 and del Arenal 2003.

7. The only exception was Catalonia, where a coalition of the sister PSOE party in the region and left-wing nationalist parties took control of the government.

8. According to the authors, fluctuations of this range are quite unusual in most West European countries with exception of Portugal, France and the U.K.

9. Oficina del Censo Electoral, Instituto Nacional de Estadística: www.ine.es. According to an analysis provided by *El Mundo* and the polling firm Sigma Dos, out of the 3 million new PSOE votes, 1.5 million came from former absentee voters, more than 500,000 from new voters, almost 700,000 from the PP, and about 303,000 from the IU. See "Dos Millones de Nuevos Votantes Apoyaro a ZP," *EL Mundo*, March 19, 2004. See also Michavila 2005.

10. "Un Clic Puede Hacer la Diferencia."

11. "SMS, páginas Web y correo electrónico," www.junjan.org/Weblog/archives/2004_03 (accessed March 1, 2008).

REFERENCES

Anduiza, E., and M. Méndez. 2001. "Elecciones y Comportamiento Electoral, 1977–2000." In, *Política y Gobierno en España*, ed. M. Alcántara and A. Martínez. Valencia, Spain: Tirant Lo Blanch.

Aznar, J. 2004. *Ocho años de gobierno*. Barcelona, Spain: Editorial Planeta.

Barber, B. 2000/2001. "Which Technology for Which Democracy? Which Democracy for Which Technology?" *International Journal of Communication Law and Policy* 6 (4).

Best, S. and B. Krueger. 2005. "Analyzing the Representativeness of Internet Political Participation." *Political Behavior* 27 (2): 183–216.

Carveth, R., and S. Kretchmer. 2002. "Policy Options to Combat the Digital Divide in Western Europe." *Informing Science* 5 (3): 115–123.

CIS. 2004. *Postelectoral Elecciones Generales y Autonómicas de Andalucía, 2004*. Madrid: Centro de Investigaciones Sociólogicas, March–April.

CMT. 2002. *Informe Annual 2002*. Madrid: Comisión del Mercado de las Telecomunicaciones.

Dahlgren, M. 2005. "The Internet, Public Spheres and Political Communication." *Political Communication* 22 (2): 147–162

del Arenal, C. 2003. "EEUU y la Política Latinoamericana de España." *Política Exterior* 17:183–193.

Deutsche Bank. 2004. "GSM White Paper: Brilliant Past, Bright Future." *Global Equity Research*. February 18.

Díez Nicolás, J. 2004a. "Flashes February 2004." Madrid: Análisis Sociólogicos, Económicos y Políticos.

_____. 2004b. "Flashes March 2004." Madrid: Análisis Sociólogicos, Económicos y Políticos.

_____. 2004c. "Flashes April 2004." Madrid: Análisis Sociólogicos, Económicos y Políticos.

Di Justo, P. 2004. "Protests Powered by Cellphones." *New York Times*. September 9.

DiMaggio, P., E. Hargittai, W. Neuman, and J. Robinson. 2001. "Social Implications of the Internet." *Annual Review of Sociology* 27 (August) 307–336.

Fortunati, L. 2002 "The Mobile Phone: Towards New Categories and Social Relations." *Information, Communication and Society* 5 (4): 513–528.

Green, D. and A. Gerber. 2004. *Get Out the Vote: How to Increase Voter Turnout*. Washington, DC: Brookings Institution Press.

Guillén, M., and S. Suárez. 2001. "Developing the Internet: Entrepreneurship and Public Policy in Ireland, Singapore, Argentina, and Spain." *Telecommunications Policy* 25 (5): 349–371.

Havick, J. 2000. "The Impact of the Internet on a Television-Based Society." *Technology in Society* 22 (May): 273–287.

International Telecommunication Union [ITU[. 2001. *Telecommunication Indicators in the Eurostat Area 2001*. Geneva: International Telecommunication Union .

_____. n.d. *Free Indicators*. Geneva: International Telecommunication Union (accessed February 28, 2007, at www.itu.int/ITU-D/ict/statistics).

Ling, R. 2004. *The Mobile Connection: The Cell Phone's Impact on Society*. Amsterdam: Morgan Kaufman Publishers.

Michavila, N. 2005 "Guerra, Terrorismo, y Elecciones: Incidencia Electoral de los Atentados Islamitas en Madrid." Real Instituto el Cano, working paper no. 13/2005.

Nokia Networks. 2003. "A History of Third Generation Mobile 3G" March.

Noriega S., R., and G. Ariño Ortiz. 2004. "Liberalización y Competencia en el Sector de las Telecomunicaciones: Balance 1998–2003." In *Privatizaciones y Liberalizaciones en España: Balance y Resultados 1996–2003*, ed. G. Ariño Ortiz, 69–238. Granada: Editorial Comares.

Norris, P. 2001. *Digital Divide: Civic Engagement, Information Poverty and the Internet Worldwide*. New York: Cambridge University Press.

_____. 2002. *Democratic Phoenix: Reinventing Political Activism*. Cambridge: Cambridge University Press.

Papacharissi, Z. 2002. "The Virtual Sphere: The Internet as a Public Sphere." *New Media & Society* 4 (1): 9–27.

Pew Research Center for the People and the Press. 2003. *The Pew Global Attitudes Project*. Washington, DC: The Pew Research Center for the People and the Press.

Piven, D. 2002. "The Mobilization Calendar: The Time Dependent Effects of Personal Contact Turnout." *American Politics Research* 30 (3).

Pomfret, J. 2003. "Outbreak gave China's Hu an Opening." *Washington Post*. May 13 (accessed March 1, 2008, at http://pqasb.pqarchiver.com/washingtonpost/access /335419151.html?dids=335419151:335419151&FMT=ABS&FMTS=ABS:FT&date=May+13 %2C+2003&author=John+Pomfret&pub=The+Washington+Post&edition=&start page=A.01&desc=Outbreak+Gave+China%27s+Hu+an+Opening%3B+President+ Responded).

Putnam, R. 2000. *Bowling Alone*. New York: Simon and Schuster.

Rafael, V. 2003. "The Cell Phone and the Crowd." *Public Culture* 15 (3): 403.

Rheingold, H. 2002. *Smart Mobs: The Next Social Revolution*. Cambridge, MA: Perseus.

Smoreda, Z., and F. Thomas. n.d. "Uses of SMS (1) in Europe." *European Telecom Operator's Research Consortium* (accessed March 1, 2008, at *www.eurescom.de*).

Trenzado, M., and J. Núñez. 2001. "Los Medios de Comunicación." In *Política y Gobierno en España*, ed. M. Alcántara and A. Martínez, 493–531. Valencia, Spain: Tiran Lo Blanch.

US. Department of Commerce. n.d. "A Nation Online: How Americans are Expanding their Use of the Internet." Washington, DC: U.S. Department of Commerce (accessed March 1, 2008, at http://www.ntia.doc.gov/ntiahome/dn)..

Van Aelst, P., and S. Walgrave. 2002. "New Media, New Movements? The Role of the Internet in Shaping the 'Anti-Globalization' Movement." *Information, Communication and Society* 5 (4): 465–93.

Yardley, J. 2005. "A Hundred Cellphones Bloom, and Chinese Take to the Streets." *New York Times*. April 25 (accessed March 1, 2008, at http://www.nytimes.com/2005/04/25/international/asia/25china.html?scp=1&sq=A%20Hundred%20Cellphones%20Bloom,%20and%20Chinese%20Take%20to%20the%20Streets&st=cse).

PART FOUR

The Latest Developments

Blogs and Social Networking Sites

Two of the most recent technological innovations–blogs and social networking sites like MySpace, YouTube, and Facebook–may be the best things that have happened to campaigns, or the worst. These innovations offer campaigns unprecedented opportunities to interact with, attract, and mobilize like-minded individuals to their cause. But they also create tremendous challenges for campaigns in that they decentralize the communication and information dissemination processes and often render campaigns completely incapable of controlling the message.

The chapters that follow explore the role of blogs and social network sites in contemporary elections. The authors describe recent developments in relation to these innovations and offer some early assessments about the impact of social network sites on election outcomes. These observations and insights are hardly definitive given the relatively recent arrival onto the political scene of online social networks (and, to a lesser extent, blogs), but they represent evaluations of an important–perhaps the most important–campaign communications phenomenon.

12

Bloggers at the Gates

Ned Lamont, Blogs, and the Rise of Insurgent Candidates

KEVIN A. PIRCH

In January of 2005, President George W. Bush kissed Connecticut Democratic Senator Joe Lieberman on the cheek as he walked to the dais to deliver the State of the Union address. What was, in all likelihood, a gesture of friendship between two kindred spirits on the Iraq war turned into a symbol of distrust and animosity toward Lieberman for many Democrats in the Constitution State. In addition to his stance on the Iraq war some Democrats were upset with Lieberman for his vote to invoke cloture on the debate over U.S. Supreme Court nominee Samuel Alito and his view on the Terri Schiavo controversy, where Lieberman supported a Republican-sponsored bill to keep a brain-damaged woman alive by denying courts the ability to allow her husband to remove her feeding tube. These and other positions led some Democrats to become frustrated with the former vice presidential candidate. "The Kiss," as it became known, was the final straw for many Connecticut Democrats, who began a grassroots search for someone to replace Lieberman as the Democratic nominee.

However Lieberman was a two-term incumbent, a former vice-presidential nominee, and a presidential contender with long-standing ties to the state Democratic Party and its affiliated interest groups. Any challenger would be forced to compete against the entire power of the Connecticut Democratic Party, a substantial war chest of campaign money, and numerous powerful national political leaders, including former presidents and current governors and senators. Despite these long odds, a relative political novice was able to upset the Democratic establishment and win the party nomination in a hotly contested primary by using the Internet in general and blogs in particular to create a "virtual" party that served the same purposes as traditional political parties.

Blogs, which originally functioned as personal diaries that were shared with the public, have evolved into an online commons where people throughout the world can read and comment on other people's opinions about the news of the day, learn about events that might be underreported by other media outlets, or simply gossip about current events. As they have grown, some of these blogs have turned into powerful political forces in their own right, forcing campaigns and the news media to monitor them, occasionally interact with them, and respond to them. This has created a particular subset of politically savvy, motivated partisans who have been able to connect with each other in ways they never have before. With blogs, geographically isolated people can instantly communicate with others regardless of distance. This technology has changed the dynamics of political participation in the United States by providing a new vehicle for information to reach people, creating new opportunities for commentary and analysis of political events, and a new way for the public to perform surveillance on both government officials and the mainstream media. Blogs have allowed people to communicate about political issues outside the boundaries of traditional political parties; because of this, blogs have taken over many of the roles of political parties.

This chapter will describe the context of the 2006 Connecticut Democratic primary and explain how blogs were able to unite like-minded individuals, vet potential candidates for office, and support challenger Ned Lamont, a multimillionaire businessman who strongly opposed Lieberman's position on the Iraq war and other issues. Once Lamont announced his candidacy the blogs continued in the role of traditional political parties by raising money for his candidacy and providing much-needed logistical assistance for his campaign for the nomination. In all of these functions many liberal blogs served the same function as a traditional political party and built the support and infrastructure necessary to mount a successful modern senate campaign.

The Role of Traditional Political Parties

Since the inception of the study of American political parties, scholars have argued about the true purpose of the organizations. For some, political parties are seen as an attempt by an organized group to gain control of the government (Epstein 1967; Schattschneider 1942). Using this explanation of political parties, the actual policies the party and its candidates represent are not as critical as winning the election. This view of parties argues that positions and policies can, and should, be abandoned if they prevent a party from winning power in the government (Downs 1957). Others have said that the purpose of political parties is to pursue a like-minded cause regardless of the success in winning elections (Burke 1897). This idea is, in many ways, the opposite of the first explanation of party politics. In Burke's view, parties demand a greater loyalty to their core philosophies and ideas and it is better for the party to lose the election and maintain its principles than to win and sacrifice those principles. However, while the goals of both of these explanations of political parties differ—one seeking victory, the other seeking specific policy outcomes—both maintain the importance of political parties in campaigns and elections.

For the candidates, political parties perform a myriad of functions during the campaigns. In two seminal works, political scientists V. O. Key (1946) and E. E. Schattschneider (1942) argued that there were three essential functions for parties during campaigns: uniting like-minded individuals, vetting all possible candidates and finding the candidate that best represents those views, and raising money for the candidates and providing the logistical support for the candidates during the campaign.

Although never envisioned or trusted by the founding fathers, political parties have become an essential part of modern political life in the United States. One of the most important aspects of the modern American political party is to unite a group of like-minded individuals so they may more efficiently attempt to affect change in the public arena (Aldrich 1995). This is done in many ways. First, political parties are adept at aggregating and articulating the policy interests of a large group of people (Wattenberg 1994). In doing this, the parties take divergent stands on the salient issues and express those views to the electorate, thus allowing the people to align themselves with the parties that they feel more closely to (Budge 1983; Sundquist 1983). Even in the modern era, when much of the popular focus is on the candidates rather than the parties they represent, voters still focus on the positions of the parties and expect that the candidates will, generally, represent the positions of the party (Snyder and Ting 2002).

If the party is successful at winning the majority, it is charged with implementing the policies it campaigned on; if it is in the minority, the political party provides an outlet for those who disagree with the governing coalition. Because of this, even when they are not in power political parties are important for creating opposition and organizing dissent (Wattenberg 1994). This organized opposition allows society to function in a more stable manner by allowing disagreement in a political arena, rather than forcing people to protest the government with less institutionalized methods of resistance. Therefore, parties allow people to express their discontent with political outcomes through the political process rather than resorting to violence (Plattner 2001).

In addition to allowing a group of like-minded individuals to unite for a common purpose, traditional political parties also are adapt at finding the most able among the group to represent them in elections and serve in office (Wattenberg 1994). Although the methods of selecting these candidates have evolved over time—changing from party leaders selecting the ideal candidate to having the party masses choose the candidate—the end result has remained the same: it is virtually impossible to win high office in the United States without having the backing of a political party (Aldrich 1980; Patterson, Bice, and Pipkin 1999). Although the primary system has altered the nature of how parties select the candidates who represent the organiza- tion, it has not changed the power or influence that parties maintain over the nomination process. It is still very difficult for a maverick to gain the nomination of the party without the support of the elite (Pomper 1998). Additionally, the primary nominations also have encouraged party regulars to become more involved in the party system and created more incentives to become ideologically distinct.

Finally, parties are adept at helping candidates during the campaigns by raising money and providing the logistical assistance candidates need to run their races. Since the inception of the Federal Election Campaign Act (FECA) of 1972, candidates have been limited in the sources they may solicit money from and the amount of money they can receive from any single individual. Finding that there were numerous ways to take advantage of the original law and contribute more money to candidates, Congress replaced the FECA with the Bipartisan Campaign Reform Act of 2002 (BCRA). Among the changes to the legal structure for financing campaigns, BCRA increased the amount of money individuals could donate to a candidate and created a mechanism to link the limit to inflation; it also prohibited the use of soft money—that is, money that is used for party building activities and is therefore unregu- lated—and also allowed candidates who are running against independently wealthy candidates to solicit more funds. Because the Supreme Court ruled in *Buckley v. Valeo* (1974) that candidates can contribute as much of their own money as they want to their own campaign, this millionaire's amendment allows the non-self-financing candidate to solicit more money for individu- als than the law allows when there are no self-financed candidates.

Because of this and other legal changes that occurred in the post- Watergate era regarding financing campaigns, there have been competing and often contradictory forces at work in the nomination process. The limits the law has created on campaign finance contributions have also created a paradoxical relationship between the candidates and the political parties. In one way the candidates have become more dependent on the political party; since candidates are forbidden from taking more than $2,300 from any individual, the political parties have become a useful way to move money from willing contributors to the candidates. Contributors can donate money to the candidate and also to the party which could pass on money to the candidate in the form of contribution. However, at the same time, candidates are less dependent on the parties because they have their own money-raising networks, which focus on their own individual campaigns. Additionally because the parties' elites have abdicated much of the vetting and nominating of potential candidates to the electorate in the primaries, candidates have a greater incentive to focusing on the voters rather than the party (Lubenow 2001; Menefee-Libey 2000).

The 2006 Connecticut Primary

As a three-term incumbent, initially Lieberman did not expect he would have to face any significant challenge in the state primary, even if there were some Democrats who were not happy with his positions. However, in January 2006, Lamont announced that he would challenge Senator Lieberman in the primary. A multimillionaire grandson of a former chairman of J. P. Morgan, Lamont had made his own fortune in cable television and had supported Democrats, including Lieberman, in the past. Lamont said he had grown frustrated with Lieberman's support of the war in Iraq and his statements that questioning the war was an unpatriotic act (Cain 2006). After an unsuccessful attempt to find another candidate to challenge to senator, Lamont decided he would run for the nomination himself despite having limited political experience.

There is a two-stage process to gain access to the ballot as a Democrat in Connecticut. First, the state party hosts a convention of 1,607 delegates from Connecticut's towns and cities; they meet to nominate candidates for various elected offices including the U.S. Senate. In many cases the delegates might overwhelmingly support a particular candidate. However, any candidate who receives 15 percent or more of the delegates' votes may later in the summer force a primary election that is open to all registered Democrats. The candidate who wins the primary goes on to the general election.

At the convention Lamont was able to get the votes of 505 of the delegates, more than 30 percent of the total, thus forcing the primary election with Lieberman. Although Lieberman announced he was happy to win two-thirds of the convention delegates, many of his supporters expressed concern about the state's primary (Pazniokas and Keating 2006). Connecticut hosts its primary in early August when many people are away on vacation or are focused on other activities besides politics (Pazniokas and Keating 2006; Yardley 2006). Many of Lieberman's advisers feared there would be a small turnout for the election and that the turnout would be composed mainly of antiwar activists who would support Lamont (Yardley 2006). The party's nomination could then be captured by a fringe segment of the party while the majority failed to turn out and vote.

The state also allows independents to register as Democrats in the weeks leading up to the primary, and many of these unaffiliated voters chose to take part in the primary. While political prognosticators thought turnout in the primary would be light, thousands of new voters signed up to participate in the election. In total, approximately 14,000 people registered to vote in the primary and another 14,000 people switched their party affiliation to the Democratic Party before the primary election (Barry 2006). This included more than 5,000 who people changed their party affiliation to vote in the primary in the month of July, when televised debates between Lamont and Lieberman aired, according to the Connecticut secretary of state's office. Those people who came to the Democratic Party late and registered for the primary during the summer were more likely to be supporters of the challenger, with Lamont getting 62 percent of the vote for people who recently registered as Democrats (CBS News 2006). The conventional wisdom about a low turnout during a summer primary turned out to be incorrect: almost 280,000 people—slightly less then 50 percent of the eligible voters—voted in the primary, which Lamont won with 52 percent of the vote (Barry 2006).

Lamont's Virtual Party

While Lamont's personal wealth would have allowed him to fund his own election if he chose to and would have bought him a certain degree of legitimacy in any campaign, he also benefited tremendously from the online political community that had developed in recent years. This community of bloggers provided him with a virtual political party that would unite people who were opposed to Lieberman and bring them to his cause, provide a place to raise money, and create easier access to organizing these people for the logistical support his campaign needed. While the number of bloggers and sites that focus on politics is vast and ever expanding—including blogs written on both Lamont and Lieberman's official campaign Web sites, this study focused primarily on only a few major blogs that focus on national Democratic Party politics and Connecticut Democratic Party politics. Specifically, the blogs DailyKos.com and MyDD.com were examined to study the national view of the Connecticut Democratic Party primary; and MyLeftNutmeg.com and the nonpartisan ConnecticutLocalPolitics.net were examined to gauge the views of people who follow Connecticut politics. The national sites were chosen primarily because of their large audience and the large number of contributors who write about politics. Additionally, both of these blogs are influential among members of the Democratic Party base who follow blogs. The two state sites were chosen because of their coverage of the campaign. In examining these sites all of the posts and comments about Lieberman and the Connecticut Senate race between November 2005 and Election Day 2006 were studied to gauge the attitudes and positions of the Democratic Party's blogging community.

Uniting Like-Minded Individuals

Originally, the role of the blogs in uniting like-minded individuals did not center on supporting Lamont. Rather, the blogs served as a forum for those who opposed Lieberman's positions to commiserate about him. It was only later that the Internet turned into a place where people began to search actively for a challenger to the incumbent. Although in the national mainstream media the most prominent issue in the primary was Lieberman's stance on the war in Iraq, there were a wide variety of reasons why people both in Connecticut and the national Democratic Party were upset with Lieberman. This included his decision to not support a filibuster of Supreme Court nominee Samuel Alito, his position on the Schiavo controversy, and his support of a new bankruptcy law (Feldmann 2006; Yardley 2006). Many bloggers also were upset with Lieberman's positions on other social issues and his position on President Bush's proposal for Social Security reform (Kirkpatrick 2005). In many of these discussions on blogs it was not only Lieberman's positions on policies that upset the bloggers, but also the belief that he had betrayed the Democratic Party by appearing too close the Republicans (Kos 2005e). Some of these instances were well documented by the mainstream media, while others were more obscure.

A post on the blog DailyKos reported Lieberman was the only Democrat who attended a birthday dinner to honor National Review founder William Buckley (Kos 2005c). According to the story, Lieberman sat at the head table at the dinner with Rush Limbaugh and Buckley, which prompted many of the commentators on DailyKos to question Lieberman's loyalty to the Democratic Party. Although this occurred more than a year before Lieberman would face reelection, a sizable number of people were already beginning to debate whether Lieberman deserved to be reelected. For many of the national blogs, such as DailyKos and MyDD, the stories and their comments became almost exclusively dedicated to those who opposed Lieberman. Those who supported the senator were not literally shut out of the debate, but they were in the decided minority.

Among the posts, many participants expressed uncertainty if Lieberman was a true Democrat or if he was a neoconservative whose positions were more closely aligned with those of Bush (Kos 2005e). The most famous example of the perceived closeness between Lieberman and the Republicans was "The Kiss," between Bush and Lieberman during the State of the Union address. This incident merited 138 separate stories on DailyKos and more than 36,400 comments on the Web site. The general Democratic disgust about the event became shorthand on blogs for those who opposed Lieberman to describe all that they believed wrong with the senator. Many of those who posted comments on the Web sites perceived "The Kiss" as an endorsement of all of Bush's policies. Occurring during a speech that was dominated by Iraq, the embrace seemed to demonstrate Lieberman's overwhelming support for a leader who is roundly unpopular with the Democratic base.

While becoming a symbol of Bush and Lieberman's perceived relationship in blogs, "The Kiss" also found other avenues of exposure on the Internet. The video of "The Kiss" spread on sites such as YouTube, where many people turned it into satirical advertisements supporting Lieberman or as a rallying cry for Lamont's campaign. The likeness also was prominently displayed on many of the anti-Lieberman Web sites that emerged during 2005 and 2006, including DumpJoe.com. It also became a campaign symbol in more conventional campaign material as Lamont supporters created a giant papier-mâché float replicating the moment; the float traveled to many town parades during the summer months to rally the Lamont supporters and frustrate Lieberman's allies. The image also was printed on bumper stickers and buttons handed out by anti-Lieberman partisans (Kantrowitz 2006).

In addition to his perceived support of Republican policy, Lieberman also had upset some Connecticut Democrats by running for both the Senate and the vice presidency in 2000 (Kos 2005d). Lamont supporters felt that in doing this he was paying little attention to the state while he ran for national office, while others believed that he was putting himself before the party and should have dropped out of the Connecticut Senate race (Kos 2005b). Had Lieberman won the vice presidency, his seat would have been filled by an appointee named by the Republican governor: because the Senate was split 50–50, the balance of power could have hung in the balance of Lieberman's decision to run for both offices simultaneously. Additionally, for many of the bloggers who remained upset about the outcome of the 2000 presidential election, the display of warm affection between Lieberman and Bush represented a betrayal of that election, similar to their belief that Lieberman was much more cordial to Dick Cheney during the 2000 vice presidential debate than he was to Democrats who disagreed with him (Kos 2005a).

Finally, some Connecticut residents believed that Lieberman had gone "national" and was more interested in a national audience than the needs of the state (Pazniokas 2006a). Simply put, while the Iraq War was an important issue among Democratic primary voters in Connecticut it was not the only issue on which voters based their decisions. Among Lamont supporters 57 percent said the reason they were supporting the challenger did not have to do with the Iraq war; rather they believed it was time for a change in leadership, did not like Lieberman's personal attributes, or did not like his relationship with President Bush (CBS News 2006). Those who supported

Lieberman were more likely to do so because of his experience, personal qualities, or some reason other than Iraq, while only 6 percent of Democratic primary voters supported the senator because of his position on Iraq (CBS News 2006). Moreover, more than 70 percent of Connecticut Democrats disapproved of the Iraq War in the summer of 2006; however, almost 40 percent of those who disapproved of the war still supported Lieberman for other reasons (CBS News 2006). In short, for a host of reasons that generally fall under the rubric of discontent with a senator who did not follow the party line, Lieberman fell out of favor with many liberals who used blogs as a place to come together and vent their frustrations about his actions and obtain new information.

Finding the Challenger

Because of the anger with Lieberman, some of the participants in blogs believed that Connecticut Democrats should try to find someone to replace him in the primary. However, although many of the bloggers were united in their dislike of Lieberman, they were not all convinced it would be wise for the resources to be spent on challenging him. In many of the early discussions, in November and December of 2005, before a challenger could be found, numerous commentators believed challenging a Democrat, and a powerful, well-connected incumbent like Lieberman at that, would be a waste of resources (Kos 2005f). These bloggers complained that Lieberman was loyal to the Democratic cause on some important issues and that money going to challenge him could have been directed to other campaigns around the nation to defeat Republicans. However, although the liberal blogosphere was resoundingly anti-Lieberman—with comments on many of the posts running less than 1 percent in support of Lieberman, a steady debate ensued about the merits of using resources to defeat a Democrat. Chief among the complaints were that the partisan balance of the senate was already close and that money should be spent defeating vulnerable Republicans in other states (Kos 2005e). Some commentators also were concerned that having a three-way race between a Democrat, a possible independent candidate, and a Republican could cause an otherwise safe Democratic seat to be lost to a Republican, who could receive a bare plurality of votes (Kos 2005f). In these debates many commentators appeared to be strategically thoughtful about the implications of supporting a challenge to a powerful Democratic senator, the prospects of losing the seat, and whether the Democratic Party should be imposing ideological tests on its candidates, of if people who are more conservative should be allowed to represent it (Kos 2005f).

A consensus eventually emerged about challenging Lieberman. Initially, former governor Lowell Weicker was mentioned as a possible challenger to Lieberman. As early as September, 2005 DailyKos and local Connecticut political blogs, such as Connecticut Local Politics, reported on stories in the Connecticut newspapers that Weicker was considering running as an independent. This provided instant fodder for bloggers given the nature of the relationship: Lieberman defeated Weicker for his Senate seat in 1988 in a closely fought campaign. In that contest Lieberman took more conservative positions than the Republican Weicker. Defeated, Weicker left the Republican Party and was elected governor as an independent (Nichols 2005). Because Weicker had been an outspoken critic of the war in Iraq, left the Republican Party, and been elected as an independent governor, numerous bloggers expressed excitement and felt he would be able to defeat Lieberman in a three-way race (Kos 2005a). Many went so far as to start a "Draft Lowell Weicker" Web site.

During this time blogs took on the traditional party role of vetting the possible candidates to determine what types of contenders they would be and if they would share the same opinions as the blogging community. On this front, because of his past affiliation with the Republican Party, Weicker was met with caution on many of the national sites where commentators expressed skepticism that he would be sufficiently progressive. However, in what became an almost-real-time conversation between the discussants, commentators from Connecticut argued that he was adequately progressive, he had left the Republican Party, and he was a more outspoken critic of Bush than Lieberman had been (Kos 2005f). After Weicker announced he would not be running against Lieberman, Lamont's potential candidacy emerged again, and again the vetting process began to determine if he was capable of defeating Lieberman and had principles similar to those of the bloggers. Questions about Lamont centered on his wealth (he is a multimillionaire from Greenwich, a wealthy New York City suburb), his experience (he only political experience was serving on the Greenwich Town Council), and his previous support for Lieberman (Kos 2006a).

After learning who he was, many commentators began to support him enthusiastically and began strategizing about his campaign. Some believed his wealth and previous support for Lieberman would be an advantage in the campaign, arguing that he could be framed as a successful businessman who understood how to handle complicated problems (Kos 2006a). Additionally, his previous support of Lieberman would indicate he was not a member of the radical left, but was a moderate supporter who had become disenchanted with Lieberman's positions. In both of these instances the bloggers took up the role usually held by the party elites and the mass media by examining the qualifications of the potential candidates, their strengths and weaknesses, and how they might best be able to frame the candidates to the public at large. The blogs looked at both Lamont and Weicker not just as extensions of their own political viewpoints (although that was explored) but as people who would be able to succeed (Kos 2006a; Kos 2005a). In short, bloggers effectively worked as their own nominating committee and vetted the possible challengers for Lieberman—not only did they try to recruit Weicker and support Lamont, but they also explored and discounted other candidates, such as a movement to draft actress Amy Brenneman and attorney Ted Kennedy Jr. (Michak 2005)

Logistical and Financial Support

Once Lamont had announced his candidacy the blogs and Internet also took on another traditional party role by providing financial, logistical, and other support for his campaign. While there was a de facto nomination of Lamont in the blogs, where commentators rallied support to him, bloggers also worked to get the challenger official endorsements from other groups. Some bloggers put forth a movement to secure the endorsement of MoveOn.org for Lamont; they eventually did so by getting 85 percent of Connecticut MoveOn members to vote for Lamont when the state group asked who to endorse in the primary (BranfordBoy 2006). Lamont also received the endorsement of the political action committee Democracy for America, which was closely aligned with some liberal blogs. The de facto endorsement of the Lamont campaign by many liberal bloggers and the official endorsements that the blogs helped ensure allowed Lamont to receive a certain degree of legitimacy among the electorate at large and the mainstream media. It also helped create the foundation for his campaign and aided his ability to raise money and communicate with potential supporters.

Using tools pioneered by John McCain during the 2000 presidential primaries and used effectively by Howard Dean during the 2004 presidential primaries, Lamont was able to raise substantial amounts of money over the Internet (Trippi 2004). Although rich enough to self-fund his campaign, Lamont actively tried to raise money because he felt it would help demonstrate to the media and the public that he had support among the voters. There were multiple ways for supporters to give money to Lamont on the Internet. People could go to Lamont's official Web site and contribute money to his campaign by filling out a form similar to a traditional online purchase, or they could go to a host of other places to give him money indirectly. Three national blogs—DailyKos, MyDD, and the Swing State Project, formed a "netroots" Web site to allow people to support many progressive candidates, including Lamont; other bloggers, including FireDogLake, Down with Tyranny, and Crooks and Liars, created a Web site to allow people to raise money for their favorite candidates. These sites acted as a clearinghouse where people could select the candidates they wanted to support and contribute directly to those campaigns. People could also give money to MoveOn.org, Democracy for America, or other political action committees that endorsed Lamont.

This fund-raising effort on the Internet was very successful for Lamont. In the first forty-five days of his campaign he raised $350,000 from more than 4,500 online contributors (Pazniokas 2006b). This included $50,000 of unsolicited contributions he received via the Internet in three days after the Democratic convention that forced the primary. Among the consortium of bloggers who created sites as clearinghouses for funding candidates, Lamont raised $453,000 from more than 8,000 contributors ("ActBlue—Netroots Candidates" 2006).

Because of the legal limits on the amount of money that people can contribute to political campaigns, there were certain limits to the degree that individual bloggers could commit to the Lamont campaign. However, because the Internet provided a convenient and efficient way for people to donate money to political campaigns, many political blogs served the role of encouraging people to contribute money to certain candidates. Additionally, blogs also served as watchdogs who monitored the amount of money opposing candidates received and who was donating money to those candidates. As a means of encouraging readers to contribute to the Lamont campaign, Lamont supporters noted the amount of money Lieberman was raising, the fact that the majority of the money was coming from outside of Connecticut—which they construed as indicating that the senator was out of touch with the Constitution State—and that some of the money was being donated by Republicans and conservative groups (Kos 2006b).

Although Lamont was able to raise a sizable number of donations in small amounts, he supplied the majority of his own campaign contributions. In total for the 2006 Senate campaign, Lamont raised approximately $20.5 million, of which $3.5 million, or 17 percent of the total, came from individuals who contributed and the remainder Lamont personally contributed (FEC Candidate Summary Reports—Lamont 2006). While Lieberman raised about $20 million, of which 87 percent or $17.5 million came from individuals and the remainder came from political action committees (FEC Candidate Summary Reports—Lieberman 2007). This indicates that while Lamont was able to gain some contributions for individuals for his Senate race, he was not able to gain the financial support that Lieberman could among the public. However, although the means by which people contribute money to a candidate are not disclosed to the Federal Election Commission, it can be inferred from many news accounts that a significant portion—at least approximately 25 percent of all of Lamont's contributions—came from online sources.

One major factor explaining why Lamont was able to go from obscurity to defeating a two-term U.S. senator in a party primary was the vast personal financial resources that he was able to contribute to his own campaign. His personal fortune was not the only reason why he was able to defeat Lieberman, however. Lamont won because he and his supporters had been able to use the beneficial attributes of blogs to help create a statewide and national network of supporters in a period of months to help his campaign. This network of supporters was first united by dissatisfaction with Lieberman, rather than desire to support Lamont; however, once they coalesced around the challenger, liberal blogs performed much the same role as traditional political parties.

In creating the virtual infrastructure to support Lamont's candidacy, the blogs were able to unite a group of like-minded individuals around an opposition candidate, provide legitimacy to the campaign, and provide logistical and financial support to the candidate. By doing the jobs that are normally the purview of the political parties, the blogs were able to unite people who felt alienated from their party's elected official and deprive that official of the party's nomination.

Conclusions

To run a successful campaign in the United States, especially at the state level, candidates need a successful organization to support them and provide assistance. Throughout history, this has required a candidate to win the allegiance of the party machine and the leaders who control the organization. Since the party elite controlled the mechanism to raise money and contact the party members, any candidate who wanted to win the party's nomination needed the blessing of the party elite. Because of this, mounting an insurgent campaign at any level has been difficult under the best of circumstances. Candidates would need to be able to raise a substantial amount of money through relatively inefficient means: by soliciting money through the mail, phone calls, or dinners, all which require a substantial amount of time, money, or both. Additionally, this insurgent campaign would need to somehow get the word out to other partisans who might feel disaffected with the current regime. This would be taking place while the forces that controlled the party apparatus worked to discourage party members from supporting the insurgent candidate and encouraged loyalty to the party standard-bearer through a combination of threats and granting favors. In practice, this meant that insurgent campaigns rarely happened, and when they did the campaign needed to be conducted by a candidate with sufficient personal wealth to finance his or her own movement and enough name recognition to either have a personal base of support or be able to build a base of support quickly.

Although name recognition and money are still valuable resources to have in a campaign, the Internet has made these attributes less important than they have been in the past. Through blogs, Web pages, and e-mail, candidates are able to contact potential supporters at virtually no cost to the campaign and find support without the benefit of the party elite. Raising money, which once required a significant capital expense to form mailing lists, craft solicitation letters, and pay postage expenses—only to find that the vast majority of the correspondents were unanswered—has become much simpler through the Internet. Political campaigns can now use their own Web sites to solicit and accept contributions, and to communicate with their supporters they may create e-mail lists, which are cheaper and more efficient to use than traditional means of contact. In addition to fund-raising, candidates can tap into online political communities to find potential supporters and to learn about the issues that are most important to those participants. By appealing to these communities, a potential candidate can find a ready-made group of supporters who would be willing to provide financial support, logistical assistance, and, ultimately, votes.

The Internet has created the ability for people to become more active in party politics and has led to, at least in the case of the Connecticut Democratic Party, a more grassroots institution. Although he had the initial support of all the state's major elected officials, Lieberman was not able to use these endorsements to persuade the rank-and-file to continue to support him. Rather, the party's leadership followed the electorate's lead in switching their allegiance from Lieberman to Lamont. In a resounding rebuke to the state Democratic Party elite, the party members did what no one expected them to do: first, people registered to vote and changed their party affiliation in large numbers; then, during the middle of the summer, a record number of Democrats turned out to vote in a primary election; finally, these voters rejected the wishes of the party leaders and elected a novice political entrepreneur.

It can be dangerous to infer too much from a single case, but it appears that the Connecticut Democratic Senate primary of 2006 could have profound implications for both party politics and electoral participation in the United States. Although Lamont had a substantial amount of money to finance his own campaign, it is very hard to imagine him being able to create the infrastructure needed to run a campaign against a three-term incumbent senator in less than five months without the benefit of the Internet. It was the Internet, and especially many national and local blogs, such as DailyKos, firedoglake, myleftnutmeg, and Connecticut Bob, that had already built the necessary logistical support for an insurgent campaign against Lieberman, which Lamont was able to take advantage of. It appears that future primary challengers will have an easier time attacking, and possibly defeating, incumbent candidates because many of the advantages inherent in incumbency are rendered moot by the Internet. As long as the challenger is able to win the support of a portion of a political blogging community he or she will have access to a ready-made financial support system and a community of people willing to help the campaign.

NOTE

An earlier version of this chapter was published in *Social Science Computer Review* (2008) 26: 275–287. Reprinted by permission.

REFERENCES

ActBlue—Netroots Candidates. 2006 (accessed February 7, 2007, at http://www.actblue.com/page/netrootscandidates).

Aldrich, J. 1980. *Before the Convention*. Chicago: University of Chicago Press.

_____. 1995. *Why Parties? The Origin and Transformation of Political Parties in America*. Chicago: University of Chicago Press.

Barry, E. 2006. "Lieberman is Defeated; Connecticut Senator, Who Supports the War in Iraq, Vows to Run as an Independent Against Ned Lamont, an Antiwar Political Newcomer." *Los Angeles Times*. August 9, p. A1.

BranfordBoy. 2006. "MoveOn Announces Its Own Connecticut Primary May 25–26" (accessed February 7, 2007, at http://www.myleftnutmeg.com/showDiary.do?diaryId=1234).

Budge, I. a. D. J. F. 1983. *Explaining and Predicting Elections: Issue Effects and Party Strategies in Twenty-Three Democracies*. London: George Allen and Unwin.

Burke, E. 1897. *Works*. Vol. 1. London: G. Bell and Sons.

Cain, K. 2006. "The Kiss of Death." *GQ*. October.

CBS News. 2006. "The Connecticut Democratic Primary" (accessed May 5, 2007, at http://www.cbsnews.com/htdocs/CBSNews_polls/ctexitpoll.pdf).

Downs, A. 1957. *An Economic Theory of Democracy*. New York: Harper and Row.

Epstein, L. 1967. *Political Parties in Western Democracies*. New York: Praeger.

FEC Candidate Summary Reports—Lamont. 2006 (accessed May 9 ,2007, at http://herndon1.sdrdc.com/cgi-bin/cancomsrs/?_06+S6CT05066).

FEC Candidate Summary Reports—Lieberman. 2007 (accessed May 9, 2007, at http://herndon1.sdrdc.com/cgi-bin/cancomsrs/?_06+S8CT00022).

Feldmann, L. 2006. "In Connecticut Race, Insurgent Left Aims at Democratic Hawk." *Christian Science Monitor*. August 2, p. 01.

Kantrowitz, J. 2006. "Kiss Float Itinerary" (accessed February 7, 2007, at (http://www.myleftnutmeg.com/showDiary.do?diaryId=4009).

Key, V. O. 1946. *Political Parties and Pressure Groups*. New York: Thomas Y. Crowell.

Kirkpatrick, D. D. a. C. H. 2005. "On Social Security, Lieberman the Centrist Ruffles Democratic Feathers on the Left." *The New York Times*, 7 March, p. A 13.

Kos. 2005a. "CT-Sen: Weicker Ponders Lieberman Challenge" (accessed May 5, 2007, at http://www.dailykos.com/storyonly/2005/12/6/2133/53245).

_____. 2005b. "Lieberman's Home-Grown Problems" (accessed February 7, 2007, at: http://www.dailykos.com/storyonly/2005/4/11/2445/98304

_____. 2005c. "Lieberman Attends National Review Bash" (accessed February 7, 2007, at http://www.dailykos.com/storyonly/2005/10/9/21278/3010).

_____. 2005d. "Lieberman is All Alone" (accessed February 7, 2007, at http://www.dailykos.com/storyonly/2005/12/9/14530/5433).

_____. 2005e. "Lieberman vs. Democrats" (accessed February 7, 2007, at http://www.dailykos.com/storyonly/2005/3/17/15322/5717).

_____. 2005f. "Looking for a Lieberman Challenger" (accessed February 7, 2007, at
    http://www.dailykos.com/storyonly/2005/12/13/12539/627).

_____. 2006a. "CT-Sen: Is Lieberman Beatable?" (accessed February 7, 2007, at http://
    www.dailykos.com/storyonly/2006/1/18/151214/197).

_____. 2006b. "CT-Sen: Lobbyists Ponying Up" (accessed May 5, 2007).

Lubenow, G., ed. 2001. *A User's Guide to Campaign Finance Reform*. New York: Rowman
    and Littlefield.

Menefee-Libey, D. 2000. *The Triumph of Campaign-Centered Politics*. New York: Chatham
    House.

Michak, D. 2005. "Liberals Hunger for Challenger for Lieberman; Weicker, Actress, Ken-
    nedy All in Speculation." *Manchester (Connecticut) Journal Inquirer*. December 9.

Nichols, J. 2005. "Run, Lowell, Run." *The Nation* (accessed February 7, 2007, at http://
    www.thenation.com/blogs/thebeat?pid=42792).

Patterson, K. D., A. A. Bice, and E. Pipkin. 1999. "Political Parties, Candidates, and Presi-
    dential Campaigns: 1952–1996." *Presidential Studies Quarterly* 29 (1): 26–39.

Pazniokas, M. 2006a. "Lamont Campaign Builds Step by Step; Candidate Makes Case as
    the Anti-Lieberman." *Hartford Courant*. March 13, p. A1.

———. 2006b. "Small Donors Aid Lamont." Hartford Courant. May 25, p. B11.

Pazniokas, M., and C. Keating. 2006. "Lamont Forces Primary; Democratic State Con-
    vention; As Lieberman Wins 2–1, His Challenger Celebrates." *Hartford Courant*. May
    20, p. A1.

Plattner, M. 2001. "The Trouble with Parties." *The Public Interest* 143:27–45.

Pomper, G. 1998. "The Alleged Decline of American Parties." In *Politicians and Party Poli-
    tics*, ed. J. Geer, 1:14–39. Baltimore, MD: The Johns Hopkins University Press.

Schattschneider, E. E. 1942. *Party Government*. New York: Holt, Rinehart and Winston.

Snyder, J. M. Jr., and M. Ting M. 2002. "An Informational Rationale for Political Parties."
    American Journal of Political Science, 46 (1): 90.

Sundquist, J. 1983. *Dynamics of the Party System: Alignment and Realignment of Political
    Parties in the United States*. Rev. ed. Washington, DC: Brookings Institution.

Trippi, J. 2004. *The Revolution Will Not Be Televised: Democracy, The Internet, and the Over-
    throw of Everything*. New York: Regan Books.

Wattenberg, M. P. 1994. *The Decline of American Political Parties 1952–1992*. Cambridge:
    Harvard University Press.

Yardley, W. 2006. "Lieberman's Support for War Leaves Him Embattled on Left." *New
    York Times*. May 19, p. B1.

13

Voters, MySpace, and YouTube

The Impact of Alternative Communication Channels

VASSIA GUEORGUIEVA

YouTube and MySpace, two social networking Web sites, featured prominently in the discourse of how technology affected elections in 2006. Social
networking sites have rapidly transformed from a niche to a mass phenomenon. Furthermore, a substantial segment of the U.S. voting age population
is using YouTube and MySpace, which make the sites relevant and important for inclusion in campaign strategies. During the 2006 election cycle,
MySpace made the news after it launched a voter registration drive for
that election, and YouTube was widely covered in the media after Senator
George Allen was caught on tape calling a college student of Indian descent
a "macaca" and the video was "tubed," causing an immediate media scandal
and quickly becoming one of YouTube's most viewed. These are just two
examples of how MySpace and YouTube have impacted election campaigns
in simple but significant ways. These sites have increased both the potential for candidate exposure at low or no cost and the ability of campaigns to
reach out to the public for campaign contributions and volunteers. In addition, they have also provided lesser-known candidates with a viable outlet
to communicate their message to voters, which is particularly significant
for local elections with incumbent participation. In conjunction with these
benefits, YouTube and MySpace have also posed a new set of challenges to
campaign staff, the most important of which is the reduced level of control that campaigns have over the candidate's image, which is of critical
importance to election outcomes. This chapter will discuss these benefits
and challenges and the impact of YouTube and MySpace on the 2006 and
future election campaigns in light of who uses these two sites and how they
use them.

Technology and Elections

The impact of the Internet on the conduct of election campaigns has been an issue of great interest in the past decade. The ways in which the Internet has affected campaigns have ranged from the use of candidate Web sites in 1996, e-mail in 1998 (the Jesse Ventura campaign), online fund-raising in 2000 (the John McCain campaign), blogs in 2003 and 2004 (the Howard Dean campaign), net-organized house parties in 2004 (the Bush-Cheney campaign), and social networking sites such as YouTube and MySpace in 2006 (Cornfield and Rainie 2006).

Previous research on the use of the Internet as a tool to promote and facilitate political participation has been conducted by Bimber (1998) and later by Bimber and Davis (2003), and the success of online social networks has attracted the attention of both the media (for example, Newitz 2003; Arrison 2004; Leonard 2004; Black 2004; Sege 2005) and researchers. The latter have focused on the existing literature on social network theory (for example, Milgram 1967; Milgram 1977; Watts 2003) to discuss its online version. Hence, studies have focused on issues of trust and intimacy in online networking (Boyd 2003); participants' strategic representation of their selves to others (Donath and Boyd 2004; Boyd 2004); and on harvesting online social network profiles to obtain a distributed recommender system (Liu and Maes 2005). No research has been conducted on the use and impact of online social networks on election campaigns, however, primarily because this application has just surfaced during the 2006 election cycle.

Research on the impact of social networking sites on the electoral process is timely since Americans are turning more and more to the Internet as a source for political news. While TV is the primary source for political news for an average of 71 percent of Americans, about 15 percent of all American adults said the Internet was their primary source for campaign news during the 2006 election, up from 7 percent in the mid-term election of 2002 and close to the 18 percent of Americans who said they relied on the Internet as their primary source of information during the 2004 presidential campaign cycle. In 1996, this figure was a mere 6 percent. Furthermore, about 25 percent of all Americans said they got information online about the 2006 elections and 10 percent of Americans said they exchanged e-mails about the candidates. Overall, about 31 percent of all adult Americans were online during the 2006 campaign season gathering information and exchanging views via e-mail and they constitute more than 60 million people, or a considerable portion of the US electorate (Rainie and Horrigan 2007).

Simultaneously with this trend, a small yet growing subset of people going online have turned to sources other than the mainstream media for political information. The Pew Center reported that about 9 percent of

Internet users said they read political blogs "frequently" or "sometimes" during the 2004 campaign (Rainie 2005). Traffic on blogs and other political sites skyrocketed on Election Day in 2004. For example, the Drudge Report, a blog maintained by Matt Drudge since 1994 with links to stories from U.S. and international mainstream media about politics and current events, had about 1 million visitors, or around 30,000 more than the New York Times on the Web (Walker 2004). In February 2005, 15 percent of Internet users and 12 percent of Americans reported that they read political blogs at least a few times a month (Saad 2005).

It is in this environment of increased use of Internet services, and of the expansion of broadband Internet access—a higher data-transmission rate Internet connection than dial-up—throughout the United States, that MySpace and YouTube have developed.[1] Both are social networking sites, but they provide different services. Social networking sites have "moved from niche phenomenon to mass adoption" (Gross and Acquisti 2005). The concept dates back to the 1960s, but its implementation was only made possible with the advent and growth of the Internet (Gross and Acquisti 2005).

MySpace and YouTube provide different services. MySpace, created in 2003, provides a place for personal profiles, blogs, and groups, as well as photo, music, and video sharing. It is one of the most popular sites on the Internet, with more than 150 million user profiles, a monthly visitor count of 54 million, and an annual growth rate of 367 percent from 2005 to 2006 (Nielsen//NetRatings 2006). It is also the leading Web site in terms of user loyalty. YouTube is a video-sharing site created in February 2005. YouTube users can create user profiles where they upload video content. They can also search, watch and leave comments on other videos and subscribe to the videos of other users. YouTube has a tagging system that allows users to add keywords ("tags") associated with the video, thus enabling keyword-based searches. The site delivers more than 100 million videos every day and has 65,000 new videos uploaded daily (Reuters 2006). YouTube videos accounted for 60 percent of all videos watched online in July 2006 and had nearly 20 million unique users per month (Reuters 2006).

Although MySpace and YouTube provide different services, they have several things in common: the extraordinary speed with which they became popular and the fact that they are representative of the next Internet generation, which is free and user-driven, i.e. users contribute as much as they consume (Boutin 2006).

Use of YouTube and MySpace during the 2006 Elections Cycle

The user-driven nature of social networking sites such as YouTube and MySpace is one of the factors that generates the importance of these sites for election campaigns. However, two other factors—how the sites are used for election campaigns and the demographic composition of their users—play an important role as well

User Demographics

Defining the demographic characteristics of the users of both these sites presents some challenges, given that social networking and user-driven environments pose the same metric problem: demographic data is as accurate as users want it to be and we therefore rely on users reporting their true demographic data. There are very few stimuli, however, for users not to report their accurate demographic data, since neither site places restrictions on age groups that can use them. YouTube has possibly the only stimulus for misreporting of personal data, which is that certain videos might be flagged as inappropriate for users under eighteen, in which case if minors want to watch these clips they have to misreport their age.

A substantial segment of the U.S. voting age population is using You-Tube and MySpace. User data shows that about half or more of YouTube's users are thirty-five or older. Several studies, using different methodologies and conducted between May and August 2006, found that between 48 percent and 65 percent of YouTube's U.S. users were thirty-five to sixty-four years old: comScore found that 48 percent of users were between thirty-five and sixty-four and Quantcast found that 65 percent of users were in that age range (Reimer 2006). MySpace's user demographic data also shows that half of its United States users (51.6 percent) are thirty-five or older (com-Score Media Metrix 2006). It is interesting to note, however, that MySpace's age demographic has shifted. The most significant shift occurred among teens aged twelve through seventeen, who accounted for 24.7 percent of the MySpace audience in August 2005 but in August 2006 represented about 11.9 percent (comScore Media Metrix 2006). Also, while in August 2005 the percentage of adult (age eighteen and above) users was about 69.5 percent, in August 2006 it was 86.4 percent (comScore Media Metrix 2006). This was mainly due to increases in the percentage of users in the twenty-five to thirty-four category (a 6.2 percentage point increase) and an increase in the percentage of users in the thirty-five to fifty-four category (a 8.2 percentage point increase).

The users' demographic data suggest several conclusions with significant consequences for campaign strategists and for candidates: as social networking has become more mainstream, it has gained an appeal across generations. It also suggests that both venues are often described in the media as catering mostly to young audiences (Lizza 2006; Jesdanun 2006), this is a misconception based on the assumption that their services do not appeal to other age groups (Jesdanun 2006). In summary, the user demographics data show that a substantial segment of the voting age population is using both YouTube and MySpace and can be reached there by candidates and their campaign ads.

In addition, the thirty-five and older segment of the U.S. population, which constitutes about half or more of the users of MySpace and YouTube, is also more politically active than the younger voting age population: during the 2004 elections, the average turnout for the thirty-five and older segment was about 70 percent, about twenty percentage points higher than the average for the eighteen to twenty-four and twenty-five to thirty-four age groups (Holder 2006). Hence, the sites are a promising venue where this politically active segment can be targeted by campaigns.

Use in the 2006 Election Campaign Cycle and Beyond

Both YouTube and MySpace became the focus of the media's and the public's attention during the 2006 election campaign cycle and were generally portrayed as the new technology fad that would affect election campaigns (Dickinson 2006; Fairbanks 2006; Keen 2006; Kiley 2006; Lizza 2006; Miller 2006). Their use in the 2006 elections demonstrated the benefits and potential they have for political advertising, fund-raising, and volunteer recruitment as well as the challenges they pose to campaigns' ability to control the candidate's image and message in these two venues, where content is user-generated and still unregulated.

YouTube

YouTube impacts several critical areas in the planning and execution of election campaigns: access to voters, advertising, fund-raising, and budget. The ability of campaigns to access voters through YouTube is potentially unlimited. "A democracy is a political system that rewards communications power" (Bryant 1995, 85), and the communications power that YouTube has is hard to overestimate. The site increased the ability of campaigns to use videos as a political advertising tool, and those videos can achieve broad dissemination via the Internet. Campaigns used videos in the past, but the practice of hiring staff to follow and film opponents has been further fueled by the advent of broadband Internet and video-sharing Web sites, which are user-friendly and have changed the use cycle by allowing the videos to be uploaded and circulated more rapidly. And, as noted earlier, the site's user demographics show that a substantial segment of the voting age population is using YouTube and can be reached there through video clips.

This communication power of YouTube was alluded to on several occasions during the 2006 cycle, when it generated controversy about the candidates by offering an uncensored look at their speeches on the election trail (New ScientistTech 2006). The effect of the videos was further augmented by the fact that the stories were picked up by the mainstream media. This is what happened to Senator George Allen, Republican from Virginia, who was caught on camera by one of his opponents' supporters using the racial slur "macaca." The video was "tubed," causing an immediate media scandal and becoming one of YouTube's most viewed. The incident was followed by a series of public apologies and media appearances by Allen. Similarly, Conrad Burns, a Republican senator from Montana, was also in the media spotlight for videos on YouTube that showed him dozing off at a bill hearing, joking about the legal status of the "nice little Guatemalan man" who works at his house, and a clip in which he warns constituents about a faceless terrorist enemy who is a "taxi driver in the daytime but a killer at night." These videos were recorded by Montana Democratic Party staffer Kevin O'Brien, who was hired to follow Burns around his public appearances and film them. Subsequently, the content of the tapes was used for press releases and YouTube videos (Johnson 2006). This was not the first time that Burns was filmed on the campaign trail. During the 2000 race against Brian Schweitzer, cameraman Matt McKenna was paid to follow Burns. The Burns campaign also occasionally filmed Burns's Democratic opponent in 2006, Jon Tester, and recorded all Democratic primary debates, but it did not have a person devoted to that activity as the Democratic campaign did (Johnson 2006).

Other election campaigns that were featured on YouTube and provide further testimony of the communication power of this site were Connecticut's, Minnesota's and Missouri's. YouTube hurt Senator Joseph I. Lieberman, who was defeated by Ned Lamont in Connecticut's Democratic primary. Pro-Lamont bloggers frequently posted flattering interviews with their candidate on YouTube and unflattering video of Senator Lieberman. The Lamont campaign even hired a staffer to coordinate the activities of the bloggers and video bloggers. Users in Minnesota posted critical clips of Democratic Senate candidate Amy Klobuchar and her Republican opponent, Mark Kennedy. In Missouri, several videos critical of Republican Senator Jim Talent were posted on YouTube by a Democratic strategist.

Overall, there is no confirmation that there was an orchestrated effort by both parties to use YouTube in 2006. However, several Democratic campaign ads and news clips favorable to party candidates were posted there. In turn, Brian Walton, the National Republican Senatorial Committee spokesman, said the party had not made a specific effort to use YouTube (Associated Press 2006); perhaps in consequence of this Republicans had fewer postings on the site than Democrats during the 2006 election cycle.

In addition to its potential as a an alternative political advertising tool to TV and radio, YouTube provides free and broad dissemination of campaign messages and ads, thus impacting the campaign budget. In 2006,

TABLE 13.1

Campaign Spending by Media
Outlet, 2002–2006 (in millions)

Media outlet	2002	2004	2006
Broadcast TV	$912	$1,450	$1,578
Direct mail	$335	$648	$707
Radio	$155	$175	$256
PR/promo	$128	$43	$254
Cable	$35	$103	$144
Newspaper	$34	$58	$104
Outdoor	$25	$34	$55
Online	$5	$29	$40
Other	$1	$2	$2
Total	$1,630	$2,742	$3,140

Source: PQ Media.

candidates and activists spent a total of $3.1 billion on political advertising, about twice as much as they had spent just four years before. Given that the site lets candidates reshow TV spots they have already produced without the expense of broadcast airtime, and considering the $1.6 billion spent to broadcast ads on TV in 2006 (see table 13.1), YouTube offers a cost-effective alternative way to get the campaign message across. Its nearly twenty million unique users per month are also a considerable audience.

By providing low- or no-cost access to voters, YouTube also allowed lesser-known candidates to disseminate their political platforms during the 2006 election cycle. This is particularly important in elections with incumbents running for office, who might have the advantage of better access to campaign financing and the media because of their incumbent status. For example, the state assembly race in New York had incumbent David Townsend running against a tech-savvy newcomer, Dave Gordon. Gordon's thirty-second spot cost $350 to make and absolutely nothing to post online.

YouTube also has potential as a fund-raising tool. The Internet provides a way for campaigns to solicit funds from more people and makes giving more convenient. In 2004, John Kerry raised $80 million in online contributions for his bid for the presidency. In addition, in 2004, about 5 percent of small political donors and 2 percent of large political donors said online videos prompted them to make their first contribution (Institute for Politics, Democracy and the Internet 2006a). In addition, more than half of the Democratic contributors and a quarter of Republican donors in 2004 made at least one online donation; in 2000, online donors were almost nonexistent. Furthermore, an analysis of response patterns to more than 300 online advertising campaigns running June to September 2006 showed that video ads generate at least twice the response (measured by clicks) as standard image (JPG or GIF) ads (DoubleClick 2007). Hence, while there are no accounts of YouTube having been used for fund-raising in the 2006 cycle, this role is worth considering for future election campaigns.

MySpace

MySpace also featured prominently in the 2006 campaign, although some-what differently. It was used primarily as a tool to promote voter registra-tion, recruit campaign volunteers, and achieve more public exposure for candidates.

One of the ways in which MySpace impacted the 2006 election was by promoting voter registration among its users. In partnership with the non-partisan group Declare Yourself, MySpace began running voter registration ads and giving members tools such as "I Registered To Vote On MySpace" badges to place on their personal profile pages. Members wishing to register were redirected to a Web site where they entered their state and zip code, after which a PDF file was generated for them to print out and send to their state election officials. Although no data are available about the proportion of registered voters who used MySpace to submit their voter registration forms, the site clearly provides an additional outreach channel for voter registration.

MySpace was also successfully used to recruit campaign volunteers. For example, in a Maryland election for state comptroller against a two-term incumbent, Peter Franchot's campaign recruited 80 percent of its volunteers online at MySpace and Facebook. Those volunteers made 15,000 phone calls and dropped 50,000 pieces of campaign literature, which helped Franchot win the September 2006 primary.

Like YouTube, MySpace provides a platform for political candidates to get their messages across to a substantial voting age population segment and at low or no cost. The demographic data for MySpace users shows that 85 percent are of voting age. In addition, MySpace users eighteen and older are three times more likely to interact online with a public official or candidate, 42 percent more likely to watch politically related online video, 35 percent more likely to research politics online, and 44 percent more likely to listen to political audio online (O'Malley 2007), which suggest that if campaigns want to reach these voters, targeting social networking sites like MySpace should be a crucial part of the election campaign strategy. During the 2006 elections cycle, this fact did not go unnoticed by Democratic and Republican campaigns: pages were set up for candidates from both parties, and each had more than 50,000 "friends" in September 2006 (Romano 2006). Some candidates, like Democratic gubernatorial candidate Ted Strickland of Ohio, even integrated YouTube videos in their profiles.

MySpace, like YouTube, also has potential for fund-raising. Chuck Poochigian, a Republican state senator from Fresno who ran for California attorney general, joined MySpace in early August 2006, and within two months the number of online donations to his campaign jumped more than 50 percent (Loveley 2006). Recognizing this potential, MySpace has launched a customized, viral fund-raising feature for the profiles of the presidential candidates for 2008.

During the 2006 election cycle, both MySpace and YouTube showed that they had substantial benefits for election campaigns; these benefits include increasing access to voters; disseminating campaign ads and messages for free or at a low cost; providing a platform for lesser-known candidates; fostering voter registration; increasing fund-raising opportunities; and facilitating volunteer recruitment. Some of those uses were not fully explored in 2006, primarily because both sites had only been set up recently. The use of these two social networking sites also presents some challenges that need to be addressed, particularly in light of the general expectation that the 2008 elections will rely much more heavily on the services that YouTube and MySpace offer.

The Challenges of YouTube and MySpace

The advent of YouTube changed the way politicians communicate with voters. Political analysts predict that YouTube will force candidates to be more natural, direct, and honest (Lizza 2006), since they might be filmed anywhere and anytime, and video can very easily be uploaded and widely distributed. YouTube's impact would also restrict the candidate's ability to test campaign messages from place to place in order to refine them, as was possible eighty years ago, and candidates would have to be prepared and camera-ready before they go on the campaign trail, rather than be a work in progress (Lizza 2006).

Both YouTube and MySpace challenge the ability of election campaign strategists to deliver a clear and consistent message and image of candidates. These sites weaken the level of control that campaigns have over the candidate's image and message since anybody, both supporters and opponents, can post a video and/or create a page on behalf of the candidates because of

the user-driven content of social networking sites. In many campaigns during the 2006 election, volunteers created MySpace profiles and/or YouTube
accounts, generally without the knowledge of the candidate. The reaction of
some campaigns, fearing an inability to deliver a unified message and lacking staff to monitor such sites, was to seek the removal of the profiles and
accounts (CBS News 2006). YouTube's impact on professional journalism is
similar as it gives the power to shape popular perception of candidates to
anybody with a PC and an Internet connection.

There are also other challenges to utilizing YouTube and MySpace for
election campaigns. Both have an element of self-selection: the people who
use them for looking up political campaign videos or join MySpace political networks have already been motivated to do so. Also, to fully utilize the
power of video streaming, campaigns still have to get the right people to
enter the right search terms and view the right videos at the right times
(Cornfield 2006). Furthermore, MySpace has a very loosely segmented audience, and proactively addressing large numbers of individual activists who
share one particular concern or demographic is difficult (Goldsmith 2006);
this also applies to YouTube.

Both YouTube and MySpace have limited functions and need to be used
in conjunction with other strategies. MySpace pages are not sites; they are
just a single page and there is no mechanism to engage visitors into opting
for e-mail list development or to provide them with comprehensive content
so these activities would be carried out at a candidate's Web page, to which
MySpace visitors would need to be redirected (Goldsmith 2006). In turn,
YouTube hosts user profiles and their video clips and allows users to subscribe to other user's clips. However, like MySpace, comprehensive content
would need to be provided elsewhere, so profiles would redirect visitors to
a candidate's Web site.

These challenges underline the importance of blended networking, or
incorporating online and offline networking, which has been emphasized
by experts (Institute for Politics, Democracy and the Internet 2006b). For
example, MySpace profiles can be used to recruit supporters who talk online
and publish content, such as blog entries or Web videos, to volunteer as
door-to-door canvassers.

The use of YouTube and MySpace could potentially be impacted by
federal regulation on political advertising. Currently, Web-only ads, or ads
circulated on a candidate's Web site and/or via e-mail, are not subject to the
Bipartisan Campaign Reform Act (BCRA) of 2002, which explicitly addresses
the scope of broadcast advertising in political campaigns. However, Web-
first ads, or ads broadcast on both the Internet and television, are subject to
the BCRA regulations. It remains to be seen whether the BCRA regulations
will be extended to Web-only ads in future election cycles.

Future Prospects

Considering the potential of YouTube and MySpace for increasing the voters' exposure to campaign ads at little or no cost, their applicability for fund-raising and recruiting volunteers, and their ability to provide lesser-known candidates with public exposure, these two social networking sites promise to be essential elements for political campaigns even in light of any challenges that may be presented now or in the future.

Online campaign strategists are predicting an explosion of video sharing during the future election cycles that will require campaigns to add online video experts to their staffs. During the 2006 election, many of the bigger campaigns already had Internet strategists, either on staff or as consultants, to maintain online communications, contact bloggers, and monitor social networking sites (Greenfield 2007). Strategists also predict that bigger campaigns will face hundreds of rogue postings each month, which would require a strategy for monitoring them and deciding how to respond. Critical elements in the responses would be to have general videos prepared during the slower season, which could be quickly edited and used as rebuttals; to post a response rapidly; to find teams of online supporters to collect, produce, and spread the video that the campaign wants others to see; and to help fight unfavorable postings through content ratings (Greenfield 2007). Recognizing the potential of social networking sites, some candidates have even created their own social networking sites. For example, Barack Obama's social networking site allows users to help him fund-raise, network with other supporters, invite friends to join the site, start and/or join groups, and find and/or host events.

The impact of the online social networks on the 2008 election cycle is already being felt: Democrats Hillary Clinton, Barack Obama, Joe Biden, and John Edwards as well as Republican Sam Brownback announced their runs for the White House not in network-news interviews but in their own online videos (Jarvis 2007). Within the first forty-eight hours after the Edwards video was released, fifty thousand people had already seen it (Cillizza and Balz 2007). For the 2008 presidential election, YouTube also set up a special feature called You Choose, a subsite dedicated to campaign-related videos. Similarly, MySpace introduced a portal—The Impact Channel—featuring presidential candidate-created profiles, voter-registration tools, job listings, videos, "friends" pages, and other political content.

In February 2007, a new Web site called techPresident was created to monitor and report on how technology and the Internet are being incorporated by candidates in the 2008 presidential campaign (see table 13.2). Table 13.2 shows the number of views that each candidate with a presence on You-Tube's You Choose channel has and the number of friends that Democratic

TABLE 13.2

MySpace and YouTube Use for the 2008
Election Cycle as of April 30, 2007

MySpace Friends

Democrats		Republicans	
	Number of friends		*Number of friends*
Obama	161,720	McCain	20,172
Clinton	41,869	Romney	11,971
Edwards	27,481	Paul	8,211
Kucinich	10,279	Brownback	4,628
Richardson	9,699	Giuliani	2,999
Biden	5,634	Hunter	2,961
Dodd	3,752	Tancredo	1,321
Gravel	2	Huckabee	1,045

YouTube Statistics

Democrats		Republicans	
	Number of views		*Number of views*
Obama	2,791,315	Romney	582,016
Edwards	517,785	McCain	304,388
Clinton	128,170	Giuliani	72,363
Kucinich	36,218	Paul	55,522
Biden	29,316	Hunter	7,744
Richardson	29,180		
Dodd	9,722		

Source: TechPresident, April 30, 2007.

and Republican candidates have on their MySpace pages. Although the percentage increases in views and new friends vary substantially across candidates, they are nevertheless indicative of the intense level of engagement that users of MySpace and YouTube have with the political ads and messages on these sites in preparation for the 2008 election. All these developments suggest that while in 2006 having a presence in social networking sites was a tangential outreach effort for election campaigns, in 2008 it is going to be a necessity.

NOTE

An earlier version of this chapter was published in *Social Science Computer Review* (2008) 26: 288–300. Reprinted by permission.

I. By August 2006, 75 percent of U.S. Internet users had broadband access at home, compared with 51 percent two years earlier, according to Nielsen//NetRatings.

REFERENCES

Arrison, S. 2004. "Is Friendster the New TIA?" *TechCentralStation* (accessed November 12, 2006, at http://www.techcentralstation.com).

Bimber, B. 1998. "The Internet and Political Mobilization: Research Note on the 1996 Election Season." *Social Science Computer Review* 16 (4): 391–401.

Bimber, B., and R. Davis. 2003. *Campaigning Online: The Internet in U.S. Elections.* New York: Oxford University Press.

Black, J. 2004. The Perils and Promise of Online Schmoozing. *BusinessWeek Online.* February 20 (accessed November 12, 2006, at http://www.businessweek.com/technology/content/feb2004/tc20040220_3260_tc073.htm).

Boutin, P. 2006. "A Grand Unified Theory of YouTube and MySpace: Point-and-Click Sites That Don't Tell You What to Do." *Slate.* April 28 (accessed November 12, 2006, at http://www.slate.com/id/2140635).

Boyd, D. 2003. "Reflections on Friendster, Trust and Intimacy." Paper presented at Intimate (Ubiquitous) Computing Workshop—Ubicomp 2003, October 12–15, Seattle, Washington.

Boyd, D. 2004. "Friendster and Publicly Articulated Social Networking." Paper presented at Conference on Human Factors and Computing Systems (CHI 2004), April 24–29, Vienna, Austria.

Bryant, J. 1995. "Paid Media Advertising." In *Campaigns and Elections American Style*, ed. J. Thurber and C. Nelson. Boulder, CO: Westview Press.

CBS News. 2006. "Candidates Flock to MySpace, YouTube: Campaigns Turn to Social-Networking, Video-Sharing Sites to Appeal to Youth." August 17 (accessed December 12, 2006, at http://www.cbsnews.com/stories/2006/08/17/politics/main1905405.shtml).

Cillizza, C., and D. Balz. 2007 "On the Electronic Campaign Trail Politicians Realize the Potential of Web Video." *Washington Post.* January 22 (accessed January 22, 2007, at http://www.washingtonpost.com/wp-dyn/content/article/2007/01/21/AR2007012101074.html).

comScore Media Metrix. 2006. "More Than Half of MySpace Visitors are Now Age 35 or Older, as the Site's Demographic Composition Continues to Shift." October 5. *Media Metrix* (accessed December 12, 2006, at http://www.comscore.com/press/release.asp?id=1019).

Cornfield, M. 2006. "YouTube and You." *Campaigns and Elections* 27 (8): 43.

Cornfield, M., and L. Rainie. 2006. "The Impact of the Internet on Politics." Pew Internet and American Life Project (accessed January 22, 2007, at http://www.pewInternet.org/ppt/PIP_Internet_and_Politics.pdf).

Dickinson, T. 2006. "The First YouTube Election: George Allen and 'Macaca.'" *Rolling Stone National Affairs Daily.* August 15 (accessed January 22, 2007, at http://www.rollingstone.com/nationalaffairs/?p=426).

Donath, J., and D. Boyd. 2004. "Public Displays of Connection." *BT Technology Journal* 22:71–82.

DoubleClick. 2007. "Doubleclick's Research Demonstrates the Benefits of Online Video Advertising." *DoubleClick.* March 20 (accessed April 28, 2006, at http://www.doubleclick.com/us/about_doubleclick/press_releases/default.asp?p=568).

Fairbanks, E. 2006. "The YouTube Election: Candid Camera." *New Republic.* November (accessed January 12, 2007, at http://www.tnr.com/doc.mhtml?i=w061030&s=fairbanks110206).

Goldsmith, J. 2006. "Adventures of a Dead Elephant on MySpace." *Frogloop.* November (accessed January 22, 2007, at http://www.frogloop.com/care2blog/2006/11/1/adventures-of-a-dead-elephant-on-myspace.html).

Greenfield, H. 2007. "YouTube Boom May Mean New Jobs on Campaigns." *National Journal.* January.

Gross, R., and A. Acquisti. 2005. "Information Revelation and Privacy in Online Social Networks." Paper presented at the Workshop on Privacy in the Electronic Society. Proceedings of the 2005 ACM workshop on Privacy in the Electronic Society (accessed July 2, 2007, at http://www.heinz.cmu.edu/~acquisti/papers/privacy/facebook-gross-acquisti.pdf).

Holder, Kelly 2006. "Voting and registration in the election of November 2004." US Census Bureau (accessed January 22, 2007, at http://www.census.gov/prod/2006pubs/p20–556.pdf).

Institute for Politics, Democracy and the Internet. 2006a. "Small Donors and Online Giving." Institute for Politics, Democracy and the Internet in collaboration with the Campaign Finance Institute (accessed January 22, 2007, at http://www.ipdi.org/UploadedFiles/Small percent20Donors percent20Report.pdf).

———. 2006b. "Person-to-Person-to-Person: Harnessing the Political Power of Online Social Networks and User Generated Content." Institute for Politics, Democracy and the Internet (accessed January 22, 2007, at http://www.ipdi.org/Publications/default.aspx).

Jarvis, J. 2007. "Why YouTube Gets My Vote for Political Punditry." *The Guardian.* February 5 (accessed January 22, 2007, at http://politics.guardian.co.uk/media/comment/0,,2005785,00.html).

Jesdanun, A. 2006. "Political Candidates Seek Youths at MySpace, YouTube." *USA Today.* August 17 (accessed January 22, 2007, at http://www.usatoday.com/tech/news/techpolicy/2006–08–17-politicians-myspace_x.htm?csp=34).

Johnson, C. 2006. Conrad Burns Being Followed by Camcorder Shadow. *Missoulian News* Online (accessed January 22, 2007, at http://www.missoulian.com/articles/2006/08/29/news/mtregional/znews07.txt).

Keen, J. 2006. "Politicians' Campaigns Invade MySpace." *USA Today.* October 17 (accessed January 22, 2007, at http://www.usatoday.com/tech/news/2006–10–16-politicians-social-sites_x.htm).

Kiley, D. 2006. "The YouTube Election Ratifies Google's Investment." *BusinessWeek.* November 8 (accessed January 22, 2007, at http://www.businessweek.com/the_thread/brandnewday/archives/2006/11/the_you_tube_el.html).

Leonard, A. 2004."You Are Who You Know." *Salon.com.* June 15 (accessed January 22, 2007, at http://dir.salon.com/story/tech/feature/2004/06/15/social_software_one/index.html).

Liu, H., and P. Maes. 2005. "Interestmap: Harvesting Social Network Profiles for Recommendations." Paper presented at Beyond Personalization—IUI 2005, January 9, San Diego, California.

Lizza, R. 2006. "The YouTube Election." *New York Times.* August 20 (accessed January 22, 2007, at http://www.nytimes.com/2006/08/20/weekinreview/20lizza.html?ex=1313726400&en=a605fabfcb81eebf&ei=5088&partner=rssnyt&emc=rss).

Loveley, E. 2006. "Politicians Try Out MySpace." *Wall Street Journal.* October 14 (accessed January 22, 2007, at http://online.wsj.com/public/article/SB116078551947392672-z5ctEb9NpsFofVV_59CVPknP2Bo_20071013.html?mod=rss_free).

Milgram, S. 1967. "The Small World Problem." *Psychology Today* 6 (1): 62–67.

———. 1977. "The Familiar Stranger: An Aspect of Urban Anonymity." In *The Individual in a Social World: Essays and Experiments*, ed. S. Milgram, J. Sabini, and M. Silver. Reading, MA: Addison-Wesley.

Miller, T. 2006. "Political Candidates Ride the YouTube, MySpace Wave." *PBS.* September 27 (accessed January 22, 2007, at http://www.pbs.org/newshour/extra/features/july-dec06/campaigns_9–27.html).

Newitz, A. 2003. "Defenses Lacking at Social Network Sites." *SecurityFocus.* December 31 (accessed 12 November 2006 at: http://www.securityfocus.com/news/7739).

New ScientistTech. 2006. "Web Clips Fuels US Election Debate." *New ScientistTech.* October 26 (accessed December 17, 2006, at http://www.newscientisttech.com/article/dn10384-Web-clips-fuel-us-election-debate.html).

Nielsen//NetRatings. 2006. "Social Networking Sites Grow 47 Percent, Year Over Year, Reaching 45 Percent of Web Users, According to Nielsen/NetRatings." *Nielsen//NetRatings.* May 11 (accessed November 13, 2006, at http://www.nielsen-netratings.com/pr/pr_060511.pdf).

O'Malley, G. 2007. "MySpace Announces Jan. 1 Presidential Election." April 4 (accessed April 5, 2007, at http://publications.mediapost.com/index.cfm?fuseaction=Articles.san&s=58191&Nid=29002&p=289069).

Pew/Internet and American Life Project. 2005. "Usage Over Time" (accessed January 12, 2007, at www.pewinternet.org/trends/UsageOverTime.xls).

Rainie, L. 2005. "The State of Blogging." Pew/Internet and American Life Project (accessed February 20, 2007, at http://www.pewinternet.org/pdfs/pip_blogging_data.pdf).

Rainie, L., and B. Horrigan. 2007. "Election 2006 Online: The Number of Americans Citing the Internet as the Source of Most of Their Political news and Information Doubled Since the Last Mid-Term Election." January 17. Pew Internet and American Life Project (accessed July 2, 2007, at http://pewinternet.org.pdfs/pip_politics_2006.pdf).

Reimer, J. 2006. "YouTube Makes the Move on TV's 'Old Rich People.'" *Arstechnica.* November 27 (accessed December 13, 2006, at http://arstechnica.com/news.ars/post/20061127–8290.html).

Reuters. 2006. "YouTube Serves Up 100 Million Videos a Day Online." *USA Today.* July 16 (accessed January 12, 2007, at http://www.usatoday.com/tech/news/2006–07–16-youtube-views_x.htm).

Romano, A. 2006. "MyBallot Box: MySpace Launches a New Effort to Bring the Benefits of Social Networking to Voter Registration." *Newsweek*. September 28 (accessed January 12, 2007, at http://www.msnbc.msn.com/id/15027829/site/newsweek).

Saad, L. 2005. "Blogs Not Yet in the Media Big Leagues." *Gallup News Service*. March 11 (accessed January 29, 2007, at www.gallup.com/poll/content/default.aspx7ci= 15217).

Sege, I. 2005. "Where Everybody Knows Your Name." *Boston Globe*. April 27 (accessed December 12, 2007, at http://www.boston.com).

Walker, L. 2004. "Bloggers Gain Attention in 2004 Election." *Washington Post*. November 4 (accessed December 17, 2007, at http://www.washingtonpost.com/wp-dyn/articles/A23628–2004Nov3.html).

Watts, D. 2003. *Six Degrees: The Science of a Connected Age*. New York: W. W. Norton.

14

"Friend" the President

Facebook and the 2008 Presidential Election

ALLISON SLOTNICK

Emerging technologies create new opportunities for reaching the public. Campaigns must not only create targeted messages, they also must communicate these messages through mediums that will resonate with the intended audience. Nowadays, it is not simply enough to place an ad in a newspaper or participate in a debate on network television. In recent years, use of the Internet for information gathering has become nearly as ubiquitous as watching a television show or reading a newspaper for the same purpose. Despite this widespread acceptance of the Internet as a mainstream media outlet, organizations have struggled with finding the right balance of Internet strategies to include in their overall communications plans. The Internet is still considered a new medium, so there hardly exist enough data to determine its true effectiveness as a meaningful way to target a group and communicate a message. When it comes to politics, campaigns have sought to go beyond mere communication of a message in their use of the Internet. The interactivity offered by the Web provides candidates with unprecedented opportunity to communicate to audiences who were previously disengaged with politics (ages eighteen to twenty-five). In so doing, they are able to communicate, mobilize a voter base, and fund-raise simultaneously. The trick throughout, though, is making use of the medium in a way that seems authentic and credible to its user base, a tech savvy and skeptical generation.

Context: Navigating Uncharted Territories

In 2003, Howard Dean came onto the national political scene as the governor of Vermont and a presidential wannabe. While initially many thought he didn't stand a chance, he was able to set himself apart from the rest of the contenders through his seemingly risky online tactics. Never before had a candidate embraced the Internet with such an open mind. For some time, Dean appeared to be the frontrunner . . . (and then he fell from grace. While he was able to ride the wave of support provided by the Internet, it produced a false sense of security. Dean may have mobilized the Web as no one ever had before, but merely relying upon its buzz was not enough to sustain a presidential campaign. ("Campaign 2.0" 2007) After one overly enthusiastic yell, often dubbed as the "I Have a Scream Speech," was repeatedly rebroadcast by the traditional media outlets and "remixed" by the young generation of voters whose support Dean had solicited on the Internet (Morrison 2004, his political demise was imminent.

Dean's rapid rise and fall resulted in candidates growing wary of using the Internet to bolster their campaigns. While on the one hand, the Internet had helped propel Dean to the top, it also had the ability to completely discredit him simply through instantaneous replays of one brief moment, a moment that would have had minimal, if any, impact in practically any other election cycle. The eye of the Internet, as Dean found, is inescapable. This medium presents the ability to change the rules of the political game. Rather than run from it, campaigns must find a way to integrate it seamlessly into their larger strategy plans.

While the Dean campaign took place only three years ago at this writing, the reach of the Internet has expanded at a breakneck pace since then. Joe Trippi, Dean's 2004 Internet campaign manager, admits that the tactics used just a few short years ago already seem a bit outdated: "It took our campaign six months to get 139,000 people on an e-mail list. It took one Facebook group, what, barely a month to get 200,000? That's astronomical" (quoted in Vargas 2007). Dean's team laid the groundwork for what campaigns need to accomplish via the Web—mobilization of people and money. Today's social networking sites, such as the aforementioned Facebook, have just sped along the process and provided a central space for putting this process into action.

In previous election cycles, candidates had to determine largely on their own how they wished to create an online presence. The recent advent of social networking sites, notably MySpace and Facebook, have opened the doors for current candidates and provided them with the platforms needed to venture more safely into the online world. Facebook, in particular, has evolved from an elite community of college students to a public content provider (Vara 2007). With this evolution has come increased opportunity for political candidates to explore the world of Facebook and use its innovative technologies for their own benefit.

The Origins and Evolution of Facebook

When Facebook came onto the scene in February 2004, it was met with mixed reactions. The notion of a virtual yearbook, a site where college students could meet and mingle with one another through an online space, seemed unusual yet appealing. Founded by Harvard student Mark Zuckerberg, the initial Facebook operation invited students from select colleges, at first only Ivy League schools, to join the network. Eventually, Facebook opened up to tens of thousands of recognized schools and organizations (as the floodgates opened, so too did the influence and reach of Facebook.

The site grew to be a phenomenon due largely to the fact that users perceived it to be safer than other similar sites, since a college e-mail address was required to register. With this sense of safety came a tight-knit and loyal user base, which grew to millions. "Facebook," as a word on its own, became integrated into the vernacular of college students nationwide and over time evolved into a trusted source for campus news and camaraderie.

Of course, as is the case with so many other seemingly exclusive forums, Facebook's founders decided to see how they could use the site to cast their net of influence wider and reach an increasingly vast user base. On September 26, 2006, less than three years after its launch, Facebook officially opened up to the public, and with that, the once exclusive students' club became a juggernaut for motivating political and social action. The site now has a staggering number of registered users—more than 26 million members and counting (Reece 2007). With this kind of reach, it should come as no surprise at all that presidential political campaigns have found their way into the "pages" of Facebook and tried to exploit its capabilities to the best of their abilities.

The partnership between politics and Facebook is not a new one, although the political origins of Facebook will likely come as a surprise to many. While on first glance the site appears to be all about providing students, and now the general public, with an opportunity to connect with one another, there is no escaping its political origins and the ways in which they have seeped into Facebook in its current form. In 2004, Facebook founder Mark Zuckerberg served as a field organizer for Democratic presidential candidate, John Kerry (Guynn 2007a) (as a field organizer, Zuckerberg headed up GOTV and mobilization efforts. The fact that the launch of Facebook happened to coincide with the heart of the 2004 primary season shows that there was a commingling of the two in Zuckerberg's life. Designing a platform that encourages group formation, the basic skill required to make Facebook a success, is quite similar to the ultimate goal of any political campaign—mobilization of voters behind a single candidate on Election Day.

When Facebook Actually Meets Politics: A Conflict of Interest?

The similarities between campaigning and virtual social networking are startling (at their core, they both rely upon constant communication and creating a platform for making this communication as seamless as possible. Is there a time, though, when the two worlds collide and result in a conflict of interest?

When University of California Merced student Josh Franco perused the pages of Facebook on a leisurely afternoon, he stumbled upon Barack Obama's profile and began reading up on the presidential candidate. On any given day, Franco would not have actively sought out a politician's Web page. However, thanks to Facebook, a site that is not overtly political, Franco became exposed to the world of politics. By summer 2008, at the age of twenty-one, Franco served as the California statewide coordinator of Students for Barack Obama, a political action committee consisting of about eighty chapters from universities across the country (Patton 2007). In this instance, Facebook proved itself as a catalyst not only capable of disseminating information and generating a virtual following but also of motivating real action and loyalty.

As the line between politics and social networking conflates, the resulting product can lead to scandal and a questioning of the authenticity of supposedly "non-partisan" social networking sites. In 2004, Chris Hughes was one of the Harvard students integral to Facebook's founding. Over the years, he worked on developing the Facebook site and continually expanding upon its capabilities (after graduation, Hughes continued his career as an affluent Facebook developer. Within five months, though, he temporarily put the world of Facebook behind him and set up shop in Chicago, where he accepted a "significant" pay cut to work long hours as an adviser for presidential candidate Barack Obama. "His [Hughes's] goal: to transfer the same magic that transformed the way college students interact to a presidential campaign" (Schatz 2007). Immediately, cries of foul were called, as Hughes's ties to the Obama campaign and Facebook have been perceived as a conflict of interest.

When the worlds of politics and technology collide in such a direct manner, questions arise as to whether the stakeholders can truly have a hand in each that is independent of the other. Even before Hughes officially joined the Obama camp, he had designed a Facebook profile page for Barack— a questionable practice given that the supposedly nonpartisan site was founded by at least two individuals (including Zuckerberg and his work for Kerry) who clearly displayed their party affiliations and candidate loyalties.

As a site founder, Hughes is privy to content management abilities and can thus theoretically censor information and use new developments before

FIGURE 14.1 Barack Obama Facebook Application Platform

the general public has caught on. In fact, this connection drew significant public attention when Facebook introduced its "platform" function earlier this year. This feature provided third-party developers unprecedented access to the world of Facebook, as it gave them the opportunity to build mini-applications into Facebook's framework. Despite the somewhat revolutionary opportunity provided by the platform, Obama's campaign was the only campaign to make its presence felt on day one of the platform launch, and it remained the only one there for several weeks. The platform allowed users to gain access to new videos and messages directly from the campaign and then pass them along to their friends (see figure 14.1 for a screen shot of the Obama platform). "If you're interested in exposing your network of friends to info about Barack, the campaign is making it a one-click affair that greatly simplifies the redistribution of campaign info," said Rick Klau of Feedburner (Levy and Sifry 2007). With more than nineteen thousand people registered to Obama's Facebook platform, many suspect that his early presence in the social networking space has a great deal to do with Hughes's ties.

Among Hughes's other work for Obama has been the creation of an official Barack Obama social networking site that, while it has clear differences from Facebook, also bears some striking resemblance. The result, MyBarack Obama.com (see screen shot of this site in figure 14.2), combines the social

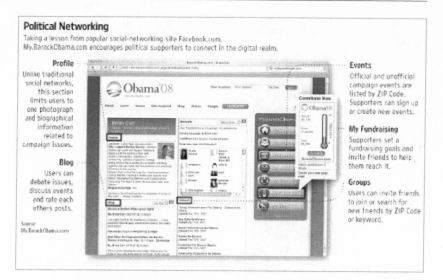

FIGURE 14.2 MyBarackObama.com

Source: http://online.wsj.com/article_email/SB118011947223614895-
lMyQjAxMDE3ODIwOTEyMTk5Wj.html; Schatz 2007.

networking of Facebook (through a profile page complete with photo and biographical information) with some of the most traditional forms of political mobilization (events and fund-raising) and finally tops them off with new media functions, such as a running blog. Through the site, visitors can make "friends" with fellow supporters and zero in on those who live in their area. This site essentially becomes a one-stop shop for any and all Obama needs— it services his campaign as it provides a tracking system for supporters and gives them the tools at their fingertips to create new networks and bring in additional supporters. This basic principle lies at the heart of Facebook, as well: to find a shared interest (a specific school in the case of Facebook, a candidate in the case of Obama) and provide users with everything they would need to build upon that network and create an authentic and mobilized force which originates from the general public, rather than the elite.

Politics Meets the Twenty-first Century

It seems so simple once it is boiled down: both politics and Facebook are essentially dependent upon strong and persistent networking. If politicians must take their campaigns on the road in order to meet the people, why shouldn't they make use of pre-created networking sites such as Facebook? While a face-to-face interaction may be more powerful, it is costly and time-consuming. Networking through a Web site like Facebook provides an inexpensive, practically free way to reach the masses. In fact, it requires absolutely none of the candidate's time, as a consultant can handle creating and monitoring the profile page.

In past decades, campaign networks relied on personal interaction, whether through campaign volunteers going door to door or participation in a town meeting. Nowadays, this sense of local and personal relationship building has been largely replaced by a global network of individuals who in many cases will never actually meet face to face. These virtual communities are formed with the help of sites on the Internet, which provide the framework needed to connect these individuals. Social networking sites such as Facebook and MySpace take this framework and create niche platforms that allow for like-minded individuals to come together. The evolution from personal networks to virtual ones has permeated nearly all aspects of life (according to Chris DeWolfe, MySpace chief executive, "Our digital candidates banner [a political application on MySpace] will be the yard signs of the 21st century and our political viral videos and vlogs [video blogs] are the campaign ads of the futures" (Aun 2007). While this transition has not been quite as smooth and wholly accepted as DeWolfe makes it seem, it certainly is underway, and candidates are finding themselves playing a game of catch-up in order to adapt.

Why has this shift on the part of political consultants to accept the Internet been so slow to develop? While the Internet is clearly the wave of the future and a growing necessity for political campaigning, there still remains a premium on more traditional means of political communication. "Most political media consultants still get paid as a percentage of the media buys they recommend for television and radio, so there's no clear incentive for them to recommend spending online," according to Andrew Rasiej, cofounder and publisher of TechPresident.com, a site solely dedicated to tracking the presence of the presidential candidates on the Web (Guynn 2007b) (as long as there is an incentive for consultants to stick to television and radio buying, they will continue to focus their efforts in this arena. Politics is a career where making money is a key component. Online campaigning has yet to prove itself as a surefire moneymaker and thus does not provide the promised income that television or radio buying do. This imbalance means that there will be less of an incentive to test the Internet waters.

How Does Social Networking Fit into the Bigger Picture?

Although there may not yet be a direct correlation between adoption of an Internet strategic plan and ultimate success, a baseline Web presence has come to be expected of the candidates. For instance, it has become a necessity to build an official campaign Web site. The site, whose URL address typically takes the candidate's name, essentially serves as the round-the-clock central campaign headquarters. If anybody wants to learn about the candidate, including biographical information, issue stances, recent news and events, and photo gallery, this is the place to go. Other forms of online engagement, such as social networking, have been only marginally embraced by the campaign teams. Even once these social networking tactics have been adopted, it is interesting to note the attention the campaign teams choose to give them. Since the candidate's official Web site acts as the hub of all of their Internet activities, it would make sense to prominently feature links to any other related sites, such as social networking profiles, in this "virtual campaign headquarters." These links would demonstrate that the candidates place an importance on all aspects of their Web presence and that their overall Internet communications strategy is acting in accord.

For the purposes of this chapter, the Facebook pages of the six perceived mainstream frontrunners in the 2008 race—Democrats Hillary Clinton, John Edwards, and Barack Obama and Republicans Rudolph Giuliani, John McCain, and Mitt Romney—will be examined. An examination of these candidates' activities should reveal the typical Internet strategies that are being employed by the "most successful" campaign teams.

Of these six candidates, a vast majority—five of them—have incorporated the interactive social networking resources into their larger Internet strategies by featuring prominent links on their official homepages. These links demonstrate a more integrated approach and show an appreciation for the importance that social networking sites can have within the campaign. The official Web sites of Obama, Clinton, Edwards, McCain, and Romney all feature clear links to four major social networking sites (Facebook, MySpace, You Tube, and Flickr). Together, these sites encompass resources for video (You Tube) and photo sharing (Flickr) along with tools to encourage mobilization (Facebook, MySpace). Although the added benefit that these sites provide has not yet been quantified, using an integrated approach such as this one allows for the ability to supply potential supporters with a wealth of various types of media through a simple click of a button.

While YouTube, MySpace and Facebook have seemingly emerged as the core of political social networking, Obama has demonstrated his dedication to networking sites by also featuring links to two event organization sites, Party Builder and Eventful, on his Web page. These sites add a further dimension to the possibilities for social networking, extending beyond the virtual space and inviting potential supporters to rally together in the "real world" to mobilize their support and, of course, their money, as well. By merging the Internet with these events, Obama is taking the first steps needed to successfully translate online support into meaningful campaign action:

"Obama's 5,000 'house parties,' which helped bring his overall fundraising total to $25 million by March 31, were set up through his Web site" (Malone 2007).

Obama may have been testing the online waters more than his opponents, but Rudy Giuliani had largely decided to remove himself from the Web-based strategies. He remained more private in his Internet choices, electing to create a minimal, and in some cases nonexistent, presence through social networking profiles. Through his main home page there was not one link to a social networking site. This decision is questionable, as social networking is intended for creation of a more public and interactive face; a private profile page means that the campaign team has to approve any "friend requests" and creates a perception of elitism and, perhaps, something to hide. By forgoing these networking sites, the Giuliani campaign took on a more traditional approach. The only indication of Giuliani embracing the wave of interactivity was the ability to download official Giuliani "widgets" that could be linked to through one's blog. These widgets, though, hardly demonstrated support of interactivity and openness, as the essential function of the widgets was to serve as an advertisement—there was no two-way communication in action. The only risk involved was the possibility that Giuliani would not approve of or agree with the content on the blog on which the widget was featured. However, there were ways to monitor the sites on which the widget was posted so that complete control was maintained.

Other than Giuliani's widgets, the only other interactive offering made available through his official Web site was the information needed to call into certain talk radio programs. Talk radio is traditionally perceived to be a conservative mode of communication, so it is logical that this offering would be found on a Republican's page. Giuliani's minimal presence, along with the ways in which Edwards and Obama emerged as proponents of the interactive social networks, should be of little surprise considering the ways in which the two parties have traditionally chosen to run their respective campaigns. "Republicans have traditionally been masters at controlling their message delivery and this is a very difficult way to be within the culture of the Internet," said Andrew Rasiej, co-founder and publisher of TechPresident.com (Guynn 2007b).

Losing Control

As the Republicans, and Howard Dean, have discovered, the Internet and its social networking capabilities provide unbridled possibilities for communicating with the general electorate, but participation also opens the candidates to criticism and uncensored comments. Once the campaigns put up their official content, which is no doubt carefully crafted, they must be prepared for users to respond in any way they choose—and this feedback can include praise or criticism and even lead to reproduction or discussion of the content through various other channels of interaction. "One of the things that's appealing to the candidates is that they get to choose the face that they get to show. Once they put it out there though, then they lose control over who's going to list them as a friend. So, there is also a piece of giving up control. It's a double edged sword," says Grant Reeher, associate professor of political science at Syracuse University ("Candidates Use Facebook" 2007). "Friending" is just the beginning of the loss of control, though. Facebook in particular provides opportunities to post on a candidate's "wall," which is essentially a message board that appears on the person's profile. While candidates can remove a wall posting if they do not feel it is appropriate, they cannot do so until it has already been posted on the profile—there is no approval mechanism in place. A further concern lies in the rapid pace of information transmission online. For instance, if a candidate did try to censor a message put on his or her profile, there would likely be backlash in the blogosphere and the message would further spin out of the campaign's control.

Control issues extend beyond worries over outsiders posting to the pages. Candidates must pay attention to the individuals they charge with creating and maintaining content on their pages. There is a generally unspoken understanding that the candidates do not personally create and update their own Web sites and social networking pages. Teams of campaign workers are assigned the responsibility of putting forward content and messaging consistent with the candidate's larger campaign strategy. Candidates trust that their campaign workers, who are primarily salaried employees, have their best interest in mind. However, once the control extends outside their immediate campaign team, doubts begin to surface.

Maintaining a candidate's site presents unique opportunities to reposition the candidate in the public eye. These opportunities are powerful, and the campaign team therefore seeks to control all channels related to the candidate. "We've had some profiles set up for politicians that they haven't wanted and we've taken them down, but that's a pretty rare occasion," says Chris Kelly, Facebook's vice president of corporate development and chief privacy officer (Baldinger 2007). The Obama campaign, however, had a run-in with the designer of its MySpace page, who was a volunteer, not a staffer. For two and a half years, Obama's page had been run by Joe Anthony, a supporter from Los Angeles (Pickler 2007). The campaign worked with Anthony and agreed to let him maintain the site despite the fact that he was a "campaign outsider." Once the 2008 race heated up, though, the campaign team decided it was time to step in and take control of the page. Obama's campaign clearly acknowledges the power of these social networking sites and wanted to take the steps necessary to directly oversee all content so that it could more effectively manage its Internet strategies. Anthony was willing to agree to give up control over the site in exchange for $49,000, which would have covered his time spent on maintaining the site over the years. Given that "the Internet is essentially a free-for-all that is treated differently than any other method of communication" (Kirkpatrick 2007), there had been little precedent in terms of how to handle such a situation.

While other forms of media bear a specific price tag, the Federal Election Commission (FEC) has yet to enforce such exact costs on the Internet. It is for this reason that the conflict between Anthony and Obama was unique and so difficult to handle. Whether it comes down to consultants not being paid a percentage of their "online media buys," or Facebook not being "fined" for presumably giving Obama's campaign access to the platform function before the other candidates, or even extending into this MySpace case, the Internet remains fuzzy territory (a 2002 FEC ruling deemed that Web sites would be excluded from the restrictions on campaign giveaways that other media outlets are subjected to. Since that ruling, the FEC has begun to recognize the influence of the Internet in elections, but it has found it difficult to establish clear guidelines.

Because of this lack of guidelines, the Obama MySpace case presented an interesting dilemma. In an unprecedented move, Obama's team refused to pay the fees, and MySpace management eventually stepped in to settle the dispute. Their decision was a split one, ruling that Obama's team did not have to pay Anthony for his work on its behalf, but that he "had the right to take all of the friends who signed up (over 160,000) while he was in control" (Pickler 2007). This issue will set the framework for future Internet campaigning in terms of both the notion of putting a price on social networking maintenance and the idea of being able to "take friends away from a candidate." Campaign teams will no doubt pay careful attention early on to who has control of pages bearing their candidate's name and image, knowing it could come back to haunt them.

The 2008 Candidates—What Face Do They Show on Facebook?

Once a team of consultants has been tasked with designing a social networking page for a candidate, it must then map out a strategy. What will these pages say? Which sites will they be posted on? "Given that Facebook has more than 20 million members, is growing by 150,000 a day, and members spend an average of 20 minutes a day on the site" (Levy and Sifry 2007), it becomes a natural assumption that anyone seriously considering a run for the presidency will ensure that his or her presence is felt on that site.

Although Facebook has opened to the general public, its core base remains with college-age individuals, the youngest and perhaps most mysterious voter demographic. Despite the fact that more than half of Americans age eighteen to twenty-four who are eligible to vote typically don't go to the polls on Election Day, recent statistics show that this age group is becoming more engaged in the political process. Voter turnout among young people rose from 36 percent to 47 percent from the 2000 to the 2004 presidential election (Guynn 2007b). It is with this encouraging trend that candidates find themselves drawn to the "pages" of Facebook.

An examination of candidate pages shows that the medium is now being used to disseminate a well thought out message and image. With this use, though, Facebook's pages clearly become a product of commercial and political interests. Each candidate's profile provides a telling look into his or her overall campaign strategies. Figures 14.3 through 14.7 present several screen shots from the various candidate Facebook pages.

The Content of the Profile Pages

Hillary Clinton's profile page is perhaps the most simplistic of those of the major candidates on Facebook. "I was raised in a middle-class family in the middle of America," Clinton's "About Me" begins. She goes on to position herself as "one of America's foremost advocates for children and families . . . (an attorney . . . (a bestselling author . . . (a champion for health care . . . (and a champion of women's rights and human rights around the world," but she provides little else. These grandiose titles are just the type that one would expect to hear from someone running for president, but they do not fit within the model of Facebook and social networking. If the candidates are going to employ social networking as part of their campaign, it is imperative that they adapt to the environment and mimic its style and tone—and this all requires a more casual and personal approach. Ironically, one of the most consistent criticisms of Clinton throughout her campaign has been that she appears to be staged and stiff. These characteristics clearly shine through when juxtaposed with the other candidate's profiles.

While Clinton's profile reveals only minimal information, she does make use of the multimedia sharing capabilities of Facebook by uploading nearly thirty videos to her profile. These videos may be nothing more than advertisements that have been scripted and rehearsed, but they do show that a presence on Facebook can consist of far more than a simple profile.

Barack Obama's page has a different look and feel. He chooses to forego the "About Me" section, which Clinton used, and instead provides some more offbeat tidbits, including his favorite books (*Moby Dick*, the Bible), favorite TV show (ESPN *Sportscenter*), and interests (basketball, writing,

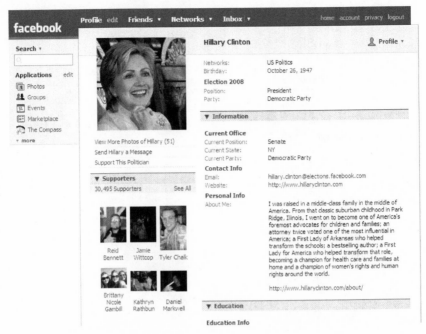

FIGURE 14.3 A Snapshot of Hillary Clinton's Facebook Page

loafing with kids). Furthermore, in line with Obama's all-encompassing online campaign, he makes sure to include links to several of his other social networking sites and has also posted more than four hundred "notes" that include opportunities to participate in online polls and text messaging. In this way, his campaign demonstrates its understanding of the virtual space and the need to integrate as many interactive means as possible, which should be no surprise considering Hughes's presence on the campaign.

John Edwards's profile represents a mix of the components used by Obama and Clinton and demonstrates perhaps the most complete use of Facebook to evoke a traditional presidential message while at the same time integrating as many "new media" components as possible. Like Clinton, Edwards describes himself in terms of his past accomplishments and upbringing, which gets across his main platform in as few words as possible—perfect for the "instant gratification" generation: "My dad was a millworker. I went to public schools . . . (as a lawyer, I stood up against the powerful (as a Senator, I stood up for you. Currently fighting poverty." Edwards also chooses to highlight his key campaign issues in the "Interest" ' section of his profile, which seems to be a somewhat odd and unnatural fit: "Fighting poverty. Raising the minimum wage. Stopping the genocide in Darfur." However, beyond these brief statements, there lies little similarity

FIGURE 14.4 A Snapshot of Barack Obama's Facebook Page

to Clinton's bare-bones page. Like Obama, Edwards list his favorites: books (*The Working Poor, Invisible in America*—no doubt chosen for their ties to Edwards's main platform, the fight against poverty); movies (*The Shawshank Redemption*); and activities (basketball and running) (also like Obama, Edwards makes use of his other interactive ties, but he does so in an even more encompassing manner. From inviting "friends" to submit their favorite quotes to him via e-mail to requesting them to text him to "stay in touch," Edwards is encouraging this generation to contact him in the ways that are most familiar to them (additionally, he uses the calendar function so that users can track his whereabouts and incorporates other well-known sites, Flickr and YouTube, as well as lesser-known Twitter, into his Facebook page.

Romney, more than any of the other candidates, tells a complete bio-graphical story on Facebook. However, it does not seem appropriate for this medium in that he writes long-form prose that fits more into a traditional print format. Romney's "About Me" section consists of four long paragraphs detailing his journey from childhood to the present. Similarly, he lists more than ten books as his favorites and ten musical artists as his favorites, as well. The Internet, and this generation in particular, are all about instant gratification and quick information. Using Facebook to connect to these voters is only one step of these process, the candidates must also master speaking in a way that is familiar to them, as well—long lists and paragraphs are not the way to gain attention and support. Romney does attempt to do this through his links to photos on Flickr, YouTube skins, and a section called "Web presence," where he provides an easy reference point for figuring out where to find Romney on the Web.

McCain's Facebook page makes an attempt at integrating other social networking sites by providing links to his official site, as well as MySpace, YouTube, and Eventful. Other than these links, though, there is very little to show that McCain truly understands ways to use the features of these sites through Facebook. Other than the links, McCain's site is rather basic, as he lists some favorites, most of which do not seem nearly as contrived and focused on campaign messaging, as did Edwards's picks. His favorite TV shows are *Seinfeld* and *24*, while his favorite book is *For Whom the Bell Tolls.*

Romney and McCain's other Republican opponent, Rudy Giuliani, not surprisingly, "doesn't exist on Facebook" (All 2007). Considering that he features no links to social networking sites via his official Web page, his lack of presence on Facebook should be expected. Yet it is surprising given the influence that Facebook has on the eighteen-to-twenty-five demographic, as

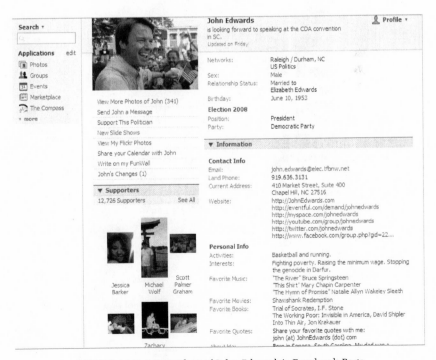

FIGURE 14.5 A Snapshot of John Edwards's Facebook Page

FIGURE 14.6 A Snapshot of Mitt Romney's Facebook Page

well as its ever-widening reach to the larger public. It seems counterproductive to neglect such an inexpensive and seemingly influential outlet in favor of more traditional campaigning, but there is little indication that this tactic greatly impacted Giuliani's standing in the polls ("Republicans Shun Debate" 2007). This strategy of disregarding interactive tactics falls in line with the overall Giuliani campaign strategy and plays into maintaining his target and proven voter base: "It is interesting that Rudy has a very small online presence, does not get many contributions from the average American, and does not even allow unrestricted comments on his videos. It is becoming increasingly obvious that Rudy is the choice of the elites who think he can beat Hillary, and that the average American wants nothing to do with him ~ religious conservatives don't like his socially liberal views, liberals don't like his Iraq stance" (All 2007).

Table 14.1 provides a comparison chart of the five candidate pages by the numbers. Obama and Romney clearly come out on top. Obama dominates in the categories that indicate support, the number of friends and wall posts. These high numbers prove that he has garnered a great deal of grassroots support from Facebook users. These supporters not only sign on as friends but also take added initiative by posting comments of support on his profile

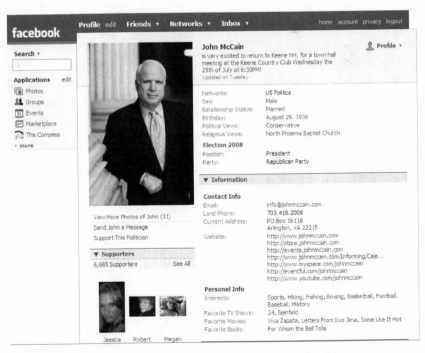

FIGURE 14.7 A Snapshot of John McCain's Facebook Page

TABLE 14.1

Basic Comparison of Facebook Sites by the Numbers

Facebook sites	Clinton	Obama	Edwards	McCain	Romney
Number of friends	30,495	118,194	12,726	6,685	13,100
Number of wall posts	5,269	12,690	1,851	670	2,223
Number of groups	11	16	—	32	76
Number of photos	51	9	341	31	1304

page. In fact, Obama's numbers are not even in the same realm as his competitors. With 118,194 friends, he has nearly four times more than does his closest opponent, Clinton. Similarly, Clinton is his closest competitor in wall posts, but Obama has more than double her 5,269 postings. Obama's integration of all of his Internet outlets (by plugging each one through links on each page) helps him recruit supporters from various sites.

When it comes to the categories that indicate a priority put on updating the Facebook page, Romney leads the way. His campaign team has put forth the greatest effort in ensuring that he is a member of more groups than any of his opponents (seventy-six , compared to McCain's thirty-two), and he has also posted significantly more photos than any others who are in the running—more than four times as many as his closest opponent in this category, Edwards. Romney makes use of Flickr to post photos on his Facebook page, which demonstrates the way in which these various Web-based sites can work with one another to further expand their reach and capabilities. Considering Romney's apparent acceptance of this new wave of technology, it is surprising to note that he shies away from groups that do not have anything to do with his candidacy. Given the fact that Facebook groups run the gamut from entertainment to sports to politics and everything in between, it is surprising that every one of Romney's seventy-six groups explicitly supports his candidacy in some way or another. Group membership can offer new networks to recruit supporters from, but by sticking to the groups of individuals who already support him, Romney takes the safe road and hopes to capitalize upon his already established support.

Vote on the Book: The Anomaly of Ron Paul

The Facebook pages of the six major candidates tell one story. They each, some more directly than others, tell the story that their candidate has chosen to tell. Clinton's is one of a carefully controlled message, an accomplished and professional woman. Giuliani's lack of presence shows a disregard for the Facebook generation. Beyond these pages, though, lies another political story embedded within Facebook—the story of Ron Paul.

If you mention Paul's name to most people, they likely have no idea who he is, let alone that he was in the running to be resident ("CNN/WMUR" 2007). Yet somehow Paul managed to dominate his opponents, both fellow Republicans and Democrats, in a virtual election on VoteOnTheBook.com and made a name for himself "among the young and the wired" (Caldwell 2007).

Vote on the Book (VOTB), a simulation of the 2008 election, provides Facebook users with an opportunity to "cast a vote" through this application. Voteonthebook.com then monitors these results and recalculates them every five minutes on its site. Eliot York, a Cornell student, designed VOTB and in the process created an interesting Facebook subculture. Although the Web site does represent a simulation of the 2008 election based upon "votes" by Facebook users, it also serves as a fund-raising vehicle and an educational tool.

At the end of the VOTB election, the site will distribute its earnings to the candidates based upon the percentage of votes they have received (additionally, the site provides a complete storehouse of information about each candidate, including their stances on the issues, the latest headlines, recent YouTube videos, and a message board that allows "voters" to explain why they support a particular candidate.

So, if VOTB is supposedly a simulation of the election, who is this Ron Paul who garnered over 60 percent of votes cast for the Republican candidates, and why didn't this dominance translating into the mainstream race? Paul is not a newcomer to the political scene by any stretch: he's a ten-term Texas congressman. He stood out from his Republican opponents primarily because of his opposition to the Iraq war, publicly putting partial blame on Vice President Cheney and thus eliciting a very public response from opponent and Republican frontrunner Rudy Giuliani.

It's ironic that Paul garnered such a following on the Web considering his otherwise traditional political campaigning: "There is something homespun about Paul, reminiscent of *Mr. Smith Goes to Washington*. He communicates with his constituents through birthday cards, August barbecues and the cookbooks his wife puts together every election season" (Caldwell 2007). Yet it was his "radical thinking," his libertarian views—antiwar, pro–gun control, pro-life, pro–state sovereignty—that generated a following for him on the Web among the more "radical" young voters. Paul recognized that his chances of winning the Republican nomination were slim to nonexistent, yet his methods were precisely why he towered above all other candidates in the VOTB race. "In Paul's idea of politics, spreading a message has always

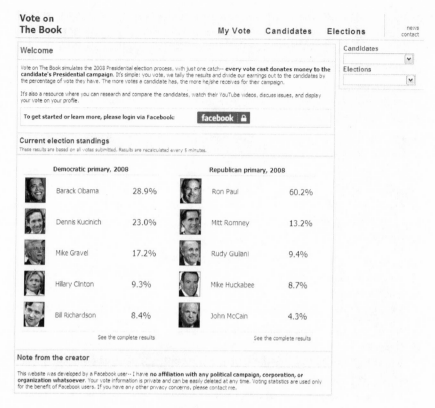

Vote on The Book

My Vote Candidates Elections

news
contact

Welcome

Candidates

Elections

Vote on The Book simulates the 2008 Presidential election process, with just one catch-- **every vote cast donates money to the candidate's Presidential campaign.** It's simple: you vote, we tally the results and divide our earnings out to the candidates by the percentage of vote they have. The more votes a candidate has, the more he/she receives for their campaign.

It's also a resource where you can research and compare the candidates, watch their YouTube videos, discuss issues, and display your vote on your profile.

To get started or learn more, please login via Facebook: facebook

Current election standings

These results are based on all votes submitted. Results are recalculated every 5 minutes.

Democratic primary, 2008		Republican primary, 2008	
Barack Obama	28.9%	Ron Paul	60.2%
Dennis Kucinich	23.0%	Mitt Romney	13.2%
Mike Gravel	17.2%	Rudy Giuliani	9.4%
Hillary Clinton	9.3%	Mike Huckabee	8.7%
Bill Richardson	8.4%	John McCain	4.3%
See the complete results		See the complete results	

Note from the creator

This website was developed by a Facebook user-- I have **no affiliation with any political campaign, corporation, or organization whatsoever.** Your vote information is private and can be easily deleted at any time. Voting statistics are used only for the benefit of Facebook users. If you have any other privacy concerns, please contact me.

FIGURE 14.8 Vote on the Book

been just as important as seizing office. 'Politicians don't amount to much,' he says, "but ideas do.'" His loyalty to ideas, and not politics, elevated his popularity among the "Facebook generation." He may be a seventy-one-year-old great-grandfather, but he has a certain authenticity that the others seem to lack, and this translated to a lead in the "virtual polls."

Facebook Politics Gets Personal

With such an emphasis being placed on the virtual presence of the presidential candidates, it is easy to forget that a Facebook profile page has real world implications. Candidates may be front and center, but they do have personal lives and families that naturally get pulled into the political process regardless of whether or not they choose to be involved. Most recently, Rudolph Giuliani found his relationship with his children thrust into the spotlight. It is well known that Giuliani is on shaky ground with his kids. Both his son and daughter remained off the campaign trail but handled the public eye in different ways. His son, in particular, has been vocal regarding his disdain toward his father and his new wife. He has chosen to go through traditional media (both print and broadcast) outlets to express his feelings toward Giuliani. Giuliani's daughter, on the other hand, has remained largely out of the limelight and elected to express herself through more personal means of communication, ones that are more associated with college-age students, such as Facebook. On her Facebook page, she reveals that her political views are "liberal."

Engaging the Next Generation of Voters—An Ongoing Process

"It's easy to sit at a computer, click 'Join this group' and feel a part of a political movement. However, it's hard to gauge if that armchair point-and-click translates into votes at the ballot box" (Stone 2007). Only time will tell what, if any, influence sites such as Facebook will ultimately have on the 2008 election. Even those behind the Facebook site question whether or not its users will feel compelled to translate their virtual action into real activity: "Remember to register to vote; the Facebook polls won't matter unless you show who you support on Election Day." Actual political action and engagement require much more than simply participating in Facebook and other social networking activities. By encouraging users to register to vote, the site creators are openly admitting that Facebook advocacy only means so much and the further action is necessary.

Facebook and similar sites are only the first step in an ongoing process of education and action. Knowledge is power—and these sites provide a central storehouse for accessing this information and interacting with it as well. It's yet to be seen whether the enthusiasm of Facebook users will translate on a consistent and meaningful basis into actual votes and action come Election Day. The hope is that the key to producing an engaged electorate lies in opening the door at an early age and communicating through a familiar medium. No one knows whether these tactics will prove effective in the long run, but for now they appear to be game changing. Just as the Nixon-Kennedy debate has now gone down in the books as historic for its use of television, the recent CNN/YouTube Democratic debate will likely go down for its innovative use of the Internet. The elections of the past will soon transform into "e-lections"—with social networking and electronic mobilization at the core.

REFERENCES

All, D. 2007. "Five Tips for Rudy Giuliani." *Techpresident*. July 22 (accessed March 1, 2008, at http://www.techpresident.com/node/3518).

Aun, F. 2007. "MySpace Aims to 'Impact' Presidential Race." *TechNewsWorld.com*. March 21 (accessed March 1, 2008, at http://www.technewsworld.com/story/social-networking/56424.html).

Baldinger, A. 2007. "Candidate Profiles Pop Up on Facebook." *Washington Post*. June 19, p. B01 (accessed March 1, 2008, at http://www.washingtonpost.com/wp-dyn/content/article/2006/06/18/AR2006061800727.html).

Caldwell, C. 2007. "The Antiwar, Anti-Abortion, Anti-Drug-Enforcement-Administration, Anti-Medicare Candidacy of Dr. Ron Paul." *New York Times* magazine. July 22 (accessed March 1, 2008, at http://www.nytimes.com/2007/07/22/magazine/22Paul-t.html?_r=1&oref=slogin).

"Campaign 2.0." 2007. *Webspace at University of Texas at Austin*. April 25 (accessed March 1, 2008, at https://Webspace.utexas.edu/btt59/Webcampaign/home.html).

"Candidates Use Facebook to Reach Internet Generation." 2007. *KentNewsNet.com*. Kent State University. February 16 (accessed March 1, 2008, at http://media.www.stateronline.com/media/storage/paper867/news/2007/02/16/ScienceAndTech/Candidates.Use.Facebook.To.Reach.Internet.Generation-2724094.shtml).

"CNN/WMUR Granite State Poll, New Hampshire Primary Poll (February 2007)." USAElectionPolls.com. 2007. May 18 (accessed March 1, 2008, at http://www.usaelectionpolls.com/2008/articles/ron-paul-unknown-in-new-hampshire.html).

Guynn, J. 2007a. "Changes in Facebook: Web Plan Hopes to Boost Activism." TheFoundersFund.com. May 25 (accessed March 1, 2008, at http://www.thefoundersfund.com/news_releases/07–0525a.html).

_____. 2007b. "Growing Internet Role in Election." SFGate.com, *San Francisco Chronicle*. June 4 (accessed March 1, 2008, at http://sfgate.com/cgi-bin/article.cgi?f=/c/a/2007/06/04/BUGI6Q5LI8I.DTL).

Kirkpatrick, D. 2007. "Facebook Free-for-all." The Caucus, *New York Times* blog. June 12 (accessed March 1, 2008, at http://thecaucus.blogs.nytimes.com/2007/06/12/facebook-free-for-all).

Levy, J., and M. Sifry. 2007. "Did Facebook Play Favorites with Obama?" *Techpresident*. June 4 (accessed March 1, 2008, at http://techpresident.com/node/382).

Malone, J. 2007. "Obama's Online Organizing Far Outpaces Competitors." Washington Bureau, Cox News Service. April 9 (accessed March 1, 2008, at http://www.coxwashington.com/hp/content/reporters/stories/2007/04/09/POLITICS_NET09_1stLD_COX.html).

Morrison, B. 2004. "Dean Scream Gaining Cult-Like Status on Web." usatodaycom. January 21 (accessed March 1, 2008, at http://www.usatoday.com/news/politics/elections/nation/2004–01–22-dean-usat_x.htm).

Patton, V. 2007. "UC Merced Student President Uses Internet Rally for Obama." Merced SunStar.com. February 26 (accessed March 1, 2008, at http://www.mercedsunstar.com/local/story/13325137p-13951023c.html).

Pickler, N. 2007. "Obama Takes MySpace Page from Backer." President2008blog.com, Associated Press. May 2 (accessed March 1, 2008, at http://www.president2008blog.com/2007/05/02/obama-takes-myspace-page-from-backer).

"Republican Shun Debate, And the Right Cries Out." 2007. FreeInternetPress.com (accessed March 1, 2008, at http://freeinternetpress.com/story.php?sid=12952).

Reece, C. 2007. "Facebook Fever Grips SA." News24.com. June 14 (accessed March 1, 2008, at http://www.news24.com/News24/Technology/News/0,,2–13–1443_2129757,00.html).

Schatz, A. 2007. "BO, U R So Gr8." *Wall Street Journal*. May 26 (accessed March 1, 2008, at http://online.wsj.com/public/article/SB118011947223614895-iSeQ_DC8SbZxiNLht HwJyIftJN0_20070625.html?mod=tff_main_tff_top).

Stone, M. 2007. "Poke Your President!" *The Wildcat Online*. University of Arizona. February20 (accessed March 1, 2008, at http://media.wildcat.arizona.edu/media/storage/ paper997/news/2007/02/20/Opinions/Poke-Your.President-2729990.shtml).

Suderman, P. 2007. "Jacked In." NationalReviewOnline.com. March 21 (accessed at http://article.nationalreview.com/?q=MDRmZmZjYWQxY2MyYmQIMGM4OThmY TczOGZmZmZjODc=#more).

Vara, V. 2007. "Facebook Opens Its Pages as a Way to Fuel Growth." *Wall Street Journal*. May 21 (accessed March 1, 2008, at http://online.wsj.com/public/article/ SB117971397890009177-wjdKPmjAqS_9ZZbwiRp_CoSqvwQ_20070620.html).

Vargas, J. 2007. "Young Voters Find Face on Facebook." *Washington Post*. February 17 (accessed March 1, 2008, at http://www.washingtonpost.com/wp-dyn/content/ article/2007/02/16/AR2007021602084.html).

Wilkie, D. 2007. "Candidates' New Soapbox for 2008: Social Networking, Video Web Sites." SignOnSanDiego.com, Copley News Service. April 9 (accessed March 1, 2008, at http://www.signonsandiego.com/news/politics/20070409-9999-1n9 youtube.html).

15

The Political Impact of Facebook

Evidence from the 2006 Elections
and the 2008 Nomination Contest

CHRISTINE B. WILLIAMS

GIRISH J. "JEFF" GULATI

With the institutionalization of campaign Web sites and increasing standardization of online content and function, many campaigns are looking to distinguish themselves from each other by employing the Web in ways that promote participatory democracy and re-energize grassroots political organizing.[1] The online tool that emerged in 2006 with the potential of accomplishing these objectives was the social networking site. Although the media directed most of their attention to MySpace (Kelly 2006)[2] and YouTube (Fairbanks 2006; Wasserman 2006),[3] it was Facebook that was most prominently used by the candidates. In 2006 Facebook created entries for all U.S. congressional and gubernatorial candidates, which the candidates could personalize. Their profiles became available for members to view, register votes supporting specific candidates, and share their support of candidates with friends. Almost one-third of the candidates running for the Senate, and about one of every ten candidates running for the House, updated their Facebook profile in some way.[4] In contrast, only 12 percent of the Senate candidates and only 2 percent of the House candidates had their own profiles on MySpace. And even fewer candidates campaigned on YouTube: only 13 of 130 Senate candidates created their own "channels," and none of the 1,102 House candidates had their own channel.[5]

Noting the potential of social networking sites, all of the presidential candidates in 2008 have established some sort of presence on Facebook and have acquired a significant number of supporters. As of January 6, 2008, Senator Barak Obama had drawn the most support from the Facebook community, acquiring more than 200,000 supporters. Among the other Democrats, Senator Hillary Clinton was the second most popular candidate, but trails far behind with just over 60,000 supporters. Among Republicans, the leading candidate was Congressman Ron Paul, who had over 65,000 supporters, followed by Governor Mike Huckabee with over 30,000 supporters and Mitt Romney with just over 25,000.

The question that concerns scholars, campaign professionals, and journalists alike is what impact does vast online support have on election outcomes? The flip side of the question is likewise of interest: is weak online support or inattention to online media a liability for candidates such that it negatively affects their electoral prospects? The sticking point has been the difficulty of collecting adequate, reliable data on how social networks have been used by both campaigns and voters that would allow a careful examination of the relationship between online activity and vote shares. These networks are relatively new and were not designed for the purpose of supporting off-line political organizing and activities. Candidates are just beginning to experiment with and develop campaign applications for social networks, largely through trial and error or imitating others. Facebook in particular is rooted in an age demographic whose political participation is moving into uncharted waters—historically weak, but now evidencing rapid growth.

Social Networks and Political Campaigns

Social networking sites are now widely accessible to the general public and have established a significant presence on the Web. Indeed, the most popular social networking Web sites—MySpace, Facebook, and YouTube—all rank among the ten most visited sites on the Web.[6] MySpace, launched at the end of 2003, allows its members to create personal profiles and share photos, journals, and interests with other group members and their own personal network of friends. MySpace had 60 million unique monthly U.S. Internet visitors to its site in fall 2006 and has added another 5 million over the past year. Facebook, which launched in February 2004, supports similar applications but had restricted its membership to people within the .edu domain until fall 2006. As a result, its audience is significantly smaller, but growing, from about 15 million in fall 2005 to just over 30 million a year later. YouTube made its debut in February 2005. Its primary applications are the watching and sharing of original videos and video clips, but users also may post commentary and discuss content with other members. YouTube had close to 30 million unique visitors at the time of the last election and has grown to just over 55 million in 2006.[7]

In terms of both audience reach and public acceptance, social networks have become a medium to which campaigns must attend. However, their objectives differ from those of political campaigns, and as a result they introduce different opportunities and challenges. A major dilemma for campaigns has been how to control both Web site content and how users interact with it. To date, there are limited data to directly assess and demonstrate whether and how much benefit candidates are reaping from online campaigning.[8] Social network supporters do not (because of their platforms) and may not (because of personal motivation and individual opportunity costs) readily convert into participants in traditional off-line campaign activities and events. Social networks are seen as a vehicle for reinforcing a campaign's core message and increasing the commitment of its active supporters (Bimber and Davis 2003).

In contrast, the objective of social networking sites is to cultivate a sense of community among members. Their users contribute and even control content as well as initiate contact with other users, which together create opportunities that can empower the individual. This is of electoral benefit to campaigns if core supporters are thereby transformed into advocates, contributors, volunteers, and, ultimately, votes for the candidate. It also can introduce unanticipated distractions and force campaigns to respond in ways that take them off message or offend key activists.[9] How campaigns can leverage social networking sites as a strategic resource is an open question that we are seeing candidates experiment with in 2008.

Facebook's 2006 Election Pulse

In 2006 Facebook responded to its growing popularity as a space where candidates and voters could interact and addressed several limitations of its software platform that had affected their use of it by creating within the main site a complementary section called Election Pulse.[10] This feature provided generic profiles to candidates running for a congressional or gubernatorial seat, with the candidate's name, office, state, and party affiliation already posted to the profile. Specific candidates could be located easily by members using a listing of candidate profiles grouped by state and congressional district. Facebook reported that in 2006, 2.64 percent of its users supported a candidate, with 1.5 million members (about 13 percent of the total user base) connected either to a candidate or to an issue group.[11] After the 2006 elections, Facebook redesigned its election sites, allowing current officeholders at all levels of office to establish personal profiles.

Facebook's efforts with Election Pulse and its streamlining of the process for connecting candidates and supporters seemed to encourage a substantial number of candidates to integrate the site into their online strategies. Almost one-third of the candidates running for the Senate (32 percent) and about one of every ten candidates running for the House (13 percent) updated their Election Pulse profile in some way (see table 15.1). In contrast, only 21 percent of the Senate candidates and only 2.7 percent of the House

TABLE 15.1

Facebook Presence in 2006 by Party

	Senate %	House %
Overall	31.5	12.8
Party		
Democrats	60.6	16.9
Republicans	39.4	13.6
Libertarians	21.4	7.5
Greens	22.2	12.2
Other 3rd parties	9.5	4.3
Independents	5	0
N	130	1084

candidates had profiles on MySpace. Only 13 of 130 Senate candidates and no House candidates created their own "channels" on YouTube. Although MySpace and YouTube received considerably more attention from the press in 2006, the candidates clearly directed more of their attention to Facebook when considering how to use online social networking sites to mobilize supporters.

On each 2006 profile, Facebook displayed the number of supporters for each candidate and provided a continuous snapshot of each candidate's percentage of "votes" in his or her race. Candidates need not have accessed their profiles to gain supporters. Among Senate candidates, each had at least one supporter in his or her tally. Most had supporters in the triple digits, with an average of 2,146 supporters for the Democratic and Republican candidates. Senator Hillary Clinton (D-NY) had the most support, with 12,038 Facebook users having registered themselves as supporters. While no one other candidate was nearly as popular as Senator Clinton, four other Democrats—Bob Casey (PA), Harold Ford (TN), Sherrod Brown (OH), and Ned Lamont (CT)—exceeded 5,000 supporters. Moreover, nine of the top ten candidates were Democrats. The most successful Republican candidate and sixth overall was Senator Rick Santorum (R-PA), who registered support from 4,981 Facebook users.

Among Democratic and Republican candidates for the House, the average number of supporters was 125. As was the case for the Senate, House Democratic candidates were more popular than Republican candidates with the Facebook community. The House candidate with the most supporters

TABLE 15.2

2008 Facebook Supporters, Pre- and Post- Iowa, New Hampshire

	Pre-Iowa: mid-December	Post-Iowa January 1–7	% change pre/post Iowa	Post-NH January 7–14	% change pre/post NH
Democrats					
Obama	171,205	205,872	20.25%	222,812	8.23%
Clinton	56,209	61,360	9.16%	67,414	9.87%
Edwards	25,743	33,067	28.45%	34,698	4.93%
Kucinich	18,233	21,911	20.17%	22,727	3.72%
Biden	8,772	8,534	−2.71%	8,296	−2.79%
Richardson	8,188	8,801	7.49%	8,816	0.17%
Gravel	7,615	7,687	0.95%	7,867	2.34%
Dodd	2,371	2,309	−2.61%	2,258	−2.21%
Total:	298,336	349,541	17.16%	374,888	7.25%
Republicans					
Paul	44,738	67,677	51.27%	70,411	4.04%
Romney	22,661	25,437	12.25%	26,610	4.61%
F. Thompson	19,290	18,479	−4.20%	18,610	0.71%
Huckabee	16,308	33,637	106.26%	37,813	12.41%
McCain	15,058	19,219	27.63%	21,971	14.32%
Giuliani	12,548	16,357	30.36%	16,964	3.71%
Hunter	1,270	1,542	21.42%	1,620	5.06%
Total:	131,873	182,348	38.28%	193,999	6.39%

was Representative Tammy Baldwin (D-WI), who had 913 members registered as supporters even though she had not personalized her profile by October. Others who were among the most popular were Representatives Dennis Moore (D-KS), Patty Wetterling (MN), Dennis Kucinich (OH), and Marion Berry (AR). The Republican with the most support and ranked ninth overall was then-Speaker Dennis Hastert (R-IL), with 580 supporters.

In the first week of January 2008, which included the Iowa caucus date, Democratic Senator Obama had the most supporters on Facebook, with 205,872, a big bump up from mid-December's 172,205 (see table 15.2). The next highest candidate was Republican Congressman Ron Paul at 67,677, which represents an even larger percentage increase over his mid-December numbers of 44,738. Republican Governor Huckabee experienced the largest surge, moving from 16,308 to 33,637.[12] Among Democrats, third-place Senator John Edwards received the greatest percentage increase in Facebook supporters, moving from 25,743 to 33,067. The three top-ranked Democrats (Obama, Clinton, and Edwards) held their respective positions throughout 2007, as did the two top-ranked Republicans (Paul and Romney). Democratic candidates as a group register more than double the number of supporters that Republicans as a group have on Facebook.[13] However, Republican candidates experienced a much larger percentage increase in supporters from mid-December to the first week in January. They started from a much smaller base, and also may have benefited more from the Iowa caucus results and attendant press coverage.

Our data from 2006 show that Democratic candidates not only were more popular with Facebook members, they also were more likely to embrace the Facebook community than Republicans that year. In 2008, Republican Ron Paul has led his party's Facebook support numbers, and on a par with second ranked Democrat Clinton. With two years' worth of experience to draw upon and a 2008 nomination contest that entails a higher level of office and greater campaign professionalization as well as resources, it is not surprising that all the presidential candidates have created social network profiles. The differences we currently find in total number of supporters for each party's candidates on Facebook and MySpace might well reflect partisan differences in their mobilization strategies and political base. Democrats appear to be more eagerly embracing the Internet as a communication and campaign vehicle than are Republicans.

Data and Methods

We assessed the impact that a Facebook campaign had on the election outcomes in 2006 in a regression model where the dependent variable is the candidate's final vote percentage and the independent variable is the natural log of the number of Facebook members who registered as a supporter of the candidate and the natural log of the number of members who registered as a supporter of the opponent.[14] We simultaneously control for other independent variables that have been shown to affect the outcomes of congressional elections (Herrnson 2004; Jacobson 2004).

Because the explanatory model for races with an incumbent running is different from races where there is no incumbent, in 2006 we estimated one set of models for incumbents who ran for reelection and had a major-party opponent and another set of models for all major-party candidates running for open seats.[15] We also focused solely on House races since there were only 29 Senate incumbents running for reelection and 8 major-party candidates running in open seats. Although we could have simply folded these races in with the House races, we rejected this strategy because of past research indicating that there is a different model for Senate races (Jacobson 2004).

For the incumbent models the control variables were (1) the incumbent's partisan advantage in the district, (2) the incumbent's voting record relative to the district's preferences, (3) a scandal associated with the incumbent, (4) the presence of a quality challenger, and (5) the ratio of challenger-to-incumbent net receipts.[16] We also expected that running as a Republican would be a liability because of the unfavorable poll ratings registered by President Bush and the Republican-led Congress throughout the fall. Thus, we included a dummy variable for party, with Republicans assigned a "1" and Democrats assigned a "0." For the open seat models, the controls were (1) party, (2) the candidate's ideological advantage in the district, (3) the ratio of candidate-to-opponent net receipts, and (4) relative experience.[17]

Estimating the impact that a Facebook campaign is having on the outcomes of the 2008 presidential nominating contests presents considerable methodological difficulties. For each contest, there are only a limited number of cases to analyze. For the Iowa caucuses, results were tallied and reported for eight Democrats and seven Republicans. While fifteen candidates constitute a large field contesting the presidential nominations of the two major parties, this is a small sample for purposes of multivariate statistical analysis. It limits the number of independent variables that simultaneously can be estimated in a model. Furthermore, many crucial factors that matter in nominating contests, such as organizational resources and tactics, face-to-face interactions between candidates and voters, and targeted media messages, are difficult to measure. Yet we do know that the results of the "invisible primary," which includes initial measure of viability, have been highly predictive of Iowa caucus outcomes (Mayer 2004). After the first contest, reassessments of viability, current resources, and results of the most recent contest are able to predict the winners in subsequent contests (Bartels 1988; Norrander 1996; Steger, Dowdle, and Adkins 2003).

We assess the impact that a Facebook campaign had on the outcome of the Iowa caucuses in a regression model where the dependent variable is the candidate's final vote percentage and the independent variable is the candidate's share of Facebook supporters among members listing Iowa as their home state.[18] To take into account resources, organizational strength, and initial viability, we simultaneously control for (1) the natural log of the dollar amount spent on television advertising on broadcast stations in the state, (2) number of campaign visits to the state, and (3) national poll standing in the December 14–16 Gallup poll, Gallup's most recent poll before the caucuses. We adapt the same model to New Hampshire except that we substitute the reported results of the Iowa caucus with the last Gallup poll as a way to measure New Hampshire voters' perceived viability of the candidates. Finally, because the vast majority of Facebook's members are under thirty years old, we estimated two additional models where we changed the dependent variable in each contest to the candidates' shares of the vote among the youngest age cohort as estimated from the Iowa entrance (eighteen to twenty-nine-year olds) and New Hampshire exit (eighteen to twenty-four-year olds) polls, respectively.[19]

Analysis and Findings

The results of the multivariate regression analyses of House incumbents' final vote percentage are presented in table 15.3. The estimates from the model predicting impact on vote share show that controlling for traditionally relevant electoral variables, the natural log of the number of the incumbents' Facebook supporters and the challengers' supporters had a significant effect on the incumbent's final outcome. The coefficients for the log-transformed variables indicate that a 1 percent increase in the number of Facebook supporters for incumbents increased their final vote percentage by .011, while the same increase in number of Facebook supporters for challengers reduced incumbents' vote percentage by .015. Put another way, an incumbent who had 100 percent more supporters than another incumbent (that is, twice as many supporters) would have finished with a vote share that was 1.1 percent higher than the other incumbent. At the same time, if the incumbent's opponent had twice as many supporters as the other incumbent's opponent, he or she would have finished with a vote share that was 1.5 percent lower.

While these results suggest that the impact of Facebook has the potential to be substantial, it is important to note that there is a diminishing return associated with adding more supporters. Increasing the number of supporters from 100 to 200, would add 1.1 percent to an incumbent's vote share. But to add another 1.1 percent, 200 more supporters would need to be added. Another 1.1 percent increase would require 400 additional supporters. Moreover, no candidate is adding supporters in a vacuum. Presumably, the challenger also is adding supporters, making the net effect, like other campaign effects somewhat minimal (Finkel 1994).

Similarly, we estimate two multivariate regression analyses of House open-seat candidates' final vote percentage (see table 15.4 for details). These results suggest that social networking sites may have an even larger impact in open-seat races. The coefficient representing the effect of the number of Facebook supporters is significant and quite substantial. Candidates who doubled the number of supporters (that is, increased their support by 100 percent) increased their final vote share by 3 percent. At the same time,

TABLE 15.3
Multivariate Regression Analysis of Incumbents'
Vote Shares, 2006 House Races

Independent Variables	Model 1 (Updating activity)	Model 2 (Number of Supporters)
Party (Republican = 1)	**−9.675*** 0.699	**−8.64*** 0.781
Incumbent's partisan advantage	**0.103*** 0.024	**0.098*** 0.025
Incumbent's voting record (centrism)	**0.122*** 0.026	**0.121*** 0.027
Incumbent scandal (Yes = 1)	**−2.886* 1.737	**−2.655** 1.736
Contributions received (challenger/incumbent ratio)	**−9.833*** 1.064	**−7.95*** 1.266
Quality challenger (Yes = 1)	**−3.556** 1.248	**−3.091** 1.262
Incumbent updated Facebook profile (Yes = 1)	**−0.884** 0.962	— —
Challenger updated Facebook profile (Yes = 1)	**−0.324** 0.911	— —
Number of Facebook supporters, incumbent (ln)	— —	**1.056* 0.54
Number of Facebook supporters, challenger (ln)	— —	**−1.541*** 0.513
Intercept	**81.831*** 1.420	**80.419*** 2.607
N	341	329
Adjusted R2	0.645	0.653

Note: OLS. Bold entries are unstandardized regression
coefficients; standard errors are in italics.

$*p < .10$ $**p < .05$ $***p < .01$

TABLE 15.4

**Multivariate Regression Analysis of Open Seat
Candidates' Vote Shares, 2006 House Races**

Independent Variables	Model 1 (Updating activity)	Model 2 (Number of supporters)
Party (Republican = 1)	**−12.331***	**−5.286***
	1.773	1.890
District ideology	**0.314***	**0.338***
	0.037	0.042
Financial advantage (candidates/opponent ratio)	**0.301***	**0.203**
	0.094	0.098
Relative experience	**3.551***	**0.373**
	1.192	1.341
Candidate updated Facebook profile (Yes = 1)	**3.849***	—
	1.953	
Opponent updated Facebook profile (Yes = 1)	**−1.962**	—
	2.022	
Number of Facebook supporters, candidate (ln)	—	**2.975***
		1.095
Number of Facebook supporters, opponent (ln)	—	**−2.355***
		1.183
Intercept	**65.318**	**52.401**
	2.918	5.368
N	64	56
Adjusted R2	0.798	0.845

Note: OLS. Bold entries are unstandardized regression
coefficients; standard errors are in italics.

$*p < .10, **p < .05, ***p < .01.$

candidates running against challengers who doubled the number of their supporters saw their vote share decrease by 2.4 percent. In both cases, the effect of Facebook activity is more than twice the amount observed for incumbents and their challengers. Without an incumbent in the race, campaign messages and the ability to communicate that message effectively become much more important for winning votes. Facebook seems to be one more tool that candidates can use to connect with voters and make a favorable impression.

We conducted two similar analyses to explain candidate outcomes in the Iowa caucuses and the New Hampshire primary in 2008 (see tables 15.5 and 15.6 for details). The results in Iowa seem to indicate that Facebook matters even more than candidate visits and television ad buys in the 2008 presidential nominating contests, and together these indicators explain very high percentages of the variance in candidates' vote shares.[20] More specifically, after controlling for advertising, campaign visits, and initial viability, there is a very strong and highly significant relationship between a candidate's percentage of Iowa Facebook supporters and the percentage of the vote received in their party's caucus. The coefficients suggest that an increase of 1 percent in the share of the Iowa Facebook poll increases a candidate's final vote by .429. Thus, candidates who registered 10 percent more supporters on Facebook than their closest opponents would be estimated to increase their final actual voter share by 4.3 percent. Among voters between eighteen and twenty-nine, the increase would be even more substantial, by 10.7 percent. Both models also have high overall predictive power, explaining 79 percent of the vote for all voters and 91 percent for voters under thirty years old.

TABLE 15.5

**Multivariate Regression Analysis of Candidates'
Vote Share, 2008 Iowa Caucuses**

Independent Variables	Model 1 (All voters)	Model 2 (18–29-year-olds)
Money spend on TV ads (ln)	**1.67**	**−0.588**
	1.512	1.322
Visits to the state	**0.209**	**0.197***
	0.124	0.108
National poll standing	**0.085**	**−0.069**
(Gallup Poll, December 2007)	0.223	0.195
% support from Facebook members in Iowa	**0.429*****	**1.066*****
	0.127	0.111
Intercept	**2.785**	**−5.68**
	5.703	4.987
N	15	15
Adjusted R^2	0.794	0.907

Note: OLS. Bold entries are unstandardized regression
coefficients; standard errors are in italics.

*$p < .10$ **$p < .05$ ***$p < .01$

TABLE 15.6

**Multivariate Regression Analysis of Candidates'
Vote Share, 2008 New Hampshire Primaries**

Independent variables	Model 1 (All voters)	Model 2 (18–24-year-olds)
Money spend on TV ads (ln)	**2.371**	**2.69****
	2.426	1.259
Visits to the state	**0.124**	**−0.253**
	0.467	0.242
Results of the Iowa caucuses	**0.427**	**0.132**
	0.272	0.141
% support from Facebook members in NH	**0.295**	**0.863*****
	0.248	0.128
Intercept	**3.604**	**7.291**
	11.861	6.154
N	15	15
Adjusted R^2	0.59	0.902

Note: OLS. Bold entries are unstandardized regression
coefficients; standard errors are in italics.

*$p < .10$ **$p < .05$ ***$p < .01$

The results for New Hampshire reveal a similar, but not identical, pattern. This model suggests that an increase of 1 percent in the share of the New Hampshire Facebook supporters increases a candidate's final vote by almost 3 percent for all voters and 8.6 percent for voters under twenty-five. It is noteworthy that the predictive power of the model for all New Hampshire voters is lower than for model of all voters in the Iowa caucuses, however, and the regression coefficients for Facebook support are not statistically significant. The model for the youngest age cohort in New Hampshire is highly predictive, and there is a very strong and highly significant relationship between actual vote share and Facebook support among eighteen to twenty-four-year-olds.

A closer look at some practical difficulties attached to interpreting these coefficients underscores the complexities and limitations of measuring the impact of social networks in election campaigns and, in particular, presidential nominating caucuses and primaries. For example, Senator Obama had the support of 56 percent of the Facebook community registered in Iowa, while Senator Clinton had support from only 14 percent of

Iowa members. Based on the estimators in our model, this would suggest that Senator Obama's Facebook support would increase his vote share by 24 percent, while Sen. Clinton's voter share would increase by only 6 percent, a net advantage of 18 percent for Obama. With the actual final popular vote difference only being 8 percent, on its face, these numbers and estimated impact seem highly improbable. When the estimators from the youth-vote model are used, however, the numbers are more realistic. While Senator Obama's Facebook support would increase his vote share by 60 percent, Senator Clinton's voter share would increase by only 15 percent; this net advantage of 45 percent for Obama is strikingly similar to the 46 percent spread between him and Senator Clinton among eighteen- to twenty-nine-year-olds estimated from the Iowa entrance polls. Similarly, in New Hampshire, our model predicts that the 40 percent Facebook advantage enjoyed by Senator Obama should win him 35 percent more votes than Mrs. Clinton among young voters, very close to the 38 percent difference between the two candidates among eighteen- to twenty-four-year-olds estimated from the final New Hampshire exit polls.

Conclusions and Implications

The combined evidence from our various models and analyses makes the case that Facebook played a role in both the 2006 congressional races and early 2008 nomination contests. It offers some initial empirical confirmation that social networking sites indeed have potential to transform campaigns and the electoral process. At a minimum, it demonstrates that social network support, on Facebook specifically, constitutes an indicator of candidate viability of significant importance in races of various types for both the general electorate and even more so for the youngest age demographic. It is this youthful age demographic that seems in 2008 to be upending historical patterns and conventional wisdom about its political participation, and hence is worthy of study. This study is also a first step in demonstrating empirically that the use and success of online campaigning must be taken into account side by side with traditional indicators such as money, organizational resources, polls, and the like.

This study is the first to collect and analyze data that address how pervasive Facebook and other social networking sites are in current campaigns and to begin untangling what effects they have had on the final outcome. We have shown that Facebook had a role in the 2006 campaigns, both in terms of being embraced by a significant percentage of major-party candidates and in terms of the final vote. We also find preliminary evidence that Facebook is playing a role in the 2008 nomination contest.

Yet we are not convinced that Facebook supporters per se actually contributed to the candidates' margin of victory. Facebook's membership draws heavily from the eighteen- to twenty-nine-year-old demographic, which has a lower voter turnout rate than other age groups. In addition, Facebook members were able to support multiple candidates and live outside the candidates' district or state, as could their Facebook "friends" who were informed of their support for particular candidates.[21] Members of Facebook could indicate their support for candidates on the site even if they were not registered to vote or did not need intend to vote. Moreover, since individuals under eighteen make up 14 percent of the Facebook community, a sizable group of potential supporters were not eligible to vote.

The high turnout of young voters in Iowa (three times the number in 2004, and representing 22 percent of the total caucus turnout) may help explain why Facebook supporters had a strong and statistically significant coefficient in that model. The situation changes somewhat for the New Hampshire model, where youth turnout (only) doubled over 2004 and represented 18 percent of the total vote. This illustrates the kinds of differences in the individual state environments for each nomination contest that make it very difficult to undertake a comparative analysis of our data, models, and their interpretation for the 2008 presidential election.

To have an electoral impact, those who view candidate profiles or get communications from Facebook friends must become motivated to engage in off-line campaign activities for candidates they learned about through the network. Yet Facebook was not set up to directly facilitate off-line political activities such as transmitting campaign contributions to candidates, signing up to attend Meetup or other campaign organizing events, volunteering, or registering to vote in 2006. Candidates could not even mass e-mail their supporters to inform them of events and volunteering opportunities. Facebook's privacy policy and community norms discourage members from sending mass messages to multiple members or friends. Instead, candidates had to post notes on their profiles, which then would trigger a notification to all supporters that a friend had posted a new note. This feature was available, however, only if the supporter had not altered the privacy setting to prohibit these notifications. In 2008, the Obama campaign was the first and possibly only one to employ Facebook in an explicitly strategic way by asking his supporters whose networks included friends in Iowa to send them a reminder about attending the Iowa caucus. We anticipate that other candidates will copy or invent similar strategic uses of social networks in subsequent contests.

In light of these caveats, what other explanations of our findings might be investigated in future studies? One is that the number of Facebook supporters is capturing the underlying enthusiasm and intensity of support for a candidate. While it long has been recognized that the intensity of support for each candidate or policy proposal must be taken into account when assessing political outcomes (Dahl 1956), it has been challenging to measure intensity and estimate its effects in a statistical model. It is possible that members of any community who are more enthusiastic about their choice are more likely to want to publicize that support and then take the time to do it. In addition, the candidates who have generated more positive media coverage are more likely to perform better (Herrnson 2004), as well as finding themselves to be quite popular on the Internet.

The explanations may be different for the 2008 presidential nominating contests, however, because there is now considerable variation in how campaign organizations are integrating social networks into their overall mobilization strategies. It is possible that in addition to capturing the underlying enthusiasm for the candidate, this variation also is capturing the extent of the campaign's organizational capacity and effectiveness of their voter mobilization practices. As with Web sites and prior new technologies and online tools, after initial experimentation, campaigns begin climbing the learning curve and taking applications to the next strategic level (Williams and Gulati 2006; Foot and Schneider 2006). It is likely that campaigns with more organizational resources have given a higher priority to online organization as well. And the effectiveness of that organization most likely goes hand in hand with an effort to transform online supporters into off-line volunteers and advocates.

This explanation makes more sense in the case of Iowa than New Hampshire, since enthusiasm for Obama and Huckabee was continuing to trend up nationally, but Clinton and McCain prevailed in the New Hampshire state vote. Apparently, the number of Facebook supporters captures candidate enthusiasm only so long as there is not a generational fault line. Exit polls and postelection analyses of exit polls suggest that such a fault line emerged in New Hampshire: older voters chose experience and competence while younger ones continued to respond to inspirational calls for change. Moreover, Congressman Ron Paul is an outlier in our 2008 data. He has generated social network support that ranks him second overall on Facebook and MySpace and first on YouTube. His vote share in the general electorate was 10 percent in Iowa and 8 percent in New Hampshire, but he placed third among eighteen- to twenty-nine-year-olds in both Iowa and New Hampshire. Interpretation of the number of Facebook supporters as an indicator of candidate enthusiasm within the general electorate and the youth cohort specifically remains complex and problematic.

Another possibility is that Facebook supporters are an indicator of how effectively candidates have organized at the grassroots. National microtargeting efforts by political parties and others may have increased levels of interest among particular demographic groups, which in 2006 included several focused on young voter mobilization. Facebook supporters could be capturing a particular combination of external campaign dynamics that is missed by or other predictors, such as party, voting record or ideological advantage, quality of challenger or experience, and financial advantage. An effective grassroots campaign has been shown to increase a candidate's vote share (Green and Gerber 2004). For example, Green and Gerber find that only .5 percent of Congressman Ron Paul's Meetup groups are based in New Hampshire and only about 1.25 percent of his Meetup supporters come from the state, whose voters represented about 5.5 percent of the ballots cast in 2004.

Considerable media attention was focused on how congressional candidates in 2006 integrated Facebook and other social networking sites into their larger campaign strategies and on what impact this new campaign tool had on the final results. As the attention only intensifies among both the media and the candidates, social networking sites are poised to become "the next big thing" in the upcoming 2008 campaigns. We are only just beginning to see how this new technology plays out over multiple elections. Further empirical research is needed to confirm that online social networks are an important determinant of election outcomes, and to understand the nature of their role. This role is evolving. In 2006 only small numbers of congressional candidates were experimenting with , social networking sites in rudimentary ways; in 2008 all the presidential candidates are employing them, a few extensively and with specific strategic objectives in mind. We need to understand from these campaigns what those objectives are and how the candidates assess their effectiveness.

That said, our initial results are intriguing and worthy of note. If future research can confirm these findings and demonstrate a causal connection between online strategies and votes, Facebook and other social networking sites will be an essential tool in enhancing the democratic process. These sites go beyond simply communicating the campaign's theme and information about how to make participating easier. Active engagement by the candidate and a well maintained site can make the candidate more accessible and seem more authentic. It also can encourage a more professional discussion among supporters.[22] In addition to personalizing the candidate, Facebook puts a face on the candidate's other supporters and facilitates interpersonal connections around activities other than politics. And because Facebook organizes members by regional and organizational networks and gives greater access to profiles in one's own networks, off-line meetings and connections are a real possibility. As membership in traditional civic associations declines, we see in these networks a new frontier for cultivating social capital, which candidates, elected officials, and civic leaders can tap when they want to mobilize citizens for political action.

NOTES

An earlier version of this chapter was published in *Politics & Technology* (2008) March: 11–21. Reprinted by permission.

1. For example, the 2006 midterm elections saw a record number of congressional candidates maintaining campaign Web sites: 85 percent of those running for Senate and 79 percent of those running for the House had an online presence. Moreover, baseline informational Web content and features evidenced more standardization, and candidates of all parties integrated these Web sites more fully into their overall communication strategies (Gulati and Williams 2007).

2. Also see Judy Keen, "Politicians' Campaigns Invade MySpace," *USA Today*, October 17. 2006, p. 1A; Erica Loveley, "Politicians Try Out MySpace," *Wall Street Journal*, October 14, 2006, p. 4; and Jessica Vascellaro, "Campaign 2006 Online: New Sites Aim to Capitalize on Social-Networking Craze Spark Political Involvement," *Wall Street Journal*, September 21, 2006, p. D1.

3. Also see Linda Feldman, "Politicos Beware: You Live in YouTube's World," *Christian Science Monitor*, August 18, 2006, p. 1; Paul Farhi, "Blundering Pols Find Their Oops on Endless Loop of Internet Sites," *Washington Post*, November 3, 2006, p. C1; Ryan Lizza, "The YouTube Election, *New York Times*, August 20, 2006, p. D1; and Amy Schatz, "In Clips on YouTube, Politicians Reveal Their Unscripted Side," *Wall Street Journal*, October 9, 2006, p. A1.

4. This wide difference between House and Senate candidates is similar to what had been observed in the early days of Internet campaigning. Senate campaigns typically raise more money and are managed by a more professional staff than House campaigns and, thus, tend to be the first to experiment with new technologies and communication strategies. And out of necessity, candidates running in a more competitive race also have sought out alternative ways of reaching voters.

5. Data on the number and percentage of candidates who had a presence on Facebook, MySpace, and YouTube were collected by the authors of this chapter.

6. Traffic rankings data were obtained from http://www.alexa.com/site/ds/top_500.

7. Data from http://siteanalytics.compete.com/myspace.com+YouTube.com+Facebook. com?metric=uv. These three social networks attract a somewhat different age demographic. Data from summer 2006 show that eighteen- to twenty-four-year-olds continue to dominate the Facebook community at 34 percent. That represents twice the percentage share for that age group at MySpace and YouTube, over half of whose users are thirty-five years or older. See http://www.comscore.com/press/release.asp?press=1019 and http://www.imediaconnection.com/content/12474.asp.

8. See http://www.meetupsurvey.com/Study and recent essays on this topic by Fred Stutzman (http://www.techpresident.com/blog/entry/18681/social_networks_and_youth_voter_activation) and Mark Glaser (http://www.pbs.org/mediashift/2008/01/your_take_roundupobamas_win_re.html).

9. For example, MySpace acceded to Senator Barack Obama's request to turn over access to the profile created independently by a volunteer for the senator (Sifry 2007). YouTube pulled down a controversial video shot of Senator McCain at a

campaign stop, then admitted it had been "mistakenly removed" when liberal activists protested the removal; see Mary Anne Ostrom, "How Google, YouTube Power Their Way to Center of 2008 Campaign," *San Jose Mercury News*, June 9, 2007, p. A1.

10. For a brief history of this site and its features see Williams and Gulati (2007).

11. Chris Hughes, Personal communication to authors, November 9, 2006

12. Increases in MySpace supporters and YouTube viewers were much smaller, across all candidates. The average change on MySpace was close to 2 percent for Democrats and 7 percent for Republicans; on YouTube it was, on average, close to 8 percent for both parties' candidates.

13. The same holds for MySpace supporters; YouTube views are virtually the same total number for both parties' candidates.

14. We used the natural log transformation because we assumed a nonlinear relationship between the votes and number of supporters, with diminishing returns for each additional supporter (Kutner et al. 2004). We assume the same relationship in relation to television advertising in our presidential models.

15. Data were obtained from CNN: http://www.cnn.com/ELECTION/2006/pages/results/house. CNN continued to update results until 100 percent of precincts had been reported and recounts completed.

16. The incumbent's partisan advantage is the average of his or her party's presidential candidate's vote in the district in 2000 and 2004, then subtracting the average of the opposing presidential candidate's vote in the district from the same two years. Incumbents' voting record relative to their districts' preferences is estimated with the residual from the regression of the average of their 2005 and 2006 ADA ratings on the 2004 Democratic presidential vote. A list of incumbents associated with a scandal was obtained from the November 7, 2006, edition of the *Hotline*. A quality challenger was defined as one who had previously been elected to the state legislature, had been elected governor, lieutenant governor, or attorney general in his or her state, or was a previous member of Congress.

17. The candidate's ideological advantage in the district is the 2004 presidential vote of their party's candidate minus the 2004 presidential vote of the opposing party's candidate. To measure relative experience, this variable is coded a "1" if the candidate is a quality challenger and the opponent is not, a "0" if both are quality challengers, and a "-1" if the candidate is not a quality challenger but the opponent is.

18. Although the announced Republican totals were each candidate's share of the popular vote, the Democrats announced the percentage of precincts won by each candidate. To make the two sets of results consistent, the Democratic candidates' popular vote was estimated from the weighted results of the entrance polls. These estimates seemed valid since the entrance poll totals for the Republicans matched the announced popular vote totals.

19. Final voting percentages and summary data from entrance and exit polls can be found at http://www.cnn.com/ELECTION/2008. Data on TV ad spending was obtained from newspaper reports and supplemented by Dante Scala, professor of political science at the University of New Hampshire. Data on state visits were obtained from nationaljournal.com and The Hotline. The most up-to-date state-by-state percentages of Facebook supporters can be found at http://www.facebook.com/politics/pulse.php.

20. We note that our models for the 2006 congressional elections control for alternative and long-recognized explanations of vote share. We are much less certain about what our models for these first two 2008 presidential contests leave unmeasured since there are few established explanations that we can draw upon and test. Thus we infer that a great deal of the variance that Facebook support captures in these models is more and different than what Facebook support captured in our 2006 analyses, where we could be more certain about the effectiveness of our controls. In the future, we intend to examine the factors that explain the extent of Facebook support in order to have a more precise measure of Facebook's strength.

21. Data provided directly by Facebook indicate that it was indeed the case that many (46 percent) Facebook members supported multiple candidates. Of course, for members in a number of states, there were elections to the House and Senate and for governor in 2006 and only 10 percent registered their support for four or more candidates.

22. Ryan Alexander, interview with authors, October 18, 2006.

REFERENCES

Bartels, L. 1988. *Presidential Primaries and the Dynamics of Public Choice*. Princeton, NJ: Princeton University Press.

Bimber, B., and R. Davis. 2003. *Campaigning Online: The Internet in U.S. Elections*. New York: Oxford University Press.

Dahl, R. 1956. *A Preface to Democratic Theory*. Chicago: University of Chicago Press.

Fairbanks, E. 2006. "The YouTube Election: Candid Camera." *New Republic Online*. November 2 (accessed at http://www.tnr.com/doc.mhtml?i=w061030&s=fairbanks 110206).

Finkel, S.1994. "Reexamining the 'Minimal Effects' Model in Recent Presidential Campaigns." *Journal of Politics* 55 (1): 1–21.

Foot, K., and S. Schneider. 2006. *Web Campaigning*. Cambridge, MA: The MIT Press.

Green, D., and A. Gerber. 2004. *Get Out the Vote!: How to Increase Voter Turnout*. Washington, DC: Brookings Institution Press.

Gulati, G., and C. Williams. 2007. "Closing Gaps, Moving Hurdles: Candidate Web Site Communication in the 2006 Campaigns for Congress." *Social Science Computer Review* 25 (4): 443–465.

Herrnson, P. 2004. Congressional *Elections: Campaigning at Home and Washington*. 4th ed. Washington, DC: CQ Press.

Jacobson, G. 2004. *The Politics of Congressional Elections*. 6th ed. New York: Addison-Wesley.

Kelly, R. 2006. "Politicians Are the New Generation of MySpace Invaders." *CQWeekly Report* 64 (31): 2155.

Kutner, M., J. Neter, C. Nachtsheim, and W. Li. 2004. *Applied Linear Statistical Models*. 5th ed. New York: McGraw-Hill.

Mayer, W. 2004. "The Basic Dynamics of the Contemporary Nomination Process: An Expanded View." In *The Making of the Presidential Candidates 2004*, ed. W. Mayer, 83–132. Lanham, MD: Rowman and Littlefield.

Norrander, B. (996. "Presidential Nomination Politics in the Post-Reform Era." *Political Research Quarterly* 49 (4): 875–915.

Sifry, M. 2007. "The Battle to Control Obama's MySpace." *Personal Democracy Forum* (accessed April 20, 2008, at http://www.techpresident.com/node/301).

Steger, W., A. Dowdle, and R. Adkins. 2003. "The New Hampshire Effect in Presidential Nominations." *Political Research Quarterly* 57 (3): 375–390.

Wasserman, E. 2006. "Media: Candid Camera Campaign." *CQ Weekly Report* 64 (35): 2444.

Williams, C., and G. Gulati. 2006. "The Evolution of Online Campaigning in Congressional Elections, 2000–2004." Paper presented at the annual meeting of the American Political Science Association, Philadelphia.

———. 2007. "Social Networks in Political Campaigns: Facebook and the 2006 Midterm Elections." Paper presented at the annual meeting of the American Political Science Association, Chicago.

16

Conclusion

COSTAS PANAGOPOULOS

Not infrequently, politicians and political operatives rely on conventional wisdom, anecdotal impressions and nonscientific evidence to craft campaign strategy and tactics. The chapters in this volume present the most comprehensive treatment and evaluations of the ways in which modern communications technology is transforming the landscape of political campaigns. The authors deploy rich descriptions and rigorous empirical methods to offer readers reliable information about the uses of modern technology in campaigns and to explore the effects of these developments. Even as the individual selections tackle compelling aspects of this phenomenon, campaigns can extract some overall conclusions from the authors' insights. Following is a brief summary of the main lessons candidates and political operatives can draw from the analyses presented in the volume.

Adaptation is key. Clearly, technology is transforming the shape and design of campaigns and elections, and campaigns will need to adapt to take advantage of these new opportunities. Present-day election cycles in the United States and abroad reveal increases in the use and sophistication of candidate Web strategies that echo the rapid growth of Internet technology and new media development generally. Campaigns are utilizing video, audio, e-mail, and social networking tools to reach out to voters, connect and organize supporters, and supplement traditional advertising methods. The impact of these new media tactics on mobilization and vote choice is now being carefully scrutinized, and analysts are just beginning to realize the most effective ways to measure the positive and negative effects these new tools produce. One thing is certain: failure to acclimate to the continuously evolving digital world may seriously hinder any campaign's success.

First, the Web offers a plethora of opportunities for campaigns at all levels of government to increase their return on investment. In fact, these opportunities may be greatest for smaller campaigns that are waged for local offices. Cost- and labor-efficient online outreach tools as simple as e-mail blasts are now a standard supplement to direct mail campaigns, for example. Furthermore, the potential for interactivity yields other benefits for campaigns. Candidates can solicit useful information about their supporters, which can be used to target and customize communications efforts. Online advertising and online fund-raising campaigns offer candidates additional opportunities. Candidates can generate millions of official Web page impressions using online ads to strategically target Internet users, whether they venture to a site seeking out political information or not. As for raising money, the 2008 U.S. presidential election has shown us that online fundraising tactics have successfully tapped into a vast base of small Web donors, many of whom have never previously given to a campaign. Creative, flash-money-raising drives have proven to generate tens of millions of dollars for candidates literally overnight. With time, these tactics will become increasingly accessible to candidates across the board.

Know the limits. The chapters in this volume suggest that new media offer many new opportunities to campaigns, but there are limits to what can be accomplished online. Even as campaigns embrace technology, traditional electioneering tactics should not be neglected. New media campaign tactics are best used in combination with traditional methods like door-to-door canvassing, direct mail, and fifteen-second TV ads, since these conventional strategies are still very useful in eliciting support for candidates. Campaigns must therefore find the best way to blend and incorporate online and off-line networking and campaign tools in order to stay afloat in new-age elections.

Look abroad. Several selections in this volume highlight how campaigns abroad are incorporating technology into their campaigns. Innovative uses of technology in campaigns can be observed in campaigns all over the world, and political operatives are wise to follow these developments closely. Electioneers may discover creative and effective uses of the technology on the campaign trail or detect mistakes that can be avoided.

Stay alert. Of course, campaigns that seek to capitalize on the benefits of new technology and increase their Web presence must also be aware of the inevitable risk of losing control. One of the most celebrated products of the Internet is the proliferation of online political discourse in the form of user-driven content—a sign of a large, active, and engaged segment of the electorate. But the degree to which campaigns can control their message while encouraging democratic participation on the Web is a central concern of every new media election strategy. Campaigns clearly benefit from the Web by improving fund-raising capabilities, reducing transaction costs, organizing support, and making their platforms more easily accessible for millions of voters. But candidates also face many new and obscure challenges in the digital realm and must walk the line carefully when perfecting their Internet strategies, coexisting in a community of empowered users who can ably use the same tools against them.

Keep up. Perhaps the biggest challenge that campaigns face in the modern era is keeping up with the sheer pace of technological advancement and change, which is unlikely to slow down any time soon. Already since the 2004 election, there has been a massive overhaul of the campaign landscape. This is only likely to continue, and perhaps even intensify. Campaigns must therefore remain vigilant and strive to reach the equilibrium between embracing interactivity and digital innovation, and maintaining control over their message.

The current state of technology and new media foreshadows a future of campaigns and elections in which the tech-savvy will be rewarded. Those who embrace these advancements head-on will find themselves leading the pack, while those who do not risk being left behind.

NOTES ON CONTRIBUTORS

STEFFEN ALBRECHT is a PhD candidate at the Institute of Technology and Society at Hamburg University of Technology.

DANIEL BERGAN, PhD, is assistant professor of communication at Michigan State University.

MICHAEL CORNFIELD, PhD, is vice president, research and media strategy, 720 Strategies, and adjunct professor in political management, The George Washington University.

ALLISON DALE is a PhD candidate in political science at the University of Michigan.

JAMES N. DRUCKMAN, PhD, is associate professor of political science and faculty fellow at the Institute for Policy Research at Northwestern University.

VASSIA GUEORGUIEVA is a PhD candidate in the School of Public Affairs at American University.

GIRISH J. "JEFF" GULATI, PhD, is assistant professor of international studies at Bentley College.

RASCO HARTIG-PERSCHKE is a PhD candidate at the Institute of Technology and Society at Hamburg University of Technology.

KATE KAYE is news and special projects editor at ClickZ.

MARTIN J. KIFER is a PhD candidate in political science at the University of Minnesota.

MAREN LÜBCKE is a PhD candidate at the Institute of Technology and Society at Hamburg University of Technology.

DAVID W. NICKERSON, PhD, is assistant professor of political science at the University of Notre Dame.

COSTAS PANAGOPOULOS, PhD, is assistant professor of political science and director of the Center for Electoral Politics and the Master's Program in Elections and Campaign Management at Fordham University. He is also research fellow at the Institution for Social and Policy Studies at Yale University.

HUN MYOUNG PARK, PhD, is a statistical software analyst/programmer at the Center for Statistical and Mathematical Computing, University Information Technology Services, at Indiana University.

MICHAEL PARKIN is a PhD candidate in political science at the University of Minnesota.

JAMES L. PERRY, PhD, is associate dean and chancellor's professor, School of Public and Environmental Afairs, Indiana University.

KEVIN A. PIRCH, PhD, is assistant professor of political science at Lehman College/City University of New York.

CHAPMAN RACKAWAY, PhD, is assistant professor of political science at Fort Hayes State University.

ALLISON SLOTNICK is a graduate of the Master's Program in Elections and Campaign Management at Fordham University.

AARON STRAUSS is a PhD candidate in politics at Princeton University.

SANDRA L. SUÁREZ, PhD, is associate professor of political science at Temple University.

CHRISTINE B. WILLIAMS, PhD, is professor of government and international studies at Bentley College.

INDEX